THE NATURAL WORLD AS A PHILOSOPHICAL PROBLEM

Northwestern University
Studies in Phenomenology
and
Existential Philosophy

Founding Editor †James M. Edie

General Editor Anthony J. Steinbock

Associate Editor John McCumber

THE NATURAL
WORLD AS A
PHILOSOPHICAL
PROBLEM

Jan Patočka

Edited by Ivan Chvatík and Ľubica Učník
Translated by Erika Abrams
Foreword by Ludwig Landgrebe
Afterword by the Author

Northwestern University Press
Evanston, Illinois

Northwestern University Press
www.nupress.northwestern.edu

Translated with the support of the Australian Research Council (ARC), within
the framework of the 2010–12 research project *Judgment, Responsibility and the
Life-World.*

Printed in the United States of America

10 9 8 7 6 5 4 3 2 1

Library of Congress Cataloging-in-Publication Data

Names: Patočka, Jan, 1907–1977, author. | Chvatík, Ivan, editor. | Učník, Ľubica,
    editor. | Abrams, Erika, translator. | Landgrebe, Ludwig, 1902–1991, writer of
    foreword.
Title: The natural world as a philosophical problem / Jan Patočka ; edited by
    Ivan Chvatík and Ľubica Učník ; translated by Erika Abrams ; foreword by
    Ludwig Landgrebe ; afterword by the author.
Other titles: Přirozený svět jako filosofický problém. English | Northwestern
    University studies in phenomenology & existential philosophy.
Description: Evanston, Illinois : Northwestern University Press, 2016. |
    Series: Northwestern University studies in phenomenology and existential
    philosophy | Includes bibliographical references and index.
Identifiers: LCCN 2016021660 | ISBN 9780810133617 (pbk. : alk. paper) | ISBN
    9780810133624 (cloth : alk. paper) | ISBN 9780810133631 (e-book)
Subjects: LCSH: Cosmology. | Human beings. | Subjectivity. | Language and
    languages—Philosophy.
Classification: LCC BD516 .P3713 2016 | DDC 113—dc23
LC record available at https://lccn.loc.gov/2016021660

Contents

Foreword

Ludwig Landgrebe

To write on Jan Patočka's philosophy, for someone who was linked with him in close friendship for over forty years, can mean only to speak of him also as a person and of the world in which he lived and through which his way of understanding his task took shape. For such reminiscences, one can hardly avoid using the first person. My knowledge of his philosophical ideas and their deep-rooted impulses comes indeed not so much from what was published in German during his lifetime as rather from our debates—which took place for nights on end in my Prague years between 1933 and 1939—and from our correspondence, which reached its highest pitch in the 1970s. Having been barred by Hitler from German universities, I experienced my Prague years as a kind of exile, and during this time Patočka was not only the only discussion partner with whom, given our common philosophical background, I found myself in unique agreement, but also my indefatigable helper in all the difficulties and hardships I encountered. I cannot imagine how I could have withstood these years without him. From the very beginning—in the fall of 1933, he had just returned from his scholarship time in Freiburg with Edmund Husserl—our conversations were never purely philosophical. Talk of personal life, family, comments on the alarming political situation in Europe, common concern for the future of Germany, also a concern of his—all this was always closely connected as backdrop to the question of the specific task of philosophy. This was to remain so in our subsequent correspondence.[1] For me, the development of Patočka's philosophy is inseparably linked with the history of a friendship. It would be impossible to say on any given point which of the two of us was on the giving or receiving end—though he, in his immense humility, would not have agreed with that.

It is almost symbolic that he lived next door to the battlefield of the White Mountain, where the destiny of his native Bohemia was decided upon for nearly three hundred years. In Prague's magnificent yet disquieting Old Town below, as well as in the Castle above, nearly every stone bears witness to this tragic history. A history still so much alive among the population that even today's[2] rulers are obliged to take care to preserve the town's physiognomy. Here all ideologies come up against their limits. But hardly anyone else has been so intensely conscious of this history, hardly anyone has thought it through with such passionate love for his homeland as Jan Patočka. Like many other friends who visited him, I count his guided tours of Prague among my most precious recollections. History came alive on these occasions in its interwovenness with art and literature. It was no narrow-minded patriotism that inspired Patočka, but rather his vision and understanding of the inseparable, world-historical connection between the history of Prague and Bohemia and the political history of Germany. Located as an outpost on the borderline between Central and Eastern European civilizations, in the midst of the tensions arising from this situation, Prague—ever and again residence to the kings of Bohemia and German-Roman emperors—was thus, from the very outset of this intertwining of destinies in the thirteenth century, a seismograph catching the first tremors of future upheavals. For Hitler too, the occupation of Prague was the dawn of his downfall. This tense borderline situation has favored and furthered the wakefulness and sensitivity of the Czech people, so highly talented in every respect. Under the pressure of ever-new foreign domination, the Czechs have proven their ability to preserve their "soul," that is, their individuality, while still remaining open to the intimate connection of their destiny with the fate of Europe. Under the title "Prague's Significance for European Intellectual History," Patočka made this complex relationship the topic of his guest lectures at the University of Cologne in the winter semester of 1967–68.[3]

Given this background, one can understand that Patočka was predisposed to feel close to the work and personality of Edmund Husserl. Husserl, born and raised in Moravia, bore the stamp of the Old Monarchy much in the same way as Patočka's father, a gymnasium professor and later chief school inspector in the educational system of the Austro-Hungarian Empire. Both were shaped by the spirit of this cosmopolitan, multiethnic state, a kind of Europe in miniature, which had kept alive something of the spirit of the Josephinian Enlightenment and its ideals of tolerance. Husserl left his homeland for Germany beginning in his student days, but his quiet and modest manners always retained something of the typical Old-Austrian privy councilor. In his moving "Recollections of Husserl," published as the introductory text of his own Festschrift,[4] Patočka recalls his first acquaintance with Husserl on the occasion of the 1929 Sorbonne lectures. Patočka was at that time studying for a year in Paris and was introduced by Alexandre Koyré, one of Husserl's earliest students, then completing a state doctoral dissertation at the Sorbonne while already a teacher in his own right. Patočka came to the first lecture "with a trembling heart," having "long looked upon Husserl as *the* philosopher." Now he was attending "the inception of the *Cartesian Meditations*, which Husserl planned and intended as a systematic presentation of the entire phenomenological problematic—unfortunately, so compressed and overflowing that it was ill-suited for lectures. Nonetheless, there emanated from the lecture and the lecturer himself something that called for understanding, drawing the listener into the thought processes, no matter how unusual—one sensed the urgent need for a new foundation, a reorientation delving centuries deep—there, before one's eyes, was a philosopher who was not expounding and commenting, but sitting in his workshop, as if he were alone, wrestling with his problems, regardless of man and world." After finishing his doctorate in Prague, Patočka spent the winter semester of 1932–33 in the "Berlin witches' cauldron," witnessing the "beginning of the end of Europe," which was to mean "at the same time a tragic turn in the fate of phenomenology and so many phenomenologists." In the summer semester of 1933, he came to Freiburg to study with Husserl, whose words of greeting, when he first invited the young man to his house, were as follows: "Finally! I have had students from all over the world, but for a fellow-countryman to come to me—that has never happened."

Patočka was introduced to the problems that then held Husserl's attention through conversations not only with the professor himself, but above all with Eugen Fink. He and Fink soon became close friends. While in Freiburg, he of course attended Heidegger's lectures as well, and the question of the relationship of Heidegger's thought to Husserl's phenomenology also became one of the topics of our well-nigh daily conversations in Prague. We both believed that the relationship should be mutually complementary. The way Husserl worked with Eugen Fink made a decisive impression on Patočka: "Two philosophers were leading a life that was a novelty to me at the time. They seemed to take no heed of the oppressive political reality that surrounded them and was shaping their destiny *nolens volens*. They . . . gave me an example of how spiritual life in the true sense can prosper, despite everything, beyond the bounds of public officialdom."

This same spirit of "despite-everything" led in 1934 to the founding of the Cercle philosophique de Prague (Prague Philosophical Circle). The initiators were Emil Utitz who, barred from his chair at the University of Halle, had accepted the offer of a professorship at the German University in his Prague hometown, and J. B. Kozák, who professed at the Czech University and, shortly after, was to supervise Patočka's habilitation thesis. Kozák was a friend of the then foreign minister Edvard Beneš. Beneš, as well as Czechoslovak President T. G. Masaryk, actively supported the foundation of the Circle. Masaryk had befriended Husserl when both were students in Leipzig, advising him to study with Franz Brentano. One must imagine the situation: Prague, asylum to many refugees from Hitler's Germany, was one of the very few places in Central Europe where the voice of free philosophical thought and humanity could still make itself heard. The Cercle philosophique proposed to stand up for "the ideals of humanity"[5] in the spirit of Masaryk and the classical European tradition, and to serve as a haven for phenomenology, then outlawed in Germany. The founders also hoped in time, with the approval of Husserl, to take on the edition of his works—a plan that definitively foundered in 1939.

Patočka was the Circle's secretary. The organization's first important initiative, which he greatly contributed to prepare, was to invite Husserl to lecture at both the German and the Czech University. Husserl counted the days of his visit and talks in Prague among his best memories. After his Vienna lectures on "Philosophy and the Crisis of European Mankind" in the spring of 1935, his talks in Prague in the fall of that year were his last public appearance.[6] Patočka related the event in his "Recollections": "It was once again a great success, Husserl's personality and the solitary energy of his thinking were fantastically impressive. Never before or after has our Auditorium Maximum witnessed such an event . . . never was one so directly touched by the spirit of philosophy." "In these lectures for the first time, everything was built around the problem of the neglected life-world: one saw the crisis of reason and the crisis of humanity looming up behind the crisis breaking out in science despite all its successes, one was given to see the whole centuries-long deepening crisis of Enlightenment that cannot be overcome by turning away from reason, but rather by attaining an as yet unimagined height of reason and science." "There was here a voice calling for conversion, bringing the message of the philosopher to humanity in its utmost danger." Such impressions must have confirmed Patočka in his conviction concerning the mission of the philosopher and his responsibility for Europe. The attempt to take on and carry out this embassy, the belief in phenomenology as the means to forcefully substantiate this message in its necessity were decisive for his further life and destiny. The speech he delivered at the ceremony organized by the Circle after Husserl's death in May 1938[7] gave him another opportunity to honor Husserl and his work.

Husserl's Prague lectures were the seed out of which grew his unfinished late work on "The Crisis of European Sciences and Transcendental Philosophy." The work was also meant as a new attempt at an introduction to phenomenology which would, for the first time, have put in their inner systemic context the problems with which he had been concerned since the early 1920s: the problem of the European crisis which had broken out with the First World War, the responsibility of philosophy in this crisis, the question of its historical grounds, to be sought in the neglect of the life-world in the history of modern thought, and the relationship between transcendental phenomenology and psychology. The problem of the "natural world-concept" was familiar to Husserl from early on, but its fundamental systematic significance became clear to him only in his late phase, when the term "life-world" was introduced. In 1934 Husserl had given up his efforts to write a new systematic summary and introduction to phenomenology, and was concerned only with ordering his manuscripts for the *Nachlaß*. The success of his Prague and Vienna lectures encouraged him, however, to concentrate all his faculties on the task of further developing the contents of these lectures and giving them a written form. On leaving Prague, he had encouraged Patočka to prepare his habilitation as soon as possible. Patočka's supervisor, Kozák, was also eager for him to do so. For Patočka, it was more or less self-evident that the theme could only be the problems introduced by Husserl in his lectures. The habilitation thesis *Přirozený svět jako filosofický problém* (*The Natural World as a Philosophical Problem*) was completed in 1936. At about the same time, the first two sections of Husserl's *Krisis* were printed in Belgrade in the emigrant journal *Philosophia*. Husserl continued working on the following sections with his last ounce of strength until the beginning of his fatal illness in the summer of 1937. The complete text with the preliminary manuscripts and drafts of continuations and corrections was to be published only in 1954 as volume VI of the *Husserliana* series.

Consequently, Patočka could not then quote Husserl's lectures in his own work. He based himself mainly on his private notes and on the conversations he had had over the years with Eugen Fink and myself. The book was also conceived as an introduction to phenomenology for Czech students and other readers. So it is clear that the problems are viewed here in very different perspectives than in Husserl's work as such. The debate with Heidegger's analytics of Dasein, with Fink's independent ideas on the concept of world, with the psychological Gestalt theory, encountered in Berlin, and, last but not least, with the linguistic inspiration drawn from his participation in the Prague Linguistic Circle under the brilliant leadership of Roman Jakobson[8]—all of this went into the book. This of course does not mean that Patočka is presenting here a phenomenology entirely different from that of Husserl. Though it does indeed stand in opposition to the one and only systematic presentation of phenomenology published by Husserl during his lifetime, that is, his 1913 *Ideas Pertaining to a Pure Phenomenology*, it is a further development of phenomenology precisely in the direction pointed to by his later and latest self-critical and, in part, aporetic reflections, the direction in which the solution of these aporias must be sought. All this was brought to public knowledge only through the edition of Husserl's *Nachlaß*. Up to then, Patočka's book was the only one dealing with the problem of the life-world. It long remained practically unknown, not only because of the then prevailing circumstances—the war began a mere three years after the book was published—but also for linguistic reasons. A second edition came out in 1970, but it was soon put on the list of forbidden books in Czechoslovakia. Since the first edition, literature on the life-world problem, both within and outside the phenomenological tradition, has become so vast as to be well-nigh uncatalogable in the Western world. Patočka's book, which appeared in 1976 in French translation and is now [in 1990] available in German, has however lost none of its relevance. All the currently discussed problems about the concept of life-world are already anticipated in it and, in some cases, solved more convincingly than anywhere else.

A detailed analysis of the whole text would be necessary in order to precisely determine the relation of Patočka's transcendental-phenomenological approach to Husserl's late work. I can here point out only a few essential features. Patočka is in full agreement with Husserl's critique of "objectivism" and the related "overlooking" of the life-world, but he adds to this critique further aspects that are either missing or at least not clearly elaborated in Husserl. This becomes evident already in the historical section, dealing with the origin of the "overlooking" of the life-world in the history of modern thought. In his *Krisis*, Husserl pursues this development only up to Kant, and then proceeds with the exposition of the problem of the life-world. Patočka goes beyond this point and compares the specificity of phenomenological reflection on the apodictic certainty of the "transcendental ego" with the absolute reflection of German idealism. This not only provides an opportunity for a more precise determination of the absoluteness of transcendental subjectivity, but also sets up the beginnings of a basis for the controversial question—a question which has yet to be put in a satisfactory way—of the relation between phenomenological analysis and dialectics in general: the transcendental method of German idealism is a logical one. It should be asked, however, whether the logical process does not conceal the true nature of absolute subjectivity. Husserl, for his part, attains the transcendental dimension straightaway thanks to the *epochē*. He has therefore no use of logic as guideline for the discovery of the transcendental, since logic too implies a thesis, which, like all theses, must undergo the *epochē*. The act that opens up the transcendental dimension is thus *extralogical* and can have no parity with other cognitive acts. In the afterword written specially for the French translation, Patočka asks whether the *epochē*, which puts the world "in brackets," and without which there can be no phenomenology, should not be interpreted as the "step back from beings" of which Heidegger speaks. But Husserl, he goes on to say, did not consistently follow through with this step. We find the same idea elsewhere: "In order to reach the origin, one must not only suspend the objective in its validity, as demanded by the phenomenological reduction, but also resist the seductions of reflection, which tends to apprehend the objective after the pattern of act constitutions."[9] That means: access to the dimension of the transcendental is not obtained, as in Fichte, by an act of free self-positing of the I, leading directly to the dialectic of I and not-I. Rather the act of *epoché* is "extralogical," since formal logic is a logic of beings and hence, as Husserl shows in *Formal and Transcendental Logic,* a "logic of the world." Better, the *epoché* merely makes visible what lies before all positing, that is, "world-belief." The I does not have the world as a result of positing. All active-synthetic accomplishments presuppose the passive-receptive acts which are carried out and have always already been carried out in the sense functions of the living and feeling body. It is in relation to these that the "natural" world, the "life-world," is organized according to near and far, familiar and alien, and all the other features deriving therefrom. The world is not pregiven as a chaos of sense-data, which the spontaneity of intellect alone orders and categorizes. The world is the total horizon, and, as horizon, always relative to those whose horizon it is. In this latter quality, it is the "life-world": the world in which we live. There is no conceivable sense in speaking of any other world than this. However we fancy the possibility of another world, however we strive to fantasize it as different—we always already bring ourselves along, with the limits of our possibility of understanding.

Admittedly, Husserl himself, in the second volume of his *Ideas,* already considered the kinestheses in relation to the formation of the consciousness of space and spatial objects; but he did not take into account the consequences that necessarily follow, on a programmatic level, for the definition of the concept of transcendental subjectivity. Here too, the formulation of his program is in contradiction with his individual analyses. These contradictions had been thoroughly dealt with in Patočka's conversations with Fink, and his book is one of the first major attempts to resolve them. In his investigations, he anticipates to a large extent the problem of the body as subsequently elaborated by Merleau-Ponty—of course, without knowledge of Patočka's work. Patočka would later suggest that Merleau-Ponty had been drawing ever closer to the position of the late Husserl, especially in his posthumous writings, and that his theory of embodiment should be understood as a theory of transcendental constitution, while not along the lines of Husserl's program, nonetheless in accordance with his concrete analyses.

This brings the answer to the question of the true definition of "transcendental subjectivity" in its fullest concretion: "the transcendental, i.e., preexistent subjectivity *is* the world," and that means, of course, the world as the horizon in which we live. As universal horizon, the world is no realm of absolute being. If being is always the be-ing of beings *in* the world, then the world = transcendental subjectivity cannot be understood as a being. Husserl's talk of transcendental subjectivity as absolute being is therefore misleading, since transcendental subjectivity is nothing that one can come across as a being in the world. It exists solely for the "disinterested spectator," who discloses it through the free act of the *epochē*. Until then it remains concealed, and the subject too is hidden to itself. But even transcendental reflection discovers no absolute be-ing, since transcendental reflection itself is merely a phase of the "stream of consciousness" and hence never brings into sight the world as a whole. What is given in transcendental reflection is always only a phase, one phase of the "monadic flux of lived-experience." Transcendental consciousness is thus nothing other than the genesis of the phases. This process *gives* being. The giving is however its "derealization," since the given immediately withdraws into having-been-ness. Original time should therefore be understood as transcendental becoming. In his late period, Husserl spoke more and more no longer of transcendental subjectivity but rather of "transcendental life," the absolute "Heraclitean flux," emphasizing that the world is no being comparable to beings in the world. But he did not expose precisely in what sense one could then speak of the "be-ing" of transcendental subjectivity. Patočka is more radical here: transcendental subjectivity is essentially not a being but, on the contrary, transcends beings in totality. Transcendental reflection is thus a reminder of human freedom, something which frees us from our self-forgetfulness, from our falling captive to mundane interests. "Transcendental consciousness" is not something just floating in the air. Transcendental subjectivity is essentially intersubjectivity, but as such it is monadically set apart, individuated and specified. Transcendental reflection is a possibility of fulfillment for every individual, and, hence, the disclosure of his possible freedom.

To grasp transcendental subjectivity not as be-ing, but rather as becoming, one must analyze original time as transcendental becoming. Patočka does not approach this analysis in the same way as Husserl in his *Lectures on Internal Time-Consciousness*. These lectures were, no doubt, the first step toward the destruction of the traditional concept of time, according to which time is understood exclusively as the form of succession. Heidegger too considered this collection of lectures to be one of Husserl's most important works. But Husserl's approach reposes on an abstraction that must be overcome. In his afterword to the 1976 French translation, Patočka sums up: "What lies at the ground of the natural world is not 'internal time-consciousness,' but rather care and temporality." That means: if reflection is to make its way toward original time, it cannot start from an analysis of the temporal genesis of sense perception, but only from the temporality of our practical intercourse with things. Since this intercourse with things must from the outset be a collective dealing in which, deepest down, the common horizon of the world is formed, it follows that the constitution of the other, our fellow man, also takes place originally not in perception but in collective dealings. Heidegger too explained the genesis of temporality out of daily work in common. Patočka therefore joins Heidegger in contesting Husserl's approach to the theory of intersubjectivity in the *Cartesian Meditations*. On the other hand, Heidegger's analysis of being-with in *Being and Time* is also criticized as one-sided: for Patočka, being-with-one-another is not exhausted by solicitude (*Für-sorge*) for others, that is, by the activity of decision-making. It is not only a matter of taking action in common but also of living in common. Man is not only thrown into the world but also accepted. Acceptance is an integral part of thrownness, so much so that being-at-home in the world is made possible only through the warmth of acceptance by others. Nonetheless, the bliss of being accepted remains rooted in anxiety. In this sense, Husserl's analyses of constitution demand to be corrected by Heidegger's analytics of Dasein as exposed in *Being and Time*. But, on the other hand, the opposition of authenticity and inauthenticity, of solitary resoluteness and falling prey to publicness, is inadequate to do justice to the complexity explored by Husserl in his rich analyses of world-structures.

What Patočka is unfolding here is thus a program of mutual complementarity. In the last chapter, proposing a philosophy of language and speech, he however goes beyond this project and broaches yet another fundamental dimension, overlooked in Husserl's analysis of the life-world. This once again anticipates a debate with Husserl which was to start up in phenomenological literature only much later, irrespective of him. The whole chapter can be read as an echo of the discussions that took place in the 1930s in the Prague Linguistic Circle. Many issues of fundamental philosophical import discussed at that time have disappeared from current linguistics under the influence of the nominalist tradition in the Anglo-Saxon philosophy of language. Their restating in Patočka's book is therefore not a mere historical reminiscence but rather an important reminder today.

Patočka meant his book as no more than a first step on the way towards a fully developed transcendental phenomenology. It includes a work-scheme mapping out further research. Let us, by way of conclusion, say a few words about this program. If the "be-ing" of transcendental subjectivity, and that is to say of the world as horizon of the human Dasein, is becoming, the task of phenomenology will necessarily be to bring this becoming into sight in such an extensive way as to understand what is present at any given moment as resulting from it. Now, this is possible only on the ground of the *epochē*, of the "bracketing" of any and all positing of being (*Seinsthese*). In the "natural attitude" and the sciences grounded in the natural attitude, time is understood as the form of the succession of what is experienced and, correlatively, as the phase-continuum of the succession of our ideas concerning what is. Such an understanding—the "vulgar concept of time" as termed by Heidegger—conceiving lived-experience as a continuum of phases, leads to paradoxes similar to Zeno's. At the same time, the peculiar "internal becoming" of this "form" remains concealed. It will be laid open only through transcendental reflection. Only when this internal process is thematized can we understand time as what it originally is. It is nothing other than transcendental becoming itself as a creative process. Patočka shows that Bergson, with his idea of *évolution créatrice*, came close to discovering original time. Time takes shape originally in every individual as the time of his personal life. It is thus an essentially historical time. As such, it presupposes the awareness of our own freedom, the grasping of the tasks that fall to us in our pregiven historical situation. In this sense, the task of phenomenology can only be fulfilled in a "universal history," also including the pre-history of theoretical thought. This alone can bring about a full-fledged and concrete legitimation of the primacy of the natural-naive world over the world of science. One may add that Husserl himself, in his late reflections, was heading toward just such a concept of phenomenology.[10]

THE NATURAL WORLD AS A PHILOSOPHICAL PROBLEM

Introduction

This work develops a few simple ideas demanding a rather complex manner of exposition and demonstration.

Modern man has no unified worldview. He lives in a double world, at once in his own naturally given environment and in a world created for him by modern natural science, based on the principle of mathematical laws governing nature. The disunion that has thus pervaded the whole of human life is the true source of our present spiritual crisis. It is understandable that thinkers and philosophers have often attempted somehow to overcome it, yet they have generally gone about this in a way meant to eliminate one of the two terms, to logically reduce one to the other, to present one—usually on the basis of causal arguments—as a consequence and a component of the other. These problems are alive particularly in modern positivism, which has however never formulated or attempted to solve them in a wholly unprejudiced manner.

Yet a solution other than by means of these alternatives is possible, a solution answering to our modern historical understanding of all reality: a solution which, instead of reducing the natural world to the world of science or vice versa, converts both to a third term. This third term can be nothing but the subjective activity that shapes both worlds, in different yet, in both cases, lawful, ordered ways. The unity underlying the crisis cannot be the unity of the things composing the world; rather, it must be the dynamic unity of the acts performed by the mind or spirit.

That being said, has not the history of modern philosophy beginning with Descartes brought such a variety of conceptions of the subject and its activity that any attempt to found rigorous philosophy on a subjective basis must, at first, seem hopeless? It can be shown, however, that the main conceptions of the subject, in particular those known to us from modern idealistic systems, all have good grounds and are stages on the way toward the ultimately creative region to which we as well propose to bring our problem. Whenever we encounter in serious thinkers divergent conceptions of subjectivity, it is a sign that the subjective level has not been rigorously purified, that the distinction between the result of subjective activity and this activity itself is as yet incomplete. Another important question is that of the subjective method. Is not subjectivism a synonym of arbitrariness? Is this not confirmed, for example, by a certain fancifulness of the dialectic method? In answer to this objection, we shall try to show that there is a positive, analytical subjective method that has philosophical and not merely psychological significance. It is the method of what we call phenomenological analysis.

From these methodological presuppositions, we proceed to actual consideration of the relationship of man to the natural world. Though not explicitly aware of it, man possesses an overall schema of the universe around him. This overall schema has a typical, relatively constant structure, the main features of which we attempt to distinguish. The human world is characterized by the opposition of home and alien, by a temporal dimension and mood coloring. Things are given to us only within such a schema. The task is then to find, through reflection, the activities of the ultimate, independent subjectivity in which man's relation to the natural world is constituted. The activity that accompanies and makes possible the whole of human life is perception; however, perception itself is impossible without an extensive structure, it presupposes the original consciousness of time, in which both perceiving and the perceived take form and shape. It also proves necessary to determine and analyze the original tendencies and activities presupposed in the automatic, so to say, passive course of everyday experience, activities not necessarily bound to the intervention of the freely acting, i.e., decision-making self. The main issue here is to clarify the process of perceiving, unifying, and typifying that forms the necessary basis of all our experience. Problems of time, space, substratum, and causality in the natural world are also dealt with in this context.

After this examination of the foundations of our world, the next question is that of the activities that can be termed personal in the proper sense, those whereby the free person *rises above* what is immediately present to or immediately determining for it (above its organic tendencies). These activities are thought and linguistic expression. The fact that the person rises here above the immediately given implies that these activities are not possible in themselves, but only on such immediate foundations. Thought and language are an expression of human freedom, an expression of the fact that the world is at our disposal, that we are not purely passively determined by our environment and the tendencies emerging in it, but rather actively appropriate reality and dispose of it.

Philosophical and scientific theory becomes possible only on the basis of linguistic thought. Theoretical activity too has its objective result: theoretical concepts and judgments are cultural products, and their relation to thought-activities is similar to the relation between the realities of the natural world and activities of a receptive character (perceiving, unifying, and typifying). Theoretical thought always relates to a pregiven, natural reality, but that does not always mean that it is merely a conceptual transcription of the given world. Philosophy alone is radical theory, aiming at conscious grasping of the essential in the world process, whereas the sciences often introduce hypotheses that have to do with our practical endeavors and may or may not subsequently prove valid. In no case, however, do our theories arise on their own; all necessarily presuppose the nourishing soil of the natural world and human life. We should not therefore hold the results of theories to be independently existing beings; we should not separate them from their life-function; rather it is out of this function that they must be understood.

Such are the broad lines of a demonstration that the unity of the world is not the unity of the materials composing it but rather of the spirit that shapes and sustains it.

1

Stating the Problem

The problem of philosophy is the world as a whole. This thesis, in agreement with historical fact, arouses immediate resistance in us who have been educated by modern science. The sciences have partitioned the world among them, and specialized scientific thought alone is regarded as exact, rigorously controllable and, therefore, theoretically significant. The thinking of the whole, classical ontology, has exploded under the pressure of criticism, but nothing consistent has taken its place in our cultural awareness. It is, indeed, typical of modern existence that there is no *definite* worldview proper to our way of life and that, unlike antiquity and the Middle Ages, modern society has no one total image, or idea, of the order of reality. Such hints of a unified view as there are are of a considerably negativized and simplified complexion in comparison with other worldviews: the closure of the ancient and medieval world has been ruled out, life and mankind dislodged from the center of understanding, the lifeless has supplanted the living, God is no longer accepted as an explanatory concept. It can, of course, be said that all these changes in our picture of the world have a single aim, and, hence, one and the same orientation: the disanthropomorphization of the world. Things in the world are not to be understood in the same way as we understand other beings analogous to ourselves, fellow men or living creatures in general; on the contrary, this mode of understanding should be distrusted on principle. What has changed is not *merely* the picture of the world but rather the very principles of understanding things. And the change affects also our overall relationship to reality. Ancient or medieval man, theoretically reflecting on the world, did not doubt that his thinking referred fundamentally to the same set of things present to him in naive, theoretically unmediated sense-experiencing. We ourselves have lost this certainty, or at least it is lacking in our present society as a whole.—Can we, in this situation, still practice philosophy, and what meaning can philosophy have for us? Can our consciousness of reality be unified by something other than the fundamental rules of the natural-scientific method? Can philosophy, in this situation, also hope to have some social effect?

The answer to all these questions is yes, on two conditions: that *unity* is something we need and something we can bring about—in philosophy—by our own efforts. The need for unity is, of course, a practical requirement. The need for philosophy is profoundly related to the praxis of human life, and today's man does not come to philosophize through mere wonder, *thaumazein*,[1] but rather on account of the inner difficulties of his spiritual life, on account of his general life-attunement. We propose here to explore in this way, with respect to the existential misery of our time, the birth of one of the trends of modern philosophy. Let it be said straightaway that our interpretation of the situation does not spring from any romantic appreciation (or depreciation) of the present; it is merely an attempt, based on both historical findings and psychological analysis, at reconstructing the ideal type of the present nihilistic mood. We regard as the fundamental constituent of this mood, or life-feeling, man's overall relationship to reality, the way he comes to terms with the milieu in which he lives. There is in this relationship a peculiar duplicity, which must first be described. In order to do so, we shall have to introduce certain fundamental concepts.

1. The Naive Life-World and the World of Science

Before an explicit theoretical interest is awakened in man, he has already acquired an image of the world, which takes shape without any conscious elaboration on his part. This image itself has two components: one that can be called "givenness," the other a complementary element of explanation or interpretation. The element of givenness comprises all formed sense-material, all past and present intuitive experience of one's own and of others; we include in the explanatory element all naive and spontaneous extension of the domain of genuine experience in quasi-experiences. This naive extrapolating cannot be termed theorizing, or only *cum grano salis*, for the theoretical tendency has not yet crystallized and become differentiated from other tendencies, and the critical exigency remains dormant. Yet there is here already spontaneous thought production, which goes beyond the limits of practical utility. Before all explicit thinking, primitives and children form, on the things of the world, opinions that they are often unable to distinguish from givens, and which, as personal development progresses, may automatically give way to clearer, more elaborate views. Of course, the structure of this interpretive element differs for people at various stages of the historical process; and many believe that even the categorial structure of the element of givenness shows essential differences. Yet the fact remains—and it alone interests us here in exposing and formulating the problem—that prior to all theorizing in the sense of the explicit positing of theoretical problems, objectivity is already given to us through multifarious sorts of experience, and that we imagine that we have immediate access to this objectivity and a certain freedom in disposing of it on the basis of our personal aims and decisions; life in this naive world is life among *realities*, and though our anticipations are frequently corrected, that in no way modifies the overall character of our living with things. Since this entire domain of realities is given naturally, i.e., without our explicit theoretical intervention, calling on no theoretical efforts or skills, we call it the "natural" or naive world; its most characteristic feature is precisely that it is *there* for us without any act of our free will, by virtue of the mere fact of our experience, prior to any theoretical attitude. We call the attitude of this simple, naive experience the "natural" attitude; traditionally, it is also termed the natural worldview or world-concept.

It must be said here, with regard to a currently very widespread life-feeling, that man who has experienced modern science no longer lives simply in the naive natural world; the habitus of his overall relationship to reality is not the natural worldview. This, however, is not to be attributed to the fact of theorizing; theorizing had been going on long before man abandoned the natural worldview with its way of seeing immediately given reality and life in the heart of the real. There had, of course, been Parmenides of Elea, but also Aristotle, whose ingenious synthesis of idea and reality "saved the phenomena"[2] for over a thousand years. The reason why modern man, i.e., man having gone through the tradition of the main ideas of modern natural science, no longer lives in the natural worldview, is that our natural science is not simply a development but rather a radical *reconstruction* of the naive and natural world of common sense. It has often been pointed out that the tendency of modern natural science, in particular physics, has something in common with Eleatism. However, the analogy lies not only in the conception of being as an eternal, omnitemporal thought-object, but also in the human consequence of splitting the life-milieu in two, between life in a world of truth and life in a world of mere appearance. The naive world is similarly devalued in both cases. Descartes's struggle against "confused ideas" is not merely a fight against Aristotelianism; the historical opposition here conceals a deeper one— the conflict between the scientific world and the naive world. What had hitherto been deemed reality is real no longer; reality, at least in its ultimate root, is something else—above all it obeys mathematical laws, it is to be understood *sub specie* of a formal mathematical model. All concepts and principles contrary to this model must be—and progressively are— barred from the reflection on true reality. The one and only thing that comes into account is mathematical mechanism, the "opus quod operatur Deus a principio usque ad finem, summaria nempe naturae lex,"[3] the mathematical structure of what happens. What then is to become of the natural attitude and the world corresponding to the natural view? The question, of course, still arises. The first and, still today, most widespread interpretation is causal-psychological. The naive world is the result of a causal connection (in a broad sense that does not exclude "psychophysical parallelism") between certain "physical" and "psychical" processes; it is the subjective phenomenon of objectivity. There is a certain degree of conformity between the objective and the naive world, but it is a purely structural (having to do with the structure of relationships), by no means a qualitative conformity. What is important for us, though, is the *orientation* of this explanation: going back from the results of natural science to "subjective givens," which are lawfully correlated with them.

2. The Impact of the Scientific Worldview on Our Life-Feeling

Our purpose here is not to elucidate the genesis and essence of scientific explanation in modern times but rather its influence on our feeling of life. As is clear from the foregoing, the first and strongest effect is to mark our naive world as nonoriginal, derivative. This is not to say that we are aware, at every step, that its qualities and structures "de facto" do not exist, that they are mere "phenomena"; but the whole of our lived-experiencing of things and of ourselves is branded with a character of nonoriginality and semblance. It is a life remote from the true, creative world forces, distrustful of its own immediate understanding. To be sure, man himself, in his true essence, is also part of nature, part of an existent geometrical system obeying—though its composition often changes *in concreto* even in the eyes of science—a principle of comprehension that remains essentially the same and is merely purified from historical dross. As part of nature, man is viewed in relation to the system of possible actions he can receive and perform, i.e., of changes he can undergo and bring about, and these actions, in turn, are studied as to their objective lawfulness, in order to obtain an objective rule of the forces governing and constraining man without his awareness. From the standpoint of this understanding, the subjective feeling of freedom has no noetic value, it is a mere *effectus non efficax*. The frequently stressed contradiction between the feeling of freedom and the objective assessment of man is basically, for modern humanity, a conflict between the two worlds, the naive and the scientific. From the standpoint of scientific objectivism, of course, there is no conflict, since naive life has a priori, in competition with the principles of the scientific reconstruction of reality, no noetic value. The naive world, conceived of as a partial (albeit structural) image of nature's reality, can contain nothing that cannot be objectively categorized and explained, it can never count as an argument against objectivism. The question is, however, whether it can indeed be conceived of in this way, and whether this conception itself does not always do violence to our original, natural life-feeling, which is a distinctive experience and, as such, may have a noetic claim worth considering. Important here is the feeling and recognition that, on the basis of the objectivist explanation of humanity, I ought in fact never to feel free; at least, freedom does not have the meaning attributed to it by naive man, it is not spontaneity of decision and liberty in disposing of my possibilities of cognition and choice but rather, e.g., independence from outside constraint.[4] It is important then that, in this peculiar conflict without contact, the scientific view can induce a profound change in the very foundations of the life-feeling; man lives in the fundamental apperception of his unfreedom, he feels himself the agent of objective forces, perceives himself not as a person but rather as a thing. Without our explicit awareness, there has been a substitution of our lived-experiences, a confusion that can then easily blind us to their deeper nature. Without going outside himself, man has become reified, alienated from his natural life-feeling; he becomes—at least at the surface of his being—what he holds himself to be. We shall call this reification, this conception of man as a thing, as a complex of objective forces, *self-alienation*. Out of it follows yet another phenomenon: *self-abdication*. Self-abdication is a reliance on "nature" where man directs neither himself nor others from a *personal* standpoint but rather gives himself up to the impulses that carry him. Since he does not live out of himself—rather life is something he *receives*—the question of the *overall meaning* of life lacks all real significance; "meaning" here means following impulses, which is done automatically in any case. Reflection has no fundamental importance for life; it is wholly in the service of action, as every personal decision follows from a *vis a tergo*, a natural necessity underlying lived-experiences. Work and activity are not so much a means toward a freely grasped goal as rather, on the one hand, a means of satisfying natural or, better, nature's tendencies, and, on the other hand, an escape from the vanity of reflection[5] and other of life's temptations: partly a vital necessity, partly a distraction. The lowered sense of self carries with it a weakening of the feeling of the threat posed to man by objective forces and of the uniqueness of life, a spreading of the objective barrenness into our very lived-experience. It is as if all the diversity of life were ringing with an unvaried tone of indifferent nothingness which makes all things equal and does justice to life's pure seeming with its uneven distribution of interests and disinterest, lights and shadows.—The fact that even such consciousness of abdication leaves room for a stabbing anxiety (about the finitude of existence) is simply more evidence of the inner conflicts in which human self-alienation becomes entangled. Alienated man finds it difficult to enter into the spirit of his self-prescribed role, or rather, the role prescribed to him by the objectivist view of his essence; life within him flees this graveyard reconciliation, and as he is unable to free himself from his self-apperception, he endeavors at least to turn a blind eye and forget his situation in the thousand distractions so abundantly offered by modern life.

There is no need to further portray the consequences of this conception. Man is, to a certain extent, pliant, and he can attempt to live even in defiance of the natural order of his own being; but when this gets him entangled in dispiriting conflicts, it is clear that he does need unity. This then provides a first indication for our problem setting, showing the need for philosophy as a unity function for our splintered consciousness, blundering from the naive to the scientific world and back, living out its unfortunate existence in between the two positions experienced as opposites. The unity function has in itself a practical significance; it is clear that the conception we have just described is far too tolerant of the grosser tendencies of human nature and does not appear as suitable ground for the genesis and development of a strong self.

3. Attempt at a Historical Typology of Possible Solutions

The confusion brought about, paradoxically, by the scientific revolution, i.e., by the doctrine of "clear and distinct" ideas, was not long in leading modern thinkers to a sharper awareness of the difference between the naive and the scientized world. Some sensed quite early on that the relation between the two could not be settled with dogmatic bluntness in favor of one or the other. But a long time went by before the problem of the natural worldview was stated in more or less adequate terms, namely, in such a way that the natural worldview itself became a problem not to be dismissed by a handful of preconceived judgments. The debate on the natural worldview requires above all the apprehension, the analysis, and the restitution of the given state of affairs; the natural world must be described as accurately as possible in its fundamental structures, examined as to the mutual relationships of its various components and aspects. Until relatively recently, no philosopher had set the task of providing such a description, and when this was finally done, the means were at first inadequate. Nonetheless, we can see the problem emerging already in the early days of modern philosophy. Berkeley vehemently attacked the Cartesian cleavage between the *mundus sensibilis* of our immediate intuition and the *mundus intelligibilis* of scientific reason.[6] He set out to disarm this dualism at all costs—even if it meant sacrificing the reality of things in general. Berkeley missed the problem he was essentially aiming at because he understood it too broadly: as a matter of fact, the dualism lies not in the idea of an independent object, not in the idea of a material substance, but rather in the idea of a *mathematically conceived* material substratum. Taking the problem too broadly, Berkeley did not himself avoid the pitfalls of objectivism in his conception of psychical life as a collection of ideas, an understanding which, stemming from Locke's semi-sensualism, does not belie its historical origin in the very metaphysical dualism Berkeley was opposing. Such a self-enclosed collection of ideas, conceived of as atoms, contains nothing specifically subjective; rather, it is a simple qualitative complex.[7] Berkeley then reduces all being to this immensely impoverished and interpretatively falsified mental sphere; he thus frees himself of the dual world without devaluing science. He achieves this by means of two principles: (1) it is through our impressions that we know all we know of things, and (2) the connection of what we call things (and the same is analogously true of causes) is not real but rather semantic, a connection of signs. The impressions of "things" are nothing but signs for other impressions, lawfully connected to the former. Basically, Berkeley thus helps himself out by doing away with the naive concept of substance, or thing, by means of an artificial interpretation which has certain features in common with the substantial relation yet fails to grasp it in what is characteristic of it.[8] Like the relation of things, the semantic relation too proceeds from the sensible to that which is not directly perceived, from the apparent to the hidden, but the relation of things includes moreover other moments, it is an extremely intricate complex of significations, whereas Berkeley orders the world with geometrical simplicity. The question of the reason for the world's being structured in classes and laws then boils down for him to the question of the divine intelligence that governs the world. Things and laws are, so to say, the words and phrases of the divine language in which God communicates with his creatures. Berkeley thus solves the metaphysical problem of the nature of what is by means of the concept of a divine grammar.

Berkeley's position was soon recognized as dependent on Cartesianism. The Scottish philosophers in particular became sharply aware of this appurtenance and protested against it. Thomas Reid points out the genealogy that runs from Descartes to Malebranche, Locke, Berkeley, and Hume, and he sees the beginning of what he terms "the universal deluge" as something to be found already in Descartes.[9] It is certainly correct that the idea Reid is above all combating, i.e., the necessity to prove the existence of the "external world," has its source in the reification of the subjective that finds its first systematic expression in Descartes as representative of an elaborated system of the mathematical conception of the world: the mind here is even more radically separated from the world than in Platonism, but at the same time it becomes a nonmaterial, nonspatial *thing*. However, as to the reason for the paradoxical fact that the mind, radically separated from all the rest of reality, has to use its own ideas of the object in order to prove to itself the ontological scope of its claim to objective knowledge, Reid does not locate it correctly in Descartes's fundamental mathematicism, but rather in what he calls "the ideal system," i.e., in Descartes's subjectivism, which has a totally different and, as we shall show below, much deeper meaning. While accurately sensing the enemy, Reid thus fails to see where he can be attacked; he is concerned only with presenting a different solution to the same—ill-posed—problem. According to Reid, the pretensions of modern philosophy are absurd, since it abandons the one and only field which nurtures the growth of philosophy: the ground of common sense, containing the principles of all possible knowledge, whether in science or practical life. Reid refuses to admit that something extraordinary happened in our world with the advent of modern natural science. He asserts outright that the man who first ascertained that cold makes water freeze proceeded in the same way as Newton in discovering the law of gravity or the properties of light. He blames all the uncertainty of the human sense of self, already observable in his time, on the hubris of philosophers who disregard the demands of common sense and seek to make philosophy independent of it—a project Reid compares to the revolt of the Titans against Zeus almighty. So, though he has (like his French predecessor Claude Buffier)[10] chosen the right opponent, the true author of the disunion he proposes to remedy, Reid does not do battle with the proper weapons. If we were to look to him for positive indications, we would find his results commensurate with the method employed: Reid makes some admittedly subtle analytical observations,[11] but on the whole his analyses remain within a Lockean conceptual schematism. There is no real description of the world of common sense in Reid; he does not even acknowledge the problem.

Reid and his followers are inconsistent champions of the natural worldview, determined to defend it against the pretensions of philosophy but not against the claims of science, which has set itself up as ontology. The problem of the natural worldview was never made fully clear in the school of Scottish "common-sense" philosophy; for proof of this, we have but to consider the objections raised by Hamilton, for example, against Reid's timid leanings toward naive realism[12]—all in all, the school's standpoint does not essentially diverge from Locke's position. Nonetheless, the sharp impression that modern philosophy is somehow unnatural in its very roots is one of the determining facts of the spiritual situation of the late eighteenth century; Reid's philosophy, itself a consequence of this impression, certainly contributed in turn to reinforcing it. The openly irrationalistic philosophical trends, among which Jacobi should be singled out as an emblematic figure, follow the same line. Jacobi represents yet another typical attitude toward our problem, an attitude that can still nowadays be encountered: the natural worldview alone is in touch with reality, all rational elaboration of this world, i.e., both science and philosophy working with and in the name of scientific principles, being discredited as sterile, of purely instrumental value. Not that rational elaboration is denied binding force, but it can only deal with things that it has arranged and fitted into its own schemata. What science understands is understandable but not real; science does away with the "clear obscure" of things, their individuality, their life, the unsaid of their relations and determinations. The philosopher should not fall under the illusion that he knows how to explain the essence of things, that he can tell what being is. The essential function of philosophy is simply to *uncover* what is,[13] to pursue the analysis as far as it can go, up to what cannot be analyzed, to the ultimate phenomenon which is essentially inaccessible, unconceivable for abstract reason.—It is interesting to find almost the same formula Jacobi uses to define the task of the philosopher in the passage of Goethe's *Theory of Colors* dealing with the philosophical significance of his investigation: "vom Philosophen glauben wir Dank zu verdienen, daß wir gesucht, die Phänomene bis zu ihren Urquellen zu verfolgen, bis dorthin, wo sie bloß erscheinen und sind und wo sich nichts weiter an ihnen erklären läßt."[14] Goethe's aversion for the *more mathematico* explanation of nature is well known; yet Goethe is no advocate of anti-scientism and irrationalism in general; he does not claim, like Jacobi, that the attempt to understand nature can lead only to a mechanical conception of the world; rather, his guiding idea is a *reform of science*, which should be brought closer to the natural world, built on foundations fundamentally different from the mathematical essence of natural science. This new science of nature does not rely on the principle of clear and distinct ideas; the unfathomable remains alive in it, in the very heart of nature, and we come closest to this heart, not in the crystalline clarity of intellectual constructions, but rather in grasping the primal phenomena as means, in Hegel's words, to "lead the black Absolute . . . out into the light of day,"[15] means that are at once ideal and real, intellectual and sensible, intelligible and experientially given. It is clear that this is an attempt to recover intimacy with nature, to grasp its inner rhythm, to deepen the natural bonds that link us with it rather than severing them systematically through science. Thus, Goethe's science of nature is both a return to the Renaissance and a gateway to the scientific endeavors of the German idealist philosophers—endeavors that, notwithstanding their lack of success, are significant and symptomatic with respect to our problem, revealing of the profound crisis caused by modern objectivism and mathematicism in the economy of our spiritual life, endeavors that will one day have to be explored in depth precisely from the standpoint of this problem, evaluated in all their richness and pertinently exploited, in search of viable paths. We cannot here even outline, let alone classify this whole movement; it has, however, one common feature, shared also with Goethe, whose philosophy of nature has rightly been called an introduction to the thought-world of German idealism:[16] an insufficient awareness of the positive significance of modern mathematical natural science, the feeling that this whole episode could be overcome and forgotten once and for all, as one forgets an intellectual error. On this point even German idealism lacks a concrete view of the historical process of the spirit as creative and positive even in its nay-saying. In actual fact, the reconstruction of nature following the Galilean and Cartesian tradition went forward well-nigh undisturbed, and in the blinding light of its intellectual and practical successes, attempts at a science of a different type and orientation faded to insignificance. The problem though remained. Three possible ways out—Reid's refusal to acknowledge the problem, Jacobi's irrationalism which is its own judge, and Goethe's reform of science—having been closed, there remained to try once again on the basis of the intellectual means made available by modern science itself; there remained to attempt an explanation of the naive world not only *on the basis of* but as identical with the mathematical world. As in Berkeley, we encounter here a transformation of naive experience, a reinterpretation which, this notwithstanding, sets itself the task of apprehending naive experience as it is and reinstating it in its rights.

Richard Avenarius's critique of pure experience[17] is a far-reaching attempt of this kind. According to Avenarius, it can be shown, on the basis of an analysis of the experience of our natural and human environment, that there are not two worlds, two realities. For Avenarius, the difference between the physical and the psychic[18] is not absolute, as both are part of the same reality: the psychic is merely a particular function of the "oscillations" of the nervous system (taken as a logically necessary presupposition of experience, not as a material thing in itself). Avenarius seeks to apply this standpoint consistently in examining all psychologically accessible experience. At no point does he conceal his naturalistic program; on the contrary, he displays it in nearly every line of his writings; his ideal is to introduce scientific lawfulness into reflection on what was formerly called the subject, consciousness. Avenarius does not use these terms; they are *idola* that crumble and fall given true analytical consistency, which knows only "elements," "characters," "things," and "thoughts." Avenarius is a subtle analyst of detail, but he fails to see the depths of the problem, having already solved it in the putting.[19] The same is true of his intellectual twin Ernst Mach, whose analysis of "sensations"[20] led, as is well known, to the discovery of the qualities of the form, or Gestalt; it was thus, psychologically, a very fruitful investigation, though its grounds were philosophically debatable, to say the least.—These thinkers have been criticized, not without reason, for having taken experience apart and not knowing how to put it back together again. If experience is always a manifold of elements, what is it that binds them together?[21] Clearly, it cannot be yet another element, as the same question would arise about it, etc.

Already Avenarius tried to heighten the precision and clarity of his attempted interpretation of naive experience by adopting a formal mode of expression using algorithmic formulas. The philosophers who apply logicism to the analysis of experience go much farther in the same direction. We cannot, in these pages aiming merely at a general typological characterization of the various standpoints toward our problem, discuss in detail the essence and development of Russian, English, and American neorealism. We must be content to show, by means of a few examples, how our problem retains the function of a starting point and how the already mentioned tendencies are brought to bear on its solution. Some currently influential doctrines would require a detailed analysis if we were to show how they can be reduced to a combination of such tendencies; these are doctrines aiming at a synthesis, where the radical consequences, of interest to us, tend to be less conspicuous. For this reason, we shall not discuss Bergson or Whitehead. Nor do we intend to retrace the history of naturalistic extremism in its individual proponents. May we be allowed just to briefly outline a few characteristic points. Here we meet with Bertrand Russell and his attempt to present cognition of the external world as a field for the application of the scientific method in philosophy.[22] Starting from Berkeley's critique of substantialism (a critique bearing, as we have seen, the mark of the dualism of the natural and the scientific world), Russell renews the question of inference from the "subjective" to the "objective" sphere. For this purpose, he first undertakes a rough analysis of what is given in everyday ("sensible") experience, distinguishing "hard" and "soft" data. Hard data are "sensible qualities," soft data are objects of common sense, such as furniture, tools, mountains, etc. Russell then takes hard data alone as a starting point from which to reach objects. He holds objects to be logical constructions from "hard data."

Construction in the common-sense world differs from scientific construction only by its lack of precision. The refusal of this imprecision entails the collapse first of the category of substance—replaced by the notion of a series of aspects obeying physical laws—then of the concepts of space and time as supposedly independent entities. In this way, Russell reaches a standpoint that involves only "data" and logical constructions. The *entire* world is then reduced to this standpoint; the dividing line between the subject and the object has been erased, common sense is in the right in the material respect (as concerns the data), science in the formal respect.

Russell is inconsistent in invoking simply "animal belief" when it comes down to overstepping the set of our *own* hard data, i.e., in the question of "solipsism," which, given his approach to the problem, is unavoidable and can receive no answer. Carnap[23] is more consistent here, declaring the question a pseudoproblem (since it cannot even be formulated in rigorously logical terms) and undertaking to construct ("constitute") the world on a private-psychical basis. Most important for this whole thought style are, however, Wittgenstein's considerations on the nature of the world and the nature of language.[24]

Wittgenstein's treatise is, in brief, an ontological theory of logic. The nature of logic ensues here from the structure of the world, but it can also be said, the other way round, that there is nothing more appropriate than an inquiry into the essence of logic for elucidating the nature of the world. The world is the totality of facts; facts are combinations of "things"; things have content and form; form is space, time, and "color." (Color corresponds to the qualitative aspect of reality as given by the senses.) The world is not the totality of things but of facts: this is important, as every fact involves a relation and every relation has a certain formal structure. It is this formal structure that makes possible language, which is nothing other than a logical *picture* of the world. There is a logical picture where there is agreement in structure between two facts.[25] Thus, a sentence directly shows the structure of the fact that is its meaning. Sentences in general have meaning only on the general condition of it being ultimately possible to resolve even their most complex expressions into expressions that show the structure of the elementary facts of which the world is composed. If the expression is in a form such that its individual signs unequivocally correspond to the objects of the pictured fact, then we have to do with a fully analyzed sentence. Every sentence can be ultimately reduced to a fully analyzed form, thereby guaranteeing agreement between the thing and its picture. The entire world is expressible, but on the condition that the expression itself is part of the world, subject to the same general laws. A sentence has meaning only if it can be verified by the direct comparison of two facts: the sentence and its object. The whole of logic follows simply from the rules of picturing. "In logic it is not we who express, by means of signs, what we want, but in logic the nature of the essentially necessary signs itself asserts."[26] The so-called laws of logic are tautologies, i.e., combinations of sentential signs valid for all possible combinations of the truth-values of the elementary propositions. In logic, something of the very essence of the world is shown simply because the fundamental structure of nature is logical. One can never resist logic, nor sin against logic. A thought is always logical.

Wittgenstein's theses, which look like wholly unprejudiced logical considerations and yet, as we see, in fact contain, implicit in their starting point, an entire objectivist, mathematical theory of being, were to provide the basis for a new polemical campaign ardently waged by certain members of the "Vienna Circle" against all "metaphysics." It is a polemic which denies the so-called metaphysical propositions, those featuring concepts such as "principle," "God," "the absolute," "nothingness," etc., not only truth but—on the basis of Wittgenstein's considerations on language as a logical picture of things—any meaning whatever. It must be emphasized here that these logicists take the word "meaning" in an uncommon acceptation, which presupposes their specific metaphysical theses (the logical atomism described above) as well as their theses on the nature of language. Nowhere, however, has there been a sustained attempt to show that this concept of meaning coincides with common, everyday use; these thinkers themselves are far from such a position. Up against the fact that people have for thousands of years taken propositions containing metaphysical names to be meaningful, they resort to a doubtless too facile comparison of metaphysics to music evoking emotions and moods; these authors deny that there is on any account thought going on here.[27]

Starting with Wittgenstein, the consideration of the role of language in the economy of world-representations becomes fundamental to the objectivists. From this angle, the problem of a unified worldview presents itself as the question of a unified language of science. Modern advocates of scientistic objectivism affirm that knowledge in all possible scientific fields can be expressed in the language of mathematical physics; such is the thesis of "physicalism," which thus rules out "subjective" experiences, once and for all, from the province of objects of clear and distinct knowledge. It cannot be denied that one of the fundamental tendencies of modern science is indeed thought through here to its conclusions: the universality of physics as a unified theory opposed to the sphere of "mere data" (it too now unified and leveled) brings to completion, in the thesis of a unified language of physics, the mathematical reconstruction of the world begun by Galileo and Descartes. It is a consistently constructed thesis, unlikely to be shaken by any criticism from within. One can, however, recall its historical origins and the dogmatic metaphysical character thereby attached to it. It can be shown, in addition, that the physicalist system can never encompass the world of naive lived-experience, which must always be somehow abstractively preserved so as to measure up to the image of immediate experience conceived by the "empiricist." How is he to prove that this so bountiful naive world, always a whole, with all its articulations, practical characters, features of familiarity, mood coloration, etc., is merely some sort of inarticulate physics? Physicalism can ascertain a lawful correspondence but by no means the identity of the two worlds, that of construction and that of experiencing. After passing through the hands of the physicalist, our problem is thus back where it was to begin with—and man goes on reeling between two essentially different views of reality with all the practical consequences of this discrepancy, as indicated above.

4. Anticipating Our Own Proposed Solution

As the reader will have gathered from our portrayal of the attempts at achieving the unity of reality, these initiatives have not been successful. We believe that the reason for their failure is that all without exception begin by considering the nature of the object and go on from there to explain lived-experience, dispensing with the descriptive and analytical work necessary to apprehend such experience in its original form and its naive world. We shall attempt here to go the opposite way. We shall try to rediscover, under the sediments of modern objectivism, a concept containing a real key to the sought-for unity. For us, this concept is subjectivity. Certainly it has already been suggested centuries ago that subjectivity should be considered the fundamental level of philosophy, but let us make no mistake: the meaning of the Cartesian reflection is still a partially unsolved problem.[28] The following investigation pursues this meaning along the path followed by modern philosophy in its characteristic representatives. We must, however, first attempt to state what we expect from this philosophical anamnesis and why we look upon the subjective orientation as a way to reestablish the world's unity, the breaking of which threatens modern man in that which, according to Dostoyevsky,[29] is most precious to him: his own self.

Let it be said to begin with that we do not understand subjectivism after the manner of Berkeley, who approached the reduction of objective entities to real finite subjects through a formal reinterpretation of experience. Our starting point considers the nature of experience in general, which is always the experience of something real, something existing in the broadest sense of the word, be it "subjective" or "objective," real or ideal, originarily given or present merely in an improper sense, etc. All that exists in all its variety is an object of experience. What then is *experience* in its ultimate essence? If, as we believe, its essential feature is that it has to do with what is, we can say that the function of understanding being surely appertains to it. Understanding the genesis of the experience of the existent would then mean inquiring into the function of understanding being. This, however, cannot be accomplished by the usual psychological method that can guide us only to certain immanent realities which, in their meaning, refer back to the objective world. Whenever we accomplish psychological reflection, we move within a certain limited domain of the existent, and so cannot trace the origin of the function of being as such. If such a task is to have any hope of success, we must resort to a deeper subjectivity, one that is not existent in the common sense of the word, one that is not a being among beings but rather constitutes in itself the universe of being in a lawful manner, each stage of this process lawfully presupposing the others. It thus becomes clear that we must distinguish two subjectivities, one creative, the other created (roughly speaking), and only regarding the latter will it be possible to say unequivocally with Descartes: *cogito-sum.*

We claim that such a methodical procedure is possible and that on its basis it becomes clear that the transcendental, i.e., preexistent subjectivity *is* the world. The task of philosophy is the reflective apprehension of this process. From that which is given us beforehand as human beings in the world we must proceed to the structures of transcendental subjectivity in which reality is formed. This, however, presupposes the apprehension and fixation of the structures of givenness itself. And that raises the task of describing the given world in the essential structures of all its regions. At the same time, it implies a certain privilege of the naive universe over the universe created in theoretical activities, and the naive universe is thereby legitimated to a large extent. However, the world, as universe, is no longer for us a dead object. Rather, it is a meaning created in an eternally flowing activity whose main modalities will be the theme of our analyses, feeling their way toward the center; thus we can no longer see being as a *fatum* but rather as a law drawn from our innermost core, as a creation which offers a certain space of freedom also to upsurges of new creativity. This, we believe, is what makes it possible to legitimize as well the scientific universe with its reconstructive tendencies; in any case, the universe of science should be explained on the basis of the common-sense universe and not vice versa.

Guided by this understanding, we shall have to break the deep-rooted thought habits and intellectual clichés that so often lead us to gloss over fundamental questions of the analysis of experience with excessively simplified formulas. Sensualism, the doctrine of the atomistically objective character of sense-data, the nominalist theory of abstraction, and the positivist notion of thought as purely reflective, noncreative (a notion which brings with it the conception of language as a "logical picture of the world") should be considered as clichés of this kind. Our attempt has thus both a positive and a negative side: a positive theory of the existent in its essential historicity, it is also, in a negative respect, a critique of the positivist conception of the world, which seems to us to make excessive use of such clichés handed down through history.

On the other hand, if we reject positivism as a philosophy building naively and uncritically on the results and the methodical assumptions of science, we cannot but criticize in the same way any attempt at absolutizing prescientific being. The most radical and thorough such attempt today is doubtless to be seen in the metaphysical and gnoseological theories of N. O. Lossky, his doctrine of intuition, the transsubjectivity of sense-qualities[30] and ideal being, etc. Here, the problem of the apprehension of the naive world is too quickly dismissed, and the problem of its understanding is not even posited; the naive attitude to the world is not taken as a *theme* for philosophical scrutiny but rather *presupposed* straightaway, and not systematically enough analyzed, in constructing a picture of the world. The philosophizing I has taken the a priori given of the naive world as an ontological norm and ground. We regard also this kind of ontologism—which, moreover, cannot ever raise the ontological question, since it has been answered in advance—as philosophically dangerous.

Should the philosophical program outlined here seem excessively poor, we believe our reflection warrants our holding things themselves to blame. The end result of our analyses is the thesis that metaphysics is possible only as a conscious reliving of the whole of reality; in our human situation, we can carry out this enormous task only in a region that may not even include the whole of human history. Indeed, when can we be certain to have truly understood extrahuman life? Yet the task we set ourselves is in itself endless, and it will never be converted to definitive formulas, since the activity of creative life will go on in us forever. The present work too is merely the first step in a program that is not proposed for the short term. It seeks but to present an orientation in the ideal prehistory of theoretical thought, without entering its realm as such. Between these two considerations there lies, as middle term, the consideration of human history, the philosophy of history, which will have to be made the foundation of a consideration regarding the development and creation of theoretical consciousness. Only once we are able to provide an outline of the history of theorizing shall a full-fledged and concrete demonstration of the primacy of the naive world over the world of science be possible; at present, we must be content with an analysis of what we hold to be the first stage of theoretical consciousness, i.e., language.

2

The Question of the Essence of Subjectivity and Its Methodical Exploitation

1. Descartes's *Cogito Cogitans* and *Cogito Cogitatum*

Against the objectivism that culminates in modern positivism, we have set a philosophical anamnesis of subjectivity. Our task now is to concretize and determine, on the one hand by adumbration with regard to other conceptions of subjectivity, on the other hand by applying an analytical procedure, what we understand by subjectivity and what method is appropriate for research in this field.

We have distinguished above two *cogitos*: for one the proposition *cogito-sum* is valid, for the other it is not. Descartes ignores the problem of this duality, for him *cogito* and *esse* are *essentially* correlative; the dependence of the two ideas is such that wherever there is *cogito* there must be *esse* (but not vice versa). Descartes thus *objectifies* the experience of the *cogito*, presenting it as a relationship between innate ideas; the truth of the proposition *cogito ergo sum* is guaranteed by the clear and distinct *perception of the relationship between the ideas* of one's own thought, certainty, and existence. Descartes's theory of the *absoluta* or *simplices*[1] finds immediate application in his theory of self-consciousness: among the *simplices* given in "intuition" (i.e., *mentis purae et attentae non dubius conceptus*)[2] Descartes mentions side by side: I exist, I am thinking, a triangle has three sides, a sphere is bounded by a single surface, etc. Descartes's methodical mathematicism is thus responsible for his passing over the actual problem of self-consciousness. Nonetheless, the *cogito* has an exceptional priority over all other ideas: it is the first idea, implying existence, it is, so to say, a generator of certainty about what is. So Descartes, too, differentiates two *cogitos* (in a different way from us, though the two ways are related). The first *certainty* is not *quicquid cogitat, est* but rather *cogito, ergo sum*. The *cogito* as an idea must be distinguished from the *cogito* as a living certainty. As long as we remain in the purely mathematical order, we attain neither being nor absolute certainty—not even by the thought *quicquid cogitat, est.* Only the *cogito-sum* is totally guaranteed against the possibility of total lack of freedom for truth suggested by the idea of a *Deus malignus*. Thus, though there are more originary *simplicia* in the logical-mathematical order, the *cogito* is first in the order of certainty.[3] Descartes himself distinguishes the *cogito cogitans*, *source* of all certainty, from the *cogito cogitatum*, which is an *objectified result* of the former. It is the *cogito cogitans* that contains the guarantee of its objects, so to say the source of living water from which they draw their life; and in the *cogito, ergo sum*, this life-giving consists evidently in the identity of the *cogito cogitans* with the *cogito cogitatum*. Whenever I reflect on my own activity, I can convince myself of my identical existence. The *cogito cogitans* turns here toward its own—past—activity. It alone can furnish a criterion of indubitable knowledge, yet what does the *cogito cogitans* mean in its unreflectedness? This question did not interest Descartes, it finds no answer in his work; in Descartes, the *cogito* remains unanalyzed.

2. Kant's I of Transcendental Apperception and Empirical I

With Kant, the problem of self-consciousness, broached in a novel manner, acquires fundamental philosophical dignity. As the Kantian doctrine of self-consciousness has been interpreted in a number of very different ways, we must, before assessing it, first attempt to expound it.

The doctrine of self-consciousness is, so to say, the keystone of the *Critique of Pure Reason*. It cannot therefore be presented without setting forth the main fundamental concepts of the critique. Kant's critique rests basically on two theses: (1) reality, as our empirical reality, must be interpreted on the basis of the *form of reality*, which has its roots in subjectivity, and (2) our subjectivity is a limited, finite subjectivity, which is dependent on *givenness* in its apprehension of what is.

The problem of reality is, in Kant's eyes, the problem of the possibility of knowledge of reality. The formal condition of all knowledge is consciousness.[4] Kant's understanding of consciousness is, to use a modern term, intentional. It is, so to say, my representation of my having a representation.[5] The reflection on the forms of knowledge is at the same time a reflection on the form of consciousness, since the distinction between different cognitive forms is grounded in consciousness.[6] Kant seeks to determine the form of knowledge by means of two pairs of concepts: (1) intuitiveness/nonintuitiveness, and (2) receptivity/spontaneity. By means of these two pairs one can define two basic "faculties" or "abilities" (*Vermögen*) of the soul: sensibility, which is intuitive and receptive, and understanding, which is nonintuitive and spontaneous.[7] Kant calls the difference between intuitiveness and nonintuitiveness "logical," the difference between receptivity and spontaneity "metaphysical." The "faculty" itself, though neither a concept drawn directly from inner intuition, nor the result of an elementary analysis of acts, is nonetheless a concept grounded in experience, originating in a reflection on the specific difference of acts. The concepts of receptivity and spontaneity should, therefore, also be interpreted out of the inner world of lived-experiencing: receptivity as passivity, spontaneity as activity. This is suggested, on the one hand, by the very terms "receptivity" and "spontaneity," on the other hand, by the manner in which Kant relates receptivity to affection. Receptivity is affectability by something that does not exist in experience otherwise than phenomenally.[8] This affectability, which is thus totally dependent on our being affected and, consequently, the direct opposite of creation, or production, is sensibility.[9] Causal action on receptivity gives rise to sensation (*Empfindung*). Together with consciousness, sensation gives perception.[10] The intuition that approaches the object through perception is empirical intuition.[11] In addition to the sensation itself, receptivity involves formal a priori elements, which, even coming from the subject, do not however give it an active character, as they are simply forms of *reception*, not of *activity*. Sensibility is, as it were, experienced as a pure potentiality that becomes actuality only through action from without. The mind is finite above all in its sensibility: precisely as finite, it is passive. Sensibility is of two kinds: external and internal. Internal sensibility is receptivity with regard to one's own spontaneity.[12]

Spontaneity—or, in psychological terms, activity—is comprehensible only in correlation with receptivity. Its essence is synthesis.[13] Synthesis consists in bringing together a manifold of representations in the unity of a cognition.[14] Synthesis is the work of a peculiar faculty that we have not mentioned so far, one that mediates, so to say, between sensibility and understanding, being always related to intuition,[15] and yet spontaneous. This faculty is the transcendental imagination. It must be emphasized that the relationship of imagination to sensibility and understanding is presented differently in the two editions of the *Critique*, apparently under the influence of newly brought up practical systematic considerations.[16] In the first edition, imagination is presented as an independent faculty, while in the second Kant terms it a "function of the understanding." This question, among the deepest in the *Critique of Pure Reason*, can and need not find a solution here; it has to do with insight into the innermost core of subjectivity (as Kant's says, "noumenal" insight), an enterprise which Kant himself did not deem promising, though he did attempt it. Synthesis, accomplished with the consciousness of active spontaneity, is bound by the rules of understanding. The pure concept of understanding, or category, is nothing but the representation of a necessary synthetic unity.[17]

It is one and the same synthesis that applies in judgment and intuition; this then makes it possible to systematically ascertain individual categories. A category is a necessary a priori condition, rule, or law of experience,[18] concerning in other words the synthetic unity of a manifold given in sensibility.

Synthesis is possible only on the assumption of unity;[19] combination is meaningful only as bringing together into unity; unity must therefore accompany the representation of a manifold in order for the idea of a synthesis to arise. The synthesis is synthesis with regard to a unity. This unity, which can contain no manifoldness, is a precondition of all possible synthesis and, consequently, of all possible spontaneity. It is given in the "I think," the most fundamental of acts, the fact of *self-consciousness* as an immediate act of spontaneity.[20] This act of spontaneity is one and the same in all consciousness,[21] and as the ultimate precondition of synthesis it contains the origin of all a priori determinations of experience. The unity of self-consciousness is thus a condition imposed on all synthesis. The given manifold must belong to a unified consciousness if this condition is to be fulfilled. It is then fulfilled in that there are hard-and-fast rules according to which a given intuition becomes an *object for* a unified consciousness. An object is that in the concept of which the manifold of a given intuition is *united*.[22] Now, the act that gives rise to the synthetic unity of the object is judgment; and the function of the unity of judgment, i.e., the representation of the necessary synthetic unity of a given manifold of intuition, is a category; it follows that categories are rules of objectivity in the objective unity of transcendental apperception.

What follows from this for the fact of self-consciousness? Unlike the Cartesian conception, which takes self-consciousness (the *cogito*) as a pure fact, Kant emphasizes that self-consciousness *is not an experience.* Experience is intuition; immediate self-consciousness is not an intuition, though it does give rise to intuition inasmuch as we objectify ourselves (Kant speaks of the effect of thought on the inner sense). My production is not only an act of spontaneity, which takes place regardless of time; it is also a temporal process whose stages I can intuit *ex post.* My consciousness, whether it be accompanied by pure fiction or by experiential data, is not itself an experience but rather a *transcendental consciousness.*[23] Transcendental consciousness is not subject to the condition of time, which all experience must obey; it is not subject to the conditions of experience, as it is itself the condition on which rests all use of understanding, logic, transcendental philosophy, even understanding itself.[24] Of course, if transcendental consciousness is not experience, neither can it be knowledge:

no object can be given in it. As a precondition of all synthesis, the I is a pure unity, prior to all object functions; consequently, it is also no concept that could have objective meaning.[25] As a unity, the pure I cannot be apprehended; every reflection apprehends it already in a temporal manifold, as an object of experience. Self-objectification is bound to the synthetic unity of the manifold in the pure dimension of time. For Kant, there is thus a twofold I: the I subject of apperception, and the I object of apperception, phenomenon of the inner sense, subject—like outside objects—to the rule of synthetic unity and, consequently, of objective existence, already given by the condition of the form of time, the successiveness of intuition. The I of apperception is not a phenomenon; it is the act of determining my own existence,[26] an act which, in its spontaneity, is, however, subject to the condition of sensibility.[27]

In answer to the obvious, unjustified objection that this conception makes for a double personality, Kant asserts that only the I who thinks and intuits is a person, whereas the I of the object that is intuited by me is, like objects outside me (in space), a thing.[28] The continuous production of the first I is, as it were, received, preserved in time; we do not have absolute freedom with respect to ourselves, and just as the objectified I is possible solely for the objectifying one, the objectifying I is impossible without the objectified one. Kant also calls the former the logical and the latter the psychological I.[29]

Let us once again sum up Kant's theses on subjectivity. According to Kant, the pure I of apperception is not a given reality but rather the condition of possibility of all reality, including empirical consciousness. On the other hand, one cannot say that the pure I falls out of the order of *all* reality; this is contrary to the statement that the logical I is also a *person*. We can call a person the reality that has in it the conditions of the possible apprehension of reality. Self-consciousness, the representation of the "I," can thus be at once a logical presupposition, on which all human understanding depends, and a feeling of reality: for Kant, the *cogito* and the *sum* are equivalent.[30] The person is a nonobjectifiable reality, totally different, in its essential structure, from all objective existence.[31]

Now, what is Kant's method? It consists in pointing out that for every *objective* existence there must be a rule of synthetic unity, which normatizes the course of the experience of it as a unified object. However, the apperception itself is a perfectly simple *cogito* and, as an act of spontaneity, it is not an experience; this means that there is a reality that must always be presupposed if objectivity is to be possible, that is, the reality of the person, or self. Selves are the fundamental layer of existence, beyond which philosophical explanation cannot proceed, as it runs up here against the limits of the ultimate conditions of thought in general.

So Kant is the first to found philosophy in a truly radical manner on the *cogito-sum*. The *cogito* at the basis of his philosophy is, however, a finite *cogito*: it is dependent on a givenness which it forms but does not create, and it can never look *beyond* its own givenness, as existent apperception is already presupposed in all understanding.

3. Fichte's Creative I and Finite I

The foregoing makes possible yet another question. The I does not exist as a thing among things but rather nonobjectifiably, as a pure act of self-determination. Now, what mode of "existence" is that? The I, taken in its meaning of person, is not subject to the precondition of time, it does not go by in time, though *its acts* have temporal extension. Except for the I, everything real is subject to the condition of time: our consciousness is thus a continual confrontation of the temporal with the atemporal, the latter, so to say, continually measuring the former by its own standard. But how is this measuring itself possible? Solely because in consciousness, i.e., in the I, the difference between manifold and unity clashes (and thus is present). And if this ultimate difference, presupposed by the facticity of self-consciousness, is, it too, a difference *in consciousness*, must not consciousness itself account for the difference? If this is so, one must make yet another distinction within the nonobjectified I itself, the I person in Kant's sense. Though the personal I is not an object in the sense of temporality, it is an object inasmuch as it presupposes something subjective preceding it. That wherein the personal I occurs is already a synthesis, the distinction between subject and object and their mutual correlation discussed in the "Transcendental Deduction." We can say that the personal I *feels*, as it were, in *itself* a totally unconditioned activity, which is at the basis of the distinction between subject and object, yet it remains distinct from this activity. In addition, though the personal I is in Kant the basis, the grounds of all objective reality, it is itself subject to the laws of formal logic; it is a priori clear that the nonintratemporal I must be identical by virtue of the law "A = A." Yet where lies the origin of this law itself, if not, once again, in consciousness?

Considerations of this kind induced Fichte to go on from the personal I as a *fact* to the origin and grounds of this personal I as well. This can be seen above all in his review of Schulze's *Aenesidemus*.[32] What the *Aenesidemus* denounced as an intrinsic deficiency of critical philosophy— the inability of critical philosophy to explain the genesis of synthesis as such or to vindicate logical laws—seeking thereby to prove it unreliable,

Fichte understood as positive *tasks* of critical philosophy.[33] It is thus the task of critical philosophy to overcome *all* the assumptions that are accepted as valid the moment we begin to theorize, i.e., from the very beginning of their subjective genesis. These assumptions include the logical laws and the I of apperception, living in the consciousness of spontaneous synthesis yet always already presupposing the given manifold of intuition. Philosophy must justify these assumptions if it is not to be founded on mere transcendental experience, i.e., an empirical givenness of a sort which precedes all experience yet for which is still available at least an empty possibility of being-different, as suggested in Kant when he speaks of the intuiting intellect as a logical possibility of which we have, however, no concrete understanding,[34] or yet again of the impossibility to give further reason for our mode of understanding by means of categories on the basis of the synthetic unity of apperception and the forms of intuition.[35] If, however, philosophy is not to be founded on brute experience, then its starting point should be no fact, nothing observable, ascertainable as given beforehand, prior to all philosophy. In accordance with this, philosophy must be founded on something unobservable, something brought to light by the act of philosophizing itself. Only in this manner can reality be radically founded; and what founds, in Fichte, all objective, objectifiable as well as nonobjectifiable reality, is the original *Act* (*Tathandlung*).[36] Fichte's theory of the supraexperiential Act, which does not and cannot even appear among the empirical data of our consciousness, but rather founds all consciousness and alone makes it possible,[37] then becomes, by virtue of its complete absence of prejudice, a general theory of consciousness and knowledge. Precisely this is expressed by the name Fichte gives his theory: *Wissenschaftslehre.*

Fichte thus posits the necessity of distinguishing between a *cogito cogitans factum* and a *cogito cogitans faciens*; yet this distinction is not to be understood as meaning that the *cogito factum* has nothing in common with the *cogito faciens* and is passive *with regard to it*; on the contrary, there is partial identity between the two, the *cogito factum is* the *cogito faciens* in its independently created finitizing, and since the *cogito faciens* is free, absolute creativity, the *cogito factum* too is freedom in its original limitation, bearing the mark of its own inwardness. Fichte thus reaches a standpoint where the *cogito* transcends the *esse*, insofar as the *esse* is taken in the sense of finite being—and all beings in the world are finite. If Kant's philosophy is transcendental philosophy from the standpoint of finitude, explaining the world out of the world-form,[38] in Fichte a radical transcending of all worldliness breaks through and philosophy becomes an absolute transcendental genesis.

Experience lies before us, so to say, as a finished product whose origin is hidden to us who live naively within it; transcendental philosophy sets itself the task of grasping this origin. The genesis of experience is not itself an experience, nor is that which transcendental philosophy brings to light a reality. Rather, it is the form of reality: all that must be produced in our consciousness in order for us to be able to apprehend any single thing as real. Philosophy thus writes, as it were, the transcendental history of reality.

What is the *method* employed by Fichte in his transcendental genesis? Since the matter in question is the history of consciousness, the starting point must be some concrete fact of consciousness, a fact that represents consciousness in its essential function. In this much, then, the method is based on *empirical reflection*; yet already at this stage the philosopher must be guided by a *divinatory feeling for the essential*, which shows him the way toward the needed foundation.[39] The point the philosopher seeks to attain is the foundation of the universal unity of knowledge. This aim presupposes some sort of *preknowledge*, made explicit in the course of the work as such. This work is an *abstraction* that eliminates from an originally empirical fact of consciousness, such as a judgment, all disregardable determinations, until there remains only that without which it cannot be thought. If the fact of empirical consciousness is a judgment of identity, abstraction proceeds as follows: identification is possible only insofar as there exists something identical, identity is possible only in the I, the I is possible only insofar as something existing can say of itself "I am." Fichte comes thus to the ultimate being which is because it is, and is what it is—it is both the origin and the content of its own being—i.e., the original Act.[40] The I is thought here with no limitation, without the slightest shade of objectivity, not in a concretion of experience, no matter whether or not we realize that the I cannot be thought absolutely, without at the same time thinking something that it is not.[41] Fichte repeats the same procedure for his second principle, meant to reveal a second fundamental act, a thesis no longer absolutely but merely formally unconditioned. Already here, embryonically, between these two reflectively abstractive acts, there is again an underlying divinatory guideline (the matter/form relation); what is sought for is that which lies at the basis of the fact of difference, or differentiation, as expressed in negative judgment, be it with a positive result; and the foundation lies again in an original Act of op-positing, or counter-positing, whereby the I creates something like a counterpart to itself whereby it defines the region of possible objectivity. The I posits a counterpart that does not belong to the I; the I, which is essentially *self*-positing, posits *the other*, the not-I, and here the philosopher comes to yet a third—for Fichte, the most important—Act of the method, i.e., the *uncovering* and *recovery* (healing) of *contradiction*. The contradiction now uncovered within the I is that the I has discovered itself as a nonself-positing self-positing. In order for the positing of the I to be in agreement with itself, in order for the I not to self-destruct through its own positing, the two must be reconciled, and the reconciliation presents itself as the mutual limitation and demarcation of the I and the not-I. The "divisible I" (*das teilbare Ich*)—i.e., an I that is no longer purely simple but rather activity and passivity at once, Kant's I of apperception—first arises only through this demarcation. Whereas the thesis has brought with it the principle of identity and the category of reality, the antithesis the principle of opposition and the category of negation, what emerges now, in the synthesis, is the principle of reason and the category of limitation, bounding, or determination, and this, for Fichte, is the category of quantity; in quantity, reality and negation counterbalance each other.[42] The subsequent steps of the method consist in finding once more, reflectively, in this fundamental synthesis, opposite notions, the synthesis of which—synthesis in Fichte (as we have seen in the first, most fundamental synthesis of the I and the not-I) is always a manner of reciprocal delimitation of competences—then produces in turn all the remaining categories. Fichte regards the categories as syntheses already presupposed in every opposition (since differentiation must always be identical in something, e.g., A and not-A in their contradictoriness). The category is not a product of reflection, but something discovered thereby;[43] consciousness finds categories within it in reflecting on the form of knowledge, and *dialectic* provides the guideline for their systematic order, while at the same time showing that they are acts, and acts of the I.[44] Fichte's transcendental method is thus a reflection which takes into account the synthetic, creative process of the mind.

4. Absolute Subjectivity and the Dialectical Method

Fichte's step beyond Kant finds its expression in the idea of a doctrine of knowledge (*Wissenschaftslehre*) proposing to investigate systematically the production of the form of reality in transcendental reflection. Let us now consider this idea. The doctrine of knowledge has essentially a twofold task: (1) to systematically discover all forms of experience, and (2) to make evident their mutual connection and interdependence. Since the primary form of experience is synthesis, it is understandable that the first step of Fichte's procedure is to reconstitute the original synthesis in the mutual opposition of the subject and the object; and since this constitution itself must take place in the subject, since, consequently, the not-I must be posited by the subject in the subject without ceasing to be not-I, this stage of the philosophical procedure will necessarily be dialectical.

The dialectic here is a *coincidentia oppositorum*, concerning the primary opposites, subject and object, and it brings insurmountable unrest and discord into the positing subject as such. Here, however, we must ask whether the dialectical procedure employed by Fichte (and his great successors) is indeed able to deliver what it promises, i.e., the ultimate philosophical clarification, whether themes unrelated to the ultimate philosophical problem do not come into play in it. The dialectical method can present a complete elucidation of the philosophical problem on the assumption that its procedure elucidates all syntheses, that it is an explication of all that is comprehensible in general, including, hence, the comprehending of the comprehensible; as absolute synthetic method, it is a theory of the absolute synthesis of the subject and the object, a synthesis which is no longer mere unification but rather coincidence. The dialectic is an absolute whole in which the I apprehends itself in necessary stages, not through subjective reflection but rather through logical, constructive objectification; the method is that of self-apprehension by means of self-activity, and it must proceed until the product is one with the producing, i.e., consciousness in the form of absolute knowledge, parallel to the form of absolute creation from which the procedure starts. Fichte himself observed that such a universal synthetic method, guaranteeing the absolute unity of knowledge, is a postulate,[45] and he added that the idea of an absolute justification of all knowledge in one single system is not provable, as its proof presupposes the system meant to be proved within it,[46] so that in the end it can but call upon immediate certainties in our knowledge.[47] Since the dialectical method is however synthetic-progressive, it entails a risk of constructive violence in the interpretation of the given syntheses. Though there is no doubt that it is no vain fantasy, the dialectical method *as a method of interpretation* requires that the phenomena be handled delicately;[48] and given its universally circular nature, there is no way out. How then are we to be sure that we have indeed grasped the process whereby being becomes manifest in our experience, that the logical scheme of the method has been a real apprehension of the ontological process? We can say: the method is guaranteed insofar as it gives form to all. But does that really mean anything more than that speculation can be wholly subordinated to a constructive scheme? Is it truly the way reality becomes manifest for consciousness?—This objection can be countered above all from the viewpoint of subjective genesis (proper to all idealism): subjective genesis, the idea of which we have so far developed, is always genesis for a subject which is, in its purity, an absolute presupposition. This absolute presupposition is however, in itself, wholly undetermined, it is mere identity, mere indifference, or, as Hegel puts it, pure being.[49] In this ultimate being one can no longer differentiate, it contains nothing, and hence it is impossible to proceed by analysis. Reflection here can have no other form than that of absolute synthesis, and the only way to apprehend a synthetic procedure is by *determining* the primary thesis, by enlarging and putting together, by synthesis. The subjective grounding of philosophy and the analytical method would thus seem to be mutually exclusive; if the starting point is to be absolute, it must be completely indeterminate, maximally abstract, since every analysis presupposes a pregiven which it has no choice but to take as what it gives itself to be, so that analysis cannot go beyond this presupposition. Unless it transcends its presupposition, it cannot however stand outside experience in the proper sense of the word, it cannot be an elucidation of experience.

This objection would be valid without question if we had to admit that the I in the sense of pure self-identity is the ultimate source of subjectivity, its very essence. What led to the representation of the I as the source and essence of subjectivity? Several strong motifs come into play here, but none is philosophically viable. First and foremost, there is the Cartesian motif of the *certainty* of self-consciousness; yet, in itself, certainty is philosophically no more important than uncertainty; both necessarily go together in the rule of determining being which the subject sets itself for its experience. Special sciences, such as mathematics, need *indubitable* initial theses in order to make their deductions untroubled; but in philosophy it is inadmissible for the mathematical ideal to override all criticism. The self-thinking I cannot be made the starting point of all knowledge merely because it is the first certainty. This motif then plays an extraordinarily important role, in particular in Fichte: Fichte is in search of an absolutely certain proposition to which the whole doctrine of knowledge could be appended just as mathematics depends on its assumptions.[50] Instead of propositions about indubitability, Fichte is in search of an indubitable proposition. Yet what if philosophy does not lead toward certainties but rather into the midst of uncertainties? What if the *apprehension of the origin* of all our certainties entails more considerable difficulties than the naive *acquisition* of certainties? Who can answer these questions a priori?—Another motif is that the I itself is outside of time; it appears thus to be altogether superior to its empirical contents. And finally, there is Kant's recognition, based on a truly analytic cognition, that all lived-experience is such *for* the I, that the I is not simply a representation among others, but contains an act of spontaneity which makes a unity of the entire representational content: *my* unity. This last argument was actually already surmounted in Fichte's philosophizing, by reference to the simple fact that the I of apperception is finite, always in synthesis, in the unification of difference, and hence that it must be preceded by something that makes the synthesis as such possible. Both the I and its objects are given as realities in a unified experience; what, then, makes it possible for me to say that they *are*, and that they are distinct?

In the post-Fichtean period, Schelling can be cited as the thinker who felt it impossible to retain the pure I as the ultimate ground of subjectivity, as Fichte would have it, without pursuing the analysis. Whereas Fichte regards the first antithesis, leading to the finitizing of the I, as an absolute (as regards form) and, therefore, nondeducible act, which requires no further justification, Schelling seeks to justify even this primary opposition, deducing it as a condition of the possibility of self-consciousness. The demonstration that all knowledge must be derived from the I leaves unanswered, says Schelling, the question as to *how* all being (the objective world and history) is actually posited by the I;[51] and only the answer to this question can give transcendental philosophy full certainty. For this purpose, Schelling ventures beyond the limits of self-*consciousness*[52] and seeks to establish even more original concepts. If the I is, as in Fichte, absolute activity, then its activity as such, the absolute production which, in its absoluteness, infinity, and unlimitedness, does not fall within the province of experience, must be distinguished from an activity whereby it limits itself in order for consciousness, experience, objectivity in general to arise. The act of op-position, of self-limitation, of production of objectivity, is thus, for Schelling, a prerequisite of self-*consciousness* as such; the pure unlimited absolute I can never be conscious.[53] Yet to posit this infinite unconscious activity in itself would mean to be lost in nothingness; for the I *is* all that it is only *for* itself; hence, infinite activity can be proper to the I only on the condition that there is in it another "tendency," turned inwards, which makes the I conscious, but *eo ipso* finite. The infinite can "exist" only in limiting, in finitizing itself.[54] From infinite, unlimited activity, the I rises toward consciousness in which it sees itself as infinite becoming.[55] In other words, subjectivity for Schelling is infinite life which limits itself in ceaseless becoming, thereby refining itself to ultimate self-consciousness. For Schelling, the identical I *in its consciousness of identity* is no longer the ultimate ground of subjectivity, as it still was in Fichte. We are speaking here, of course, of Schelling's period of the system of transcendental idealism, characterized by youthful speculative fervor in discovering and exploiting new problematics, as against the formalistic rigidity of the system of identity.

5. "Absolute Skepticism": Schelling, Hegel, and the Phenomenological *Epochē*

Schelling's attempt to go beyond the I as the essence of subjectivity was not meant to be set against the constructive method but rather as a prerequisite for a more perfect synthetic construction. As far as we are concerned,

it points to the question whether subjectivity might not be grasped otherwise than in absolute abstraction, whether the absolute of subjectivity
requires absolute simplicity in the starting point. We shall therefore try
starting from a preliminary, anticipatory concept of a concrete absolute
which (in accordance with the requirements of the problem as we have
defined it) is absolute subjectivity, but in which we presuppose neither
downright absolute *totality* nor a *universal* law of its structure; our intention is to separate the whole problem of transcendental philosophy from
the problem of an absolute and total synthetic construction. In German
idealism, the transcendental procedure is a *logical* one: it is a search for
an inner connection of meanings, an attempt at a *hypothesis* that would
make possible an ever clearer and more exhaustive connection. We must
ask here whether the logical procedure does not conceal the nature of
absolute subjectivity and whether its uncovering should not rather be set
about in a way that not only has no logical guideline but makes a point
of paralyzing beforehand all logical guidelines. The paralysis of logical
guidelines is not meant here as a negation of logic, whether in the formal
or the dialectical sense, but rather as a mere abstaining, i.e., what Edmund Husserl calls the *epochē*. A logical guideline always already implies a
thesis of some sort, whereas the task of transcendental philosophy is precisely to discover the origin of all theses. Opening up the transcendental
field must, then, be an extralogical act, which cannot be put on a level
with other acts of cognition.

In searching for the concrete transcendental, we do well to call to
mind the indications that can be found scattered in Schelling and Hegel.
The transcendental philosopher—says Schelling—is intent on avoiding
above all the implication of any objectivity whatsoever in the sphere of the
subject, in the purely subjective principle of knowledge. The means he
employs for this is absolute skepticism, aimed not at artificial prejudices
but rather at those instilled in us by nature itself. The first of these is the
prejudice of absolute objectivity.[56] There is, states Schelling, a contradiction in that something in need of proof, insofar as it *makes claim to existence*, presents itself as immediately certain.[57] Hegel speaks in the same
sense of skepticism as an introduction to philosophy;[58] for Hegel it is,
however, a cheerless, dissatisfying path (*ein unerfreulicher Weg*). Now, what
if this is the one and only way that can give us what we need: the concrete
transcendental field without dialectical presuppositions?

How are we to understand this "absolute skepticism"? Schelling does
not mean that the positing of absolute objectivity should be annulled, its
thesis replaced by the negative thesis, but rather that it requires justification, or clarification. The thesis as such will undergo no modification, but
it must first be made clear. *This* is the end to which "skepticism" is to be
the means. Descartes, with his methodical doubt, was on the way toward a

similar purification of experience but went astray when his search for the unconditional became a search for the first certainties, his ontological skepticism an ontic one. Methodical "skepticism," then, does not consist in that we put a not-being or being-doubtful in place of being as it manifests itself in experience; rather, we suspend judgment about the existent, we cease to live in performing the theses of being and simply observe as a datum the whole content of our experience, those theses included.[59] As a datum, this flow of experience is not for us the object of a thesis; we do not posit it as existent; rather, we regard all theses as appertaining to its content. We thus acquire a field of pure experience independent of all intuitions and theoretical presuppositions, given in an adogmatic view. The aim of this reduction is the immediate flow of life, given apodictically, i.e., with no possibility of being-other; the means to this end is the absolute adogmatism into which the transcendental method transforms ontic skepticism. Of course, the fact that the philosophizing subject is placed in a field that admits no otherness, and hence no doubt, does not mean that apodictic certainty is the aim pursued unconditionally by our philosophizing or thought to be reached here once and for all. While the field is indeed given in apodicticity, the philosophizing has only just begun: transcendental philosophizing has its possibilities of deficient viewing and inadequate interpretation, no less than those regions of being given to the naive observer. The apodicticity of the transcendental field does not mean that statements concerning the transcendental cannot be mistaken; rather, it indicates the inner character, so to speak, of this region, its pure subjective givenness as against the being of the naive attitude, which is always the *object* of positive or negative *theses*. This trait must be quite explicitly stressed, considering the many and varied attempts made from various sides at explaining the process of reduction as meant to provide totally sure, apodictically certain cognitions about what is, e.g., about real inner, psychological lived-experience.[60] All that is acquired by the reductive process is the domain of flowing life, as yet unsubjected to the law of being. Transcendental life *does not exist*, since it is what is left over after the suspension of all natural ways of positing being; the reduction is the destruction of the *natural attitude* characterized by the thetic habitus. If we call "world" the universe of what exists as the object of a possible natural thesis, then we must admit that transcendental life does not appear in the world, that among existent things it is nowhere to be found.

The reduction must proceed universally if its meaning is not to be compromised. Not only logic, sciences, and practical knowledge undergo reduction but also and above all presuppositions concerning the subject. From the standpoint of natural experience, the subject is always bound to a body, dependent on the givenness of realities outside it, and hence finite; it is a person. One can ask however: How is it, then, in pure inner psychology, which takes no account of the objective insertion of consciousness in nature and considers it only in its immanent flow? Does this too not bring us to "pure givenness"? Here too we can say that whatever is given to me must be given to me in experience and, hence, that I grasp the origin of objectivity in pure immanent reflection. What, then, is the difference between transcendental consciousness and purely inner experience? Psychological experience has an important presupposition, which cannot be simply bypassed if reduction is to be grasped in its meaning, and which must be suspended. This presupposition is that it has to do with the states of something existent, standing among other existent beings; something that knows of other beings only from its own experience yet relates to them as to independent realities in which it believes. Empirical consciousness has its object always outside itself, even if its whole knowledge of this object comes from itself; only transcendental consciousness has its object in itself; pertains to it not only all that is subjectively given but also all that is given objectively, all that can be made conscious in any manner whatsoever, as made conscious. The empirical I is essentially transcendent, it always falls short of perfect immanence, even if the something lacking is totally vague and indeterminate, a mere problem. This holds both for its activity directed at objectivity and for its reflective activity. It is true that in reflection we do not directly practice the belief in external objects, since here we are turned to ourselves; yet external objectivity is presupposed by our own existence, toward which psychological reflection is turned. If the reflecting I does not believe explicitly, it believes implicitly, *en parergō*, and *the same* I that is turned toward the inner process can at any time turn to objective belief. It is also clear that, even for empirical reflection, all the contents of reality can ultimately come only from the subject, given that nothing can enter the flow of consciousness and remain entirely alien to it: objectivity, no less than the difference between what we call "subjective" and "objective," is something we know about always only from our own acts. Yet this whole argumentation does not make empirical consciousness (be it given in pure reflection) transcendental, the ultimate ground for all ontological determination; on the contrary, it intensifies the paradox of the situation of the empirical reflecting psychologist, who is *obliged* to presuppose something that he can never prove, despite all his insight into the immanence of psychical being. As against empirical reflection, transcendental reflection is characterized by the fact that the reflecting subject no longer lives in the act of belief proper to the reflected; in fact, his object encompasses the entire sphere of theses; the transcendental onlooker turns his attention not to empirical existence but rather to transcendental preexistence.

At least one more important remark, or so we trust, should be made about the reductive procedure in order to avoid possible misunderstandings. The reductive procedure applies, of course, to each and every particular thesis, but above all to the so to say general theses, which are already presupposed in singular judgments, and so on, e.g., the thesis that the world exists with its specific real structures. The reduction applies thus not only to propositions about what is but also to propositions about the structure of what is: not only to ontic but also to ontological propositions. Reduction should not be regarded, as is sometimes the case, as a method for acquiring a priori knowledge.[61] A priori knowledge, i.e., cognitions not directly dependent on singular experience, is itself of two sorts: ontic and ontological. The propositions of mathematics are a priori and ontic; propositions concerning the nature of mathematical objects (the propositions of a philosophy of mathematics) are a priori ontological (to give a simple *example* of this distinction). The a priori of both the first and the second kind must exist *before the reduction*, and consequently cannot first be acquired through reduction; the reduction applies to it as to something implied by the particular theses, whether the subject has already become explicitly aware of it or prior to any ontological turn. Yet is transcendental consciousness not similarly implied in our ontic theses? The only way to answer this question is to clarify the manner in which the ontological a priori is implied in our particular theses. In naively performing our theses, we do not believe in ontological truths as such, they are not thematic for us in these acts. They nonetheless govern our understanding of the singular. For example, whenever we expect a certain result, our theme is not the general ontological law of cause-effect relationship between things but rather this particular result, and yet the law is what governs our experience. We can say, then, that ontological lawfulness is not originally in our consciousness as its object, or theme, but rather as a law of its functioning. Can the same be said of transcendental consciousness? Evidently not. The ontological a priori is in us, originally, not as an act of belief but rather as a working rule of beliefs (theses). Transcendental consciousness, though it imposes no laws, contains them all, as well as the whole manifold of empirical givenness. Transcendental consciousness is neither a logical presupposition nor an ontological law that could be reached by logical or ontological reflection. Admittedly, from the ontological standpoint I do not investigate any *given* reality but rather the necessarily presupposed structure of reality *per se*; nonetheless, I do in fact presuppose implicit belief in *this* reality, and no ontological analysis goes so far as to call into question this presupposition itself. Ontology in itself cannot lead to the transcendental attitude. On the other hand, the ontological problematic—the question of the necessary presuppositions of our particular theses—does not require the reductive procedure.

Inasmuch as it is a theory of the inner structure of regions of existents, ontology does not then require the reductive procedure; the reduction is however a prerequisite for the more radical question concerning the nature of being itself. In order to raise such a question, we need a field where not only existing things and their structure, necessarily presupposed by our theses, but being itself, presupposed by both, can become thematic. Something can be existent only insofar as it fulfills the conditions of *being*; being however, as we well know, is no predicate attached to things as their determination, so that things could be thought without it, or it without things. Now, the reduction to pure consciousness has shown that givenness in itself is no being, nothing existent, but rather a pure *phenomenon of being*; and this phenomenon, because it is a phenomenon, i.e., something uncovered, manifest, is no less than the existent itself, but rather *contains it* as something that has a claim to recognition. If it can demonstrate its claim to being posited, we say: it *is*; being is demonstrability. In order to ask the question concerning the nature of being as demonstrability in a truly universal manner it is however necessary to thematize the demonstrability of all fundamental regions of what is, to bring demonstrability itself to light as a unitary phenomenon having a specific structure. It is necessary, in particular, to counter the potential objection that demonstrability is itself something "subjective," anthropologically dependent, and that in addition to the human mode of being with its evidential structures there is another possibility: a completely different, absolute being, with its own, totally incomprehensible (for us) demonstrability of what is. In that case, ontology—considered as the science of what makes beings exist, what makes it possible to say of existents that they are—would be a science beyond the philosopher's pale or, as Aristotle has it, *kai tēn toiautēn ē monos ē malist' an ekhoi ho theos.*[62] This mystical skepticism is, however, essentially contradictory, for if such a transcendental ontology is to have meaning, it can take it only from lived-experiencing, outside of which nothing exists for us. The question concerning the essence of being thus requires an apodictic field, independent of anthropological presuppositions; and, as shown above, the reductive procedure alone is able to furnish such a field. Ontology in this deep sense is a transcendental doctrine of the essence and forms of thetic consciousness in general.

The answer to the question concerning the essence of being should thus be sought in thetic consciousness, and thetic consciousness pertains to the phenomenon as its essential component. The ontological question in its radical sense can consequently be answered only by the science of the phenomenon as such, or phenomenology, which reaches its objects on the basis of the transcendental reduction, i.e., transcendental phenomenology. The ontological thesis of transcendental phenomenology, drawn from the idea of the reductive procedure and from experience in the apodictic field, states: being is the universal law of demonstrability, i.e., a law of the binding belief in objectivity, a law which encompasses all experience and holds for all consciousness of objectivity. The attainments of the reductive procedure are thus twofold: on the one hand, the sphere of transcendental experience, containing in it all and every concretion of our lived-experiencing, and on the other hand, the fundamental ontological general thesis which puts transcendental consciousness above all demonstrable being, as its place of origin.[63] The phenomenological reduction makes clear that what I held, in the natural, empirical attitude for existent things are, in the transcendental attitude, *appearances of the existent*; what appeared in the natural attitude to be originary, finished givenness in itself, the legitimacy of which was not questioned, is seen in the transcendental attitude as a crystallization in the lawful processes of verifying experience.

There is another objection that can be raised against reduction, and the discussion of which may help to further clarify its nature. The reduction is supposed to place us outside *what is*; yet, in fact, if there are no things and processes for the transcendental observer, there are theses, and thus, again, something existent, albeit of a different content. The transcendental reduction is supposed to place us outside the *thesis*; yet, in fact, transcendental viewing remains thetic, since it accepts transcendental life *as a given*.

This objection can be answered as follows. It is true that in phenomenologizing, in a way, we posit, judge, etc. However, the character of our positings is different here from that of positings in the sphere of the natural attitude. The naive belief of the natural attitude is receptive, it believes in objects as independent from our turning our attention to them. The "belief" of the phenomenological observer is not reception; rather, transcendental life first *arises* and *holds good for him* in his view. The same holds for natural and transcendental being. Natural being exists always *prior to* the grasping view of the finite subject, which merely *acknowledges* it. Transcendental being arises first through reduction; it is, in its "ontic" character, *dependent* on the transcendental subject, whereas in the natural attitude it is always the subject who is dependent on being.

The answer to this objection, suitable to provoke a clarification of the foregoing, can be further specified by adding that phenomenological analysis discovers all naturally thematic being as *being in the world*, having its determinate place among other existing objectivities. In this

sense, every being posited and inquired into in the naive natural attitude is a *finite* being. (What we have in view here are not, of course, the
problems traditionally understood under the conflict between finitism
and infinitism, and most often debated in connection with Kant's antinomies.) *The* "being" uncovered by the view of the phenomenological
observer in the process of phenomenological reduction is, however, not
a being in the world, nor therefore any finite being in the sense meant
here; rather, containing the world in it as a phenomenon, it is the level
of the transcendental origin of beings in the usual, finite sense.

6. The Method of Phenomenology: Guiding Clues, Constitution, Eidetic Intuition

The result of the radical purification of experience aiming at pure givenness is, as has been shown through reduction, pure consciousness. One
of the fundamental ideas of modern empiricism, the purification of experience, is radically followed through, in this idea of reduction coined
by Edmund Husserl, to its most far-reaching consequences, where it
meets up with the philosophical intentions of constructive rationalism.
The success of philosophy depends on its ability to combine the rational-
ist's intention of radicality and consistency with the empiricist's intention
of concreteness. The method of empiricism is essentially analytic, presupposing the fullness of givenness, which must be structured and ordered.
This is precisely how we proceed now that we have acquired the transcendental field. As stated above, the transcendental field appears as flowing
life, presenting itself with the character of apodicticity; its contents
include all and every object of our lived-experiencing, all and every
being, grasped, of course, as a phenomenon. This is all given in apodicticity, but not all in the same way. When I perceive a table, there comes into
play, on the one hand, an act of perception (act of attention, act of turning toward) and, on the other hand, certain sense-qualities, and finally
the intended as such, i.e., the actually given table in the mode of certainty.
It is clear now that the act and the sense-qualities are given in a completely different manner from the intended as such. The act and sense-
qualities belong to lived-experience, they are given as its direct components, something that does not exist outside of lived-experience. The
intended table, on the other hand, *exceeds* every actual lived-experience
and, as a matter of fact, is never contained in any one. The act and the
qualitative manifold are apodictically given. What about the table? How
is *it* given? By nothing other than the fact that it is part of the intrinsic

character of the act to be the consciousness of something, and first and foremost of something distinct from itself. This particular feature of conscious acts is called (following Brentano) "intentionality": the table is in consciousness not as a component, as a moment of consciousness, but rather intentionally, as a correlate without which the act would not be what it is. Perception is here perception of the table, but the table is neither the perception nor any part of it; what does belong to perception as component pieces are precisely the act and the qualitative impressions. The view of the phenomenological observer is first turned toward concrete activity, yet it is one of the characteristics of such activity to exceed itself, to have something like a meaning outside itself. In this lies the ontologically representative feature of consciousness that can be characterized as transcendence. In describing the transcendence of consciousness as "intentionality," we use the image of an outward direction, well suited to the act of attention, which moves so to speak out of the self to reach its object; this is not, however, meant as referring to a real process, where consciousness really intervenes in things or, on the contrary, things in consciousness. Manifestly, the causal explanation—which, as Schelling once put it, can explain that the subject is affected, but cannot make clear how the subject knows about this[64]—is of no help in elucidating transcendence; philosophy is still obliged to turn to consciousness itself for an explanation. The transcendence of consciousness is transcendence *for* and *through* consciousness, hence it avails little to interpret it as the consequence of a real objective distinction between the "subject" and the "object."[65] It should be grasped by purely descriptive analysis, not on the basis of ontic analogy. Ontic analogy, i.e., the explication of transcendence by means of relations between objective beings, either discards transcendence and blinds the analyst to it, or fails to perform the assigned task. The analogy used by *empiricism* is the causal relationship (understood as a "law"); consciousness is a set of causal effects (the functioning of the central nervous system); as we know, this viewpoint leads, on the one hand, to sensualism and, on the other hand, to the paradoxical result that the transcendence we started from is conjured away, since consciousness in this theory is a closed set of real (*reell*) elements. The analogy used by *intuitive realism* is the relation of container and contained: consciousness is (nonexplicitly) conceived as an extendable and transportable recipient; from this standpoint, which cannot, moreover, do without the support of the causal model, it is impossible to explain illusion and error.—The *content* of transcendence, that is, that which is given us by transcendence, such as it is given, must be distinguished from its *essence*, that which makes possible the giving function of transcendence. It is part of the content of transcendence that the *object* is given as a *prius*, prior to the *consciousness of the object*, it is part of the essence of transcendence that it is for consciousness and through consciousness, and hence must be explained from the essence of consciousness. Transcendence lies in the fact that, *through reell*-ly, purely actually existent givenness, something is present to me that is not identical with this actually existent givenness. That toward which acts of consciousness transcend is to their own processes as unity to the manifold, and this relationship is not contingent but necessary. Consciousness does not transcend arbitrarily, but lawfully, and its transcending is essentially synthetic. A very special sort of problems, of a higher order, are raised here by the consciousness of the transcendental observer, which is at once itself synthetic and consciousness of ontic syntheses; it is both transcendentally synthetic and transcendentally thetic. The transcendence of the transcendental observer cannot be considered together with transcendence of another sort; it is not a transcendence that proceeds from consciousness to an existent object, it is not a transcendence in the world but a transcendence within transcendental consciousness, a transcendence toward being in totality, a transcendence beyond the world. Transcendence—and intentionality—is not an unequivocal term that means the same thing for thetic consciousness and for the transcendental observer; on the contrary, their unity is purely analogical. We shall concern ourselves here with the transcendence of thetic consciousness, i.e., of all consciousness except that of the transcendental observer. Thetic or doxic consciousness is possible only by virtue of the positing of a "reality"; this is analytically inherent in its essence. Thetic consciousness has essentially being as its correlate. However, this "correlation" should not be understood as a relation between two existent things,[66] since the *entire* process of relating takes place *within* consciousness. Since doxic life has, however, certain rules which govern, as stated above, the showing of the existent, the entire course of experience is governed by laws, and the laws of doxic life are rules of transcendence. The task of transcendental phenomenology is then to describe the course of the whole of doxic life, to find its laws in correlation with the given objectivities, in other words, to find the laws of the synthetic constitution of objects (existents) correlatively to the sequences of doxic experience. If this task is conceived universally, as a descriptive analysis of both real and possible lived-experiencing of all possible objectivities and as the grasping of the lawful forms of such experience, we shall also have fulfilled philosophy's task of providing elucidation of the world as a whole while, at the same time, representing a theory of knowledge in the Fichtean sense of the word, for the philosophical elucidation of the world calls above all for the exploration of all possible forms of the course of doxic life. The investigation of the lawful result of the correlation between the appearing object and the various classes of lived-experience is called an investigation of the *constitution* of the object or objectity (type of objects) in consciousness;[67] transcendental problems are problems of constitution.[68] If the immediate lived-experience, with its qualitative (hyletic) data and intentional, opining, doxic moments, is designated as the "noesis," the object of lived-experiencing as the "noema," the problem of constitution can be characterized as a matter of elucidating the noetic-noematic structures.

In speaking of constitutive laws, we have anticipated the idea of transcendental phenomenology so as to better penetrate its *method*. Let us attempt to characterize this method in more detail and, at the same time, to dissipate possible misunderstandings. What is given in reduction is, we have said, flowing life; this the observer must grasp in its full givenness, bringing to it no principles of judgment, but merely noting its course. As it has no presuppositions of judgment or discourse, the phenomenological method can be nothing other than reflective intuition. But does not reflective intuition in its purity come up against the frequently raised objections we have seen, for example, in Kant: that subjective activity, apprehended in reflection, is no longer an activity *in statu nascendi*, and hence has become *something else* than it originally was in its performing? Does not reflection alter the nature of psychical life?—But what can possibly warrant this objection if not a *knowing* of the difference between the immediate act of consciousness and consciousness in the state of reflection? And what does the difference consist in for our immediate consciousness? A priori, one of two things could be expected: the alteration concerns either the qualitative contents of activity or its mode of givenness. If the alteration undergone by activity in passing from its immediate performance to the field of vision of reflection were qualitative, we could not be conscious of an *identity* between an activity in the mode of performance and the same activity in the mode of objectification; even immediate recollection of lived-experiencing, for example, would be impossible. Yet recollection is a fact, and so is the consciousness of the identity between experiencing and what is experienced; the difference must therefore be of a nature other than qualitative. It is simply a difference as between actual and nonactual performance, and as between an act that is or is not thematic.—As we have presented it here, the refutation of the objection applies to empirical reflection; even for it, the objection does not hold. All the less so for transcendental reflection. The transcendental observer as *I* has the particularity that he is *not* performer of the acts that become an object of his reflection, whereas the empirical I lives (or can live) alternately in direct performance and in a reflection on itself, on *its own* experiences. The empirical I is never *purely* reflective, as is the I of the transcendental onlooker. With respect to this state of affairs, Husserl speaks of a splitting of the I that comes with the phenomenological reduction.[69]

The method of phenomenology is thus primarily a descriptive analysis of what is found in the reflective intuition of the transcendental onlooker, whose purely intuitive activity does not interfere with the effectuation of the act of belief in the world, the production of which is the work of transcendental life. Since, however, the method includes not only the means and the mode of cognition but also the end with regard to which cognition is accomplished (since the means must be adequate to the end), and since the end, as determined above by anticipation, is the cognition, the knowledge of constitution, the main question of the method is to acquire a guideline for the knowledge of constitution. Given, moreover, that *constitution* has been determined as the constituting of a synthetic unity, the unity of *constituted* objectivity can serve as the sought-for guideline. This means that a certain type of objects of experience (whether external or internal), as presented to us by our naive experience, will be used as the Ariadne's thread for discovering the noetic processes to which it is correlative; its unity must let us see the lived-experiential manifold it governs as a unifying pole. This point of the method, the discovery of guiding clues in the types of constituted objects, is the second essential part of its procedure, clearly attesting to its analytical character. Unlike the method of German idealism, which, since the subjectivity it *starts* from is an abstract *cogito*, a mere abstract I, proceeds necessarily in an exclusively synthetic manner, the method of guiding clues is doubly analytic. The object experience under consideration is descriptively broken down into its (nonessential as well as essential) moments, and operations of variation, which we will come back to later, are then carried out with all these moments. This entire descriptive analysis is, however, purely static, it takes both the object and the experience of it as they come, and inquires only after their structure. We can inquire thus, for example, after the specific structure of perception, recollection, valuing, etc., and receive as answers a *static* analysis of this sort. On the other hand, analysis can be taken beyond a mere structural consideration if we raise the question of how the different *concrete* formations of our experience, parallel to a certain region of objects, mutually presuppose each other, how this experience is *built*. From a static analysis we thus proceed to a transcendental-genetic, properly constitutive consideration.

The constitutive-genetic elucidation presupposes, as a rule, a twofold description: (1) the description of an objectivity given in experience, (2) the description of the experience, i.e., of all the lived-experiential modalities in which an objectivity of a certain type can be given. In addition to this descriptive task (which is naturally analytic), phenomenology also includes an ultimately explicative, i.e., constitutive component.

Unlike German idealism, constitutive analysis presupposes no other thesis concerning the essence of subjectivity than its graspability in reflection; it starts from no definitive conception of this essence, but rather aims its whole effort at the concretization of the concept of subjectivity and must always be prepared for corrections and more fitting approximations. Even where the constitutive process is described so to say historically, i.e., from the most elementary up through the highest strata, this synthetic procedure is, in fact, merely a method of exposition, not of investigation, which remains analytic. Only a divine philosopher, capable of overlooking the whole infinite richness of the constitutive processes, could proceed indifferently either analytically or synthetically in the constitutive problematic.

Another essential feature, regulating the *scope* of the methodic procedure, is the acquisition of a priori generalities. To attain a priori generalities on transcendental ground is analogous to attaining them on mundane ground. The acquisition of these generalities is not the work of mere abstraction in the sense of the doctrines of modern empiricism and Kantianism, where abstraction always means the division of a concrete represented totality and the separate consideration of its moments; rather, it presupposes an orientation toward the essence particularized in the facts we start from.[70] In this orientation, by running through a series of the possibilities of particularization admitted of by a given species or genus, we carry out the apprehension of the common ground in all the specializations considered, that to which their specific determinations are then added. *In concreto* this means that an example taken as representative of the intended generality is put through *variations*—modifications of its moments—which indicate to what extent we can still speak of *the same* and to what extent we pass into the sphere of another generality, the sphere (to use a different term, reminiscent of the Aristotelian tradition) of another *eidos*. This procedure of methodical variations on the basis of the thematization of the consciousness of generality that originally arises in us on its own is also often attacked in modern philosophy, though without going deep enough. The outward terminological coincidence with certain Platonic motifs, in particular, has more than once led to a wholesale rejection of the procedure which, roughly sketched in the *Logical Investigations*, was to be more fully elaborated later. The fact that the Husserlian operation of discerning an identical *eidos* is designated by the name of *ideation* or *eidetic intuition* (*Wesenschau, Wesenserschauung*) added to the confusion. That sounds rather like the Platonic *epistēmē*, direct viewing of "ideal being," elevated above any discursive *dianoia*, and since

Husserl himself advocated, in the first part of the *Logical Investigations*, a pure logic in the Bolzanian, i.e., Platonic-Leibnizian style, and spoke, in volume 2 of the same work, of the "ideales Sein der Spezies" (while of course protesting against any *realization* of the ideal), it was easy to take his doctrine of the cognition of ideality as identical with Plato's intuitionism (in modern interpretation!). As direct viewing, eidetic intuition would, of course, have the immediate certainty that is lacking in discursive procedures; but this postulate of an intellectual intuiting, coming after so many modern criticisms of the Platonic-Aristotelian *noēsis*, which played such a prominent part in the dogmatic philosophy of Scholasticism, is precisely what aroused suspicions concerning eidetic intuition, though few thought to ask whether the original indeed matched their interpretation.[71] In actual fact, eidetic "intuition" is itself a *discourse*, i.e., an intellectual *procedure*. According to Husserl's new investigations, three essential moments should be distinguished in ideation, three aspects of the process: (1) producing and running through the variations of an example, (2) their unitary linking by means of continuous partial overlapping, and (3) actively bringing out and identifying congruence and difference.[72] Of course, variations, e.g., of the pitch of a tone, can go on indefinitely; but essential or eidetic intuition does not require running through them *all*; it is sufficient to be conscious of the *direction* of the variation, consciousness which can be expressed as that of the "and so on"; we can then be certain that an individual of a certain *eidos* can in no actual occurrence fail to fulfill the conditions called for by the essential intuition. Felix Kaufmann puts clearly one of the main differences of this Husserlian theory of the cognition of generalities as against the traditional theory of abstraction in stating that the act of bringing out that which is general is not here an *elimination* of anything, but rather a way of *leaving open space for variation* ("kein Ausschalten, sondern ein Offenlassen");[73] the difference is not then to be found in the direction in which it is usually sought, it is not ontological but rather *descriptive*. One often forgets that the term "ideal being" in Husserl is meant not to solve but merely to signify a problem; the foregoing confirms that the being of his "ideal objects" and "ideal relations" is not to be conceived naively, as in Bolzano, as absolutely independent of the subject; rather, their *ontological meaning* implies that they can in principle be given only in the intellectual activity outlined above. The significance of eidetic cognition is evident from the fact that all our abstract general knowledge is essentially eidetic: Husserl has shown this to be so for logic and mathematics, others for other disciplines; and the neopositivist, nominalist theory of mathematics, operating with the concept of structure, cannot be considered a refutation of the eidetic essence of mathematical knowledge, since structure itself is an *eidos*.[74]

It is therefore fundamentally important for transcendental phenomenology to apply the method of ideation in its domain, in order to
be able to study the universal *laws* of constitution. That these laws cannot
be empirical is clear from the foregoing. That ideation is indeed possible
in the transcendental domain needs no demonstration; its possibility lies
in the fact that we are aware of a difference between recollection, perception, etc., and other mental acts, as well as of the identity of these
various acts through the course of time: simply, that there is a typicality
to lived-experiencing. And wherever there is a typicality, there can also
be thematization of typicality, i.e., eidetic intuition. In performing eidetic
intuition, the transcendental onlooker in fact performs yet another reduction, the reduction of transcendental facticity to transcendental eidetics; he performs abstinence not only from belief in the world but also
from factual givenness, which henceforth functions for him merely as an
example. What serves to indicate the course of transcendental life is no
longer a spontaneous creative flow, but rather the theoretical intention
of the transcendental onlooker. We pass from the sphere of transcendental empiricality to that of transcendental typicality.—In so doing, we
should keep in mind the essential differences between natural eidetics
and transcendental eidetics. Natural eidetic knowledge is a priori, i.e.,
aiming at the presuppositions of singular knowledge that must already
be at work in order for the singular knowledge to be achieved; it is, so to
say, the *recollection* of something already, though not explicitly, familiar to
us (*anamnēsis*). Transcendental consciousness, as it produces at the same
time what is a priori and what is a posteriori, has no longer any presuppositions; actually, there is no longer any difference here between a priori
and a posteriori in the mundane sense.[75]—In becoming no longer transcendentally empirical but transcendentally eidetic, phenomenology provides us with a doctrine of possible consciousness in general and, thereby,
with a doctrine of possible constitution in general; it is only with this step
that a perspective on a possible philosophical system opens up for phenomenology. Of course, the methodics of the philosophical problems
involved here is yet but nascent.

7. The Objection of Solipsism and Transcendental Intersubjectivity

Before closing our inquiry into subjectivity as the universal basis for philosophy and into the method to be employed in its domain, we shall now
consider an often raised objection against idealism of every hue, an objection that is claimed, if not to refute peremptorily, at least to relativize its

philosophical pretensions. It is the objection of solipsism. Idealism—so goes the objection—reduces being to the subject; if he is to be consistent, the idealist must restrict being to his own subject; not to do so would be to fall into the same contradiction he criticizes in realism, and postulate transcendence. As concerns specifically transcendental phenomenology, the critique would be as follows: transcendental phenomenology seeks to reduce the universe to constitutions of the transcendental ego; the sphere of reduced realities includes also the other subjects, whose experience presupposes the experience of real things; in transcendental phenomenology, the other subjects as well must therefore be reduced to constitutions of the individual transcendental subject.

It should be said first of all that even if the objection were valid, it would be no threat to transcendental phenomenology, since the theoretical system alongside which one can propose no other, fulfilling the same theoretical claims, would have to be considered unimpeachable even if it offends our most deeply rooted mental habits. In actual fact, however, the whole point of the objection is to indicate an important problem. All in all, the function of skepticism in philosophy is, as Fichte once said,[76] to reveal the shortcomings of philosophical argumentation to date and to raise new problems. The problem pointed out here can be put as follows: Is the other I merely a constitutive product of my own transcendental ego? If not, what is its status? Is transcendental experience exclusively my own experience of my own constitution?

But where are the limits of transcendental immanence?

Constitution takes place in time. Not in objective natural time, which is itself a product of constitution, but rather in a more original, internal consciousness of time. However, the fact that it is subject to time, i.e., to the law of succession, does not mean its total disappearance from the view of the transcendental onlooker. Without positing anything whatever as *being, existing in the world*, the transcendental onlooker lifts the life that produces belief in existents out of its initial anonymity and makes of it a transcendental "preexistence"; constitution is indeed not given to the originally constituting life, but solely to the transcendental onlooker. The onlooker's transcendental experience thus relates not only to actual but also to past constitution, encompassing in addition an anticipation of future constitution. Transcendental experience is not merely an experience of constituting but also of the fact that there has been and will be constitution, an experience of the constitution not actually performed by the productive flow. Part of this experience of constitution not actually performed by me, and yet *given*, is also the experience of the transcendental alter ego. The other I can be given only indirectly; it, too, is a kind of presentation,[77] whereby I "project" a lived-experiencing similar to my own into an animate body similar to my own. In the natural attitude, the presentiated other I's are as finite and limited as I am; in the transcendental attitude, the fact that my own subjectivity takes on the sense of constitution implies, however, the acquisition of a constitutive sense by the alter ego, the *other* I as well, though its constitution differs from my own. The reduction can thus be intersubjectively enlarged: it is part of the meaning of transcendental subjectivity as it appears to the transcendental observer, or monad, to constitute in parallel with other monads; constitution is co-constitution; subjectivity is thus, defined *in concreto*, a transcendental universe of monads that carry out constitution "harmonically," and *intersubjective* constitution alone then sets the rule of existence. Of course, this manner of surmounting solipsism is possible only where the process of phenomenological reduction has been accomplished, i.e., where questions of existence in the world are not at stake; the *real givenness* of the other for a particular individual remains subject to the rules of concordant constitution and is hence on the same level of presumptive certainty as any other object in the external world. On the other hand, intersubjective constitution means that a world *for me alone* would not be the real world of our experience.

We can now, summing up, state in what direction we see the essence of subjectivity and show how the standpoint of transcendental phenomenology allows us to apprehend in a unitary manner the concepts of I-ness developed, on the basis of historical material, in the introductory sections of this chapter.

The concrete concept of subjectivity reached so far by methodic analysis is the transcendental universe of monads that intermesh with one another and harmonically constitute both being and its a priori lawfulness. What is given in *immediate* transcendental experience is, however, not this universe but merely the phases of a single monadic flux of lived-experience. The monadic transcendental subjectivity has no existence properly speaking; it is not given to itself, nor is it the object of any ontic thesis; rather, it "exists" only for the transcendental onlooker who, on the basis of the process of reduction, lifts this productive subjectivity out of self-forgetfulness and transposes it into the mode of "preexistence" while developing, through ideation, the universal essence of possible constitution in general. Considering the productive character of its cognition and its typically extraexistential givenness, the I of the transcendental onlooker could be likened to Fichte's absolute I. Schelling's I, on the other hand, which Schelling proposes to conceive more concretely, would be comparable to the full constituting flow. The constituting flow produces belief in the world, yet it is not manifest to itself in this function, it loses sight of itself in acquiring the world. The concentration of the constituted around two poles, the objective and the subjective, comes about in the course of world-constitution. While there are many objective poles, the subjective pole is but one, constituted as receptor of the outside world and author of acts of comprehension. In this sense, it can be said to accompany necessarily all experience, and in this sense it can be likened to Kant's I of transcendental apperception. In its function as author of our acts, the I is nonobjectifiable; if we reflect on it, we have it no longer directly in this function, rather we objectify it. In psychological reflection, psychological activity can be explicated as to its qualitative filling, but in no case the I itself. Yet the pure I is not merely an identical pole; it is at the same time the substratum of our habitualities (convictions, attitudes, habits), and in this respect it can be determined as a *person.* Mere psychological reflection is not sufficient to determine the person without real, practical confirmation. The Cartesian *cogito,* as usually understood, is the activity apprehended in psychological reflection; diverse and sundry *cogitationis modi,* variously qualified mental states are discerned within it; eidetic abstraction leads then to psychological concepts, and analysis to propositions and laws concerning them. These concepts and laws are however no longer, or at least need not be, living experience, and they are on a level with other thought-objects; this is what makes the difference, noted by Descartes, between *quicquid cogitat, est* and *cogito, ergo sum.*

The passage through phenomenological reflection has thus made possible at least a cursory outline of continuity in various modern problematics of subjectivity, concluded here, after having reached with it, so to speak, the summit of the curve, by a look back at our starting point.

3

The Natural World

We have seen in chapter 1 that the conflict between the naive and the scientific world, revealed as one of the fundamental consequences of the modern philosophical method, can be solved in a way that fully respects the rights of the naive world and does not make it into a mere derivative aspect of true reality; it can be solved on the basis of idealist philosophy which conceives all reality in correlation with subjectivity. Objectivism, if it is to be something other than feckless fantasy, must perforce interpret the naive world from the scientific. Idealism itself, if it is to acquire internal force and consistency, cannot be content as empirical, but must assume the hubris of transcendental idealism. It is only in going beyond the concept of the empirical subject to transcendental consciousness that one can silence certain questions which, that not being the case, have always raised difficulties for idealistic tendencies in philosophy, and which show how inaccessible idealism is to both simple and philosophizing "common sense." These are questions regarding "how the subject approaches the object" and "how the subject comes out of its closure," questions echoing the entire prephilosophical manner of conceiving the explication of reality (according to the causal model), which only transcendental idealism can replace with a comprehension of a radically different orientation, one that we must first get used to, that requires us to rid ourselves of quite a few mental habits and opens the gate to metaphysics not as a doctrine of the transcendently existing in itself, but rather as a doctrine of being as such, i.e., a doctrine of constitution. At the same time, in chapter 2, we have seen that transcendental idealism is not a simple solution, proceeding from an established ground, from subjectivity presented or even intuited in some definitive way; rather, the meaning of the transcendental method can lie only in the discovery and elucidation of subjectivity itself; we have seen that subjectivity, be it the ultimate *explicans*, is far from being a simple given, but must first be disclosed and ever more deeply grasped in its achievements in the process of explication. It is an illusion to believe that the essence of subjectivity is always present, given, and known to us—an illusion nourished by the theological motif of an immortal, simple substance, by the mathematical motif of axiomatic certainty and simplicity, and by the psychological motif of the self-certainty of consciousness. And we have also seen, in thinkers who in more recent times have sought to take subjectivity as an established starting point and who have, as a result, come to adopt a constructive method in philosophy, how this concept itself tends to dissolve, leading to ever new distinctions and attempts to get at an ever deeper origin. We have characterized the philosophical discovery of the field of subjectivity in the transcendental, i.e., universal sense as *reduction*, the explication reductively made possible as constitution, and we have described the various stages of this explicative procedure. We now proceed to the work of concrete analysis on our problem. Our problem is man in his relation to the world. Such will be the theme of the following sketch, necessarily incomplete and tentative, as it points at every step to problems that have not as yet been elaborated. If we retain a synthetic procedure in the section dealing with constitutive problems, this is not in order to give our explication an appearance of system—system is nothing to be desired for a consistently phenomenological thinker—but merely to enhance the clarity of the written account. Our purpose is but to present some idea of the process of constitution; there are, we wish to make it clear directly, extremely important problems which are hardly broached here, e.g., the question of modalization (modes of certainty), closely connected with the ontological problem. Yet, as we are concerned for the moment, above all, with elucidating the manner in which man exists in and relates to his world—at what fundamental levels and in what acts of subjectivity this relationship is established—it would seem legitimate to place the accents with an eye to this aim.

1. The Situation of Man in the World

The theme we are to analyze is man in the world. The first thing to do is to define this object in a purely descriptive way, as an objective guideline. If we start from man as a fundamental term of the relation and take him objectively as part of nature, as a living creature in his manifold reactions, what belongs to him essentially, with no doubt whatsoever, is a corporeality which (as for all animals) is at his disposal and through which he is in continual interaction with the things of his environment. In the idea of embodiment we encounter one of the essential limits of the possible variation of our concept of man; I can lend him a fantastic corporeality, as has been done, in the way of a possible variation, by authors of fantasy, from Lucian to Swift and Wells; but I cannot think a human being without embodiment and bodily communication with the surrounding world. And there is still more to my consciousness of man. The body as something at our disposal is inherent in the essence of the animal in general; in our consciousness of man, however, this aspect is a mere component. It is a fundamental component of human *finitude*, since it is on the basis of his corporeality that man stands in causal interaction (broadly speaking, leaving aside philosophical theories) with the things of his environment that limit him. The things of the human environment are, however, not only causal agencies which limit man, they are also understood by man as independent causal agencies, i.e., as things; man is not merely a thing among other things, as can still be said of animals (except perhaps for the highest primates); man is above all *aware* of his situation, he *understands* his own finitude. Finitude grounded in interaction is a set situation, though its actual face keeps changing; man as man cannot step out of it. This constant situation can be further determined as a consciousness of our dependence on things and an interest in things. Things themselves are originally perceptibilities on the paths of our interests or of our acts guided by interests. Their being for us is not, however, exhausted by this function in our lives. They do not cease to exist, their function once performed, but remain in their independent being at the disposal both of our own and of others' repeated acts, as long as they are not eliminated through change or consumption. In addition, their being for us is not something hanging in the void: things refer to other and yet other connections, which can be connections of origin, of purpose, of mere contiguity, or of temporal succession. When I turn from one thing to another, what is is not lost for me—it does not become unavailable; on the contrary, there remains a fundamental connection within which all things find their place, and which "is there" even if I take no notice of it and explicate nothing from it. This connection, which is nothing determinate, no real thing, is nonetheless always present and operative in life: if not for it, we could have singular impressions, perceptions, thoughts, memories, but there would not be the so to say automatic linkage which binds them into a unified whole. If not for this unitary, unique whole, the phantasms of dreams, the representations of fantasy, and so on, would not be distinguishable from carefully observed realities, nor would we have the possibility of ordering and unifying the different phases of life. In short, we would not have that which makes us say that both we ourselves and other things are in the world: we would have individual things, but we would not have *the world*.

We are faced here with a peculiar fact. In our attempt at a descriptive analysis of the relation of man and world, we have started from one term of the relation and come to the conclusion that it can be characterized *proprio modo* only on the basis of the other: man is not only a finite being, part of the world, but also a being which *has the world*, which has knowledge of the world. On the other hand, the world we encounter here is not simply the totality of existing things but first of all something pertaining to the very essence of humanity, to the form of our existence among things: a function which makes it possible for us to have such a growing reality in our consciousness. This is the function which first allows us to possess a unitary reality, the universe of all that is. Does not this function, encompassing the possibility of the universe, deserve, then, to be called "the world" in the most original sense?

Man can now be characterized anew as a being having the world, a being who is at the same time bodily contained in the world and lives in contact, through his corporeality, with other objects of this world. He lives in the world primarily with other subjects, first of all with his fellow men and those closest to him. Man is not characterized solely by the above-mentioned features but also, especially, by his ability to understand other living beings as well and to be fully conscious of this understanding. This trait of conscious co-living with others has been traditionally emphasized as a distinguishing feature, essential for *humanitas*. Human life is not a life lived in and for itself; it is a living with others and with regard to them. At the same time the world of our actual lived-experiencing is common to us all, it is, if not the milieu of every activity of human life in particular, then a milieu actually accessible to various individuals to a varying extent and, in principle, intersubjectively, equally accessible to all. But here we must shift over to a more concrete analysis.

It is important to observe that the world, in this original sense of the term, announces itself in a whole series of concrete phenomena, that it is not an abstract unifying function, functioning in the same way in all cases and for all subjects. The unity of the original world is the unity of a style of experience, of a familiar "and so on" in the manifold of impressions, a style indicated by that with regard to which things are understood, i.e., by our interests; and since these interests are not purely individual, but rather take the form of the various communities we belong to, our world, as a concrete phenomenon, is the world of the life-community of which we are a part. The world of the townsman is different from that of the countryman, the world of the primitive different from that of the civilized, the world of the coastal dweller different from that of the inlander. Despite this basic changefulness of the world as a concrete phenomenon, it should be emphasized that it does not change in the same way as empirical objects; the world is relatively constant, and its changes cannot be *directly* observed like those of individual things. Changes in our world take place unthematically, without our conscious active participation; the eye of reflection alone is in a position to grasp and comprehend them in recollection. For that matter, the grasping of the changes of the world itself, which take place, for instance, in moving on from one age of life to the next, is a complex phenomenological problem, which re-poses, in a particularly difficult form, the whole complex of questions having to do with remembrance.

As concerns the now following description, let it be stressed once again that it is not to be viewed as if it were describing determinate, existing things in our environment, nor as a description of their essential thing-structure, but rather as a description of the specific phenomenon of *being-in-the-world* which, for common-sense reflection, is at first hopelessly concealed by individual things and the objective structure peculiar to them. One could almost say that the description of this essential "within" is a description of the *perspective* of the universe, if the notion of perspective were not suggestive of an excessive "subjectivity," a nonoriginarity of the phenomenon. Being-in-the-world is a perspective, but of a kind which first makes it possible for things to be what they are—a perspective, too, which extends beyond things and prior to them.

The structure of the world has also something else in common with perspective, inasmuch as it runs outward from a determinate center into indeterminate depth. It is part of the essence of our world to have as its central core the region with which we are most familiar, where we feel safe and there is no need for any discoveries, where every expectation has already been or can always be fulfilled in a typical way; we call this part of the world home. Home is not merely our individual home; it includes community as well, with a variety of typical structures based on the various and variously intermeshed interests of the social groups that partake in it: the narrow family home with its life-functions of everyday close contact and order, the broader home of looser social relations which one feels more or less tied to and understands on the basis of traditions and of one's own personal interests. This more broadly conceived home is then differentiated into the domains or worlds of various professional occupations in which everyone is also, in various ways, "at home," and out of which he looks upon the others; yet, in a sense, *all* these human occupations, whose function we become accustomed to within our community, belong to our broader home. The shading of the home-world, running from family to locality, community, region, nation, state, etc., recedes into the indeterminate in a mixture of known and unknown, near and far.

Yet home is not (as the analogy with perspective might wrongly suggest) a center determined by my momentary position. Home is not where I happen to be; on the contrary, I can myself be far from home; home is a refuge, a place where I belong more than anywhere else; it is impossible to experience more than one home at the same time with the same intensity. Home is the part of the universe which is the most pervaded with humanity; things are here, so to say, the organs of our life, they are *pragmata*, which we always know roughly what to do with, or at least what it is that others do with them, or *that* they do do something with them; within this comprehension, they are unsurprising and inconspicuous. Inconspicuousness is a specific feature of home, toward which it tends as toward its (albeit infrequently achieved) *telos*. At the very center of home, there is not *nature*, which makes itself known here merely as "that out of which" and "that in which" (phenomena such as night and day, the four seasons, etc., have their place here). Nature, in its proper and original sense as *phusis*, is thus not the universe of what is but rather a certain layer, a stratum, which is not central, and which allows for shading and gradations of various sorts: the nearest environment, a so to say homely nature, the nature of one's particular region, and so on . . .

The boundaries of the more remote home extend indefinitely and vanish in the undomesticated and the alien, in the distance. The distant and alien also admits of gradations and has its own specific modalities. In order to avoid the impression of a false opposition, it should, however, be stated straightaway that distance does not have a character of absolute unfamiliarity; rather, it is a specific mode of oriented comprehension, in contrast with home. The world is a whole from which no phenomenon escapes completely and which admits nowhere of radical incomprehensibility. The distant and alien (the two go together essentially) are such that surprise is possible at every step, objects and people behave or can at every step behave differently from what we are used to at home.

There are two principal modes of the alien-distant: the human and the extrahuman, and, within the extrahuman, the living and the lifeless. The human alien has to do, for instance, with the comprehension of an exotic community as human, although its relationships to the things of its environment and to its fellow men are incomprehensible to us: we cannot ourselves experience these relationships, and the type of action within the community is unfamiliar, its occupations and, consequently, its articulation of the objects of general use are not those we know; it can be that the overall relationship to life and reality is different, surprising, unexpected. This is how we stand toward exotic peoples, however high or low their cultural differentiation: we understand them only from without, intellectually; and yet this "incomprehensibility" is a contrastive kind of *comprehension*, an understanding capable of systematic organization without ceasing to be understanding of the *alien*. We may be able to feel with these people and live their life in certain very general respects, but never taken as a *whole*—unless we *alienate* or *estrange* ourselves from our own former way of life.—As a matter of fact, human strangeness as a *possible foil* is always somewhere on the outskirts of our home-world—e.g., the

strangeness of fantasy, the strangeness of fabled worlds, situated somewhere far away, with a style of experience different from that of home.
The fantastic exists here by virtue of a gradual modification of the style
of our experience of reality within one and the same world; it represents
a sort of "peripheral world"—possible, unknown, unexplored. Let us add
immediately that the overall situation of purely fantastic worlds, forming
spheres of their own, is entirely different; the relation of such fictional
worlds to the one fundamental world of reality is a specific, complex
problem.

A heightened strangeness prevails in our relationship to living
nature, unless its creatures are counted among the purely domesticated,
pragmatically understood components of home (but even in this case
there can be outbreaks of strangeness). Animals, with their life-relations,
are not just perceived things, nor are they simple citizens of our human
world. Animals impose on us their own animal relationship to us—a relationship of attack and defense; it is within this narrow frame that we encounter them (speaking of nondomesticated animals), only here and in
a few fundamental organic functions that we originally understand them.
And nature goes beyond the sphere of life in general—a purely alien,
uncomprehending, ruthless, so to say formless and threatening nature;
no longer nature as a domain fashioned to our needs, a storehouse, or
a homeland, but rather something uncontrollable, infinitely strong and
chaotic, which threatens life with disaster: the boundless indifference and
force of matter which is the ultimate *terminus ad quem* of our world in its
opening out from home into the alien.

This first dimension of the world, as outlined in the foregoing in its
tension between home and alien, is, however, but one of several; there
are, in addition, yet other world-dimensions—first and foremost, the
temporal dimension, very richly differentiated in our consciousness, especially in connection with the home-world. Time is for us the unified
domain of what is gone by, what is just now, and what is to come, in each
of which regions certain articulations can be distinguished. Past, present, and future encompass and set the rhythm of the whole of our life-
functions and occupations. Each life-function, every stage of our activity
has its time; temporal phrasing codetermines our style of life, while the
whole of this articulation rests on the periodical course of natural time
with its regular succession of day and night, the seasons, etc. Not only our
day is then articulated, by the regular course of life, into a time for rest,
for work, for food, for fun, etc., but the same principle applies to the different periods of life: youth, maturity, and old age are defined according
to the principle of a time for . . .

Uniformly and unchangingly articulated time gives us the present in a broad sense, the boundaries of which are variously subject to shifting: we speak of the present from a personal standpoint, meaning thereby the regular shaping of our actual life, but also as concerns the community and its great functions, e.g., the present-day Czechoslovak national economy or the present state of Czech literature. As far as we are concerned, the past world no longer shows complete unity of style with the present: we feel it in contrast, passing gradually, though with some breaks, into indeterminacy. Among the most important places of passage is the connection between generations; we do not take over entirely the world of our fathers, which for us always belongs to the past. There are, however, certain common tasks that subsist in the succession of generations and continue to phrase time—henceforth in a historical way. Our home-world is a world of traditions and impulses passed and carried on. The historical dimension has a fantastic ultimate edge in myth, which is thus part of the inventory of the naive world, pushed into the background only by scientific consciousness.

Natural time has a much poorer structure; just as animal life is feebly articulated in comparison with human life, the same goes for animal time, though it does have the same character of a time for something; purely objectively natural time is not of this type, but is a simple one-dimensional succession.

And there is yet another dimension that forms a necessary and essential part of our being-in-the-world and should at least be mentioned if we wish to concretize somewhat the development of this problematic. It is a dimension that could be called subjective, since it has to do with our general life-feeling in a given state of affairs. The whole of being appears to us, always, in a certain mood-coloring; though the mood is in fact always our own inner "state," it colors surrounding things at the same time, so that our objective environment, too, seems to partake of it. As we have already seen, there are entire regions of the world that have a characteristic mood-coloring, and certain moods come on us at the sight of certain things, particularly those laden with memories.

Moods and "states" are dynamic: it is part of their essence to be from something and for something; every mood is a mood for a certain activity, be it idleness. The possibility of our activities lies in our moods and "states" (in "how we are," or "how we are doing"). Each and every life is then characterized by a scale of moods, of which some alternate and periodically supplant one another in evident connection with our organic needs, while others have to do rather with the overall course of our life. Affective, or "mood" life has always a rich structure, it is never simple; one should speak rather of a dominant than of an exclusive mood—even deepest grief has its ups and downs, even here life goes through moments of satisfaction, and conversely every joy is surrounded by a horizon of pain and sorrow.

There are moods in which we are practically incapable of normal life-functions, moods that rob us of our life; there are indifferent and everyday moods in which life can function mechanically; finally, there are moods that open up a distinctive possibility of life to us. In grasping these, we seek to organize our entire life in accordance, we subordinate our life to an essential passion as determining *telos*. These are the moods in which the most essential human activities are born, from which creative life emerges; in them we relate to the whole of life and of the world, they maintain alive our marveling at the whole, a sort of prethematic comprehension of the fact of being-in-the-world.

2. Historical Development of the Problem

We have attempted, in the foregoing descriptive sketch, to conceive the problem of ontology in partial opposition to the constructive traditions in which it has the form of the problem of categories. For us, the world is not a complex or a system of categories, but rather a unitary *schema* within which the categories find their place; and this schema is not possible without the individual real things that fill it, it does not exist in itself. Perhaps the phenomenon of the world could best be characterized by the term "pure intuition"—without, of course, the rigid abstraction of Kantian pure intuition; we have seen that the world itself is in unceasing becoming and only its fundamental dimensions remain as the constant backbone of change.

Our conception of the world as an ontological schema is not given by descriptive arbitrariness; rather, as will be shown in the following historical sketch, it stands in the line of philosophical development. Kant was the first to show that the concept of the world as the universe, the totality of existent things, raises difficult problems, which he formulated as antinomies, introducing, as a result, the world-as-regulative-idea instead of the world-as-thing. For Kant, the world is an ideal concept of the one whole of reality, to which every experience contributes, but which cannot be realized in experience. Kant's conception thus differs from the notion outlined above insofar as the world, for Kant, is merely *an ideal demand for unification*, a should-be, which is, consequently, neither given nor realized. For the conception we have outlined here, the world is, on the contrary, not a demand or a goal to which experience tends but rather the preliminary whole on the ground of which it unfolds.

The idea that singular experience presupposes the world whole is one of the fundamental notions of German idealism; yet its great representatives did not speculate on the concept of the world, or at least did not take it up as one of their principal speculative themes. On the other hand, the concept of world plays an important role—though never in full philosophical clarity—in other thinkers of the same period, such as Wilhelm von Humboldt. For Humboldt, "world" designates primarily the constant and accepted milieu of a culturally living individual: world is here a historical-cultural concept, there is an essential correlation between man and world, the individual is never without the world, history is possible only through the dynamism of the world.[1] Like Kant, Humboldt too views the world as essentially correlative to the subject; for Kant, however, the world is the mere consummation of the unified form of experience, hence a purely formal concept, whereas in Humboldt it is something that has content but is ontologically indeterminate.

In connection with this peripheral branch of German idealism, we should also mention the thinkers imbued with a historical view who came up against the same problems; we have in mind Dilthey and his school. Dilthey arrived at the problem of the subjective phenomenon of world in his "philosophy of philosophy":[2] the conflict of "worldviews" originates in the *life-function* objectified in thinking of a certain kind, and not primarily in an objectively theoretical problematic (as metaphysics itself, in its naive form, holds to be the case). Dilthey is aware of the similarity of his views with Kant's attempt to overcome the old dogmatic metaphysics in subjective orientation; a certain philosophical inconsistency leads him, however, to believe that these views can be made to accord with a "noetic realism" which appears in his overall thought-style as naturalistic dross.

In the context of Kantian thought, the problem is broached yet again by Georg Simmel, in chapter 2 of his *Lebensanschauung.* Simmel's clear investigation of the vulgar concept of the world as the universe of the existent leads to the conclusion that we have to do here with a secondary phenomenon, one that presupposes a more original unifying formal function which first puts individual things together into one whole. The world, in this more original sense, is conceived here as form: "Welt im vollen Sinne ist . . . eine Summe von Inhalten, die vom Geiste aus dem isolierten Bestande jedes Stückes erlöst und in einen einheitlichen Zusammenhang gebracht ist, in eine Form, die Bekanntes und Unbekanntes zu umschließen imstande ist."[3] Simmel's achievement consists, on the one hand, in replacing the Kantian division of ontological elements (into intuitions, categories, and ideas) with a unified and unifying form of reality, and, on the other hand, in showing the world as a *concretum* of spiritual life. "Welcher Leitbegriff nun jeweils dem einzelnen Denker seine Welt als solche schafft, hängt ersichtlich von seinem charakterologischen Typus ab, von dem Weltverhältnis seines Seins, das das Weltverhältnis seines Denkens begründet"[4]—these words, in Simmel the subjectivist, should not be taken as a confession of tepid relativism but rather as a glimpse into the depths of radically creative spirituality.

Edmund Husserl, in considering the natural attitude toward reality and the world as surrounding world (*Welt als Umwelt*), was the first to show the world *as a phenomenon*.[5] Husserl distinguished here in particular the objective, practical environment, in which man lives in his naively unreflected dealing with things, and ideal worlds (especially the world of science, represented by the example of mathematics). The reflection on the "plurality of worlds" was then frequently taken up again; Simmel himself bases his conception partially on Husserl. Max Scheler, in his *Probleme einer Soziologie des Wissens*,[6] introduces the idea of "relative natural views of the world." In his later metaphysical works he arrives at the conviction that the objective structure of the world is correlative with the "spirit" of which man as a person represents the "individual self-concentration."[7] Scheler thus seizes upon the most originary motifs of Western European metaphysics; in fact, the possibility is given here for modern subjectivism to reveal itself as ontology. All these motifs will be more fully grasped and elaborated by Martin Heidegger (especially in *Sein und Zeit*, 1927). For Heidegger, the world is an ontological milieu, "das Worin des . . . Verstehens als Woraufhin des Begegnenlassens von Seiendem."[8] Heidegger in particular, with his often remarkable analyses, has drawn the attention of the broader philosophical community to the ontological concept of world.

The ideas of certain subjectively oriented biologists concerning animal worlds or the forms of lived-experience in animals should also be mentioned in this context. Karl Ernst von Baer has presented interesting views on the structure of experience in connection with the variations of possible observation in time. Uexküll's broader elaboration of a subjectively oriented biology supported by experiment works with concepts such as *Merkwelt* or *Wirkwelt*,[9] understood basically as certain lived-experiential forms. On the basis of human analogies, Uexküll determines concepts of home and homeland for certain animals as well, whose "world" is thus also characterized by this structural moment.—In some of his works, Bergson introduces motifs similar to Uexküll's (articulation of the environment according to the possibilities of action).[10]

Husserl is the author of more detailed—as yet unpublished—analyses of the "home" and other dimensions of the world.[11]

One can also make out an (albeit vague) inkling of the world motif in Spengler.[12] Authors who truly attempt to *work* with it in the field of the history of ideas and the philosophy of history include, in particular, certain thinkers influenced by Dilthey, such as Georg Misch,[13] Bernhard Groethuysen,[14] Erich Rothacker,[15] and others.

A similar intention can be detected, furthermore, in Lévy-Bruhl's attempts to discern special "thought forms" for primitive peoples[16] and in Piaget regarding the life-form of childhood.[17]

3. The Subjective Attitude

Going over now—after this attempt at a purely objective description of the phenomenon of world—to the reductive attitude, for which all experience, as well as its form, is a *pure* phenomenon of which the I makes no use as valid, binding theses, the task before us is to grasp this new field of experience by means of adequate concepts and to carry out a subjective description of the experience in which this phenomenon is given. This static analysis once accomplished, there remains to be effected another, even more fundamental operation—to clarify the genesis of the conscious formations presented to the transcendental consciousness as thetic experience. This thetic experience is simply naive, natural experience made clear and transparent for the philosophic eye: experience, not of an obscure transcendent realm, but rather of the sense of inner life.

Under the eye of reflection, psychic life shows itself to be essentially credulous. It is a dynamic process of belief that goes through a number of typical peripeties: direct experience of the thing itself, mere intuitive or nonintuitive presentiation, plain or symbolic presentation, judgment—all of this originally in the mode of certainty, then with modalizations ranging all the way to the crossing-out of the thesis. Our experience is a drama of belief (in the sense of theses); emotional experiences, too, posit determinations (values) on objects, the will itself is thetic and built on theses. Further, theses do not simply follow in time one after the other but rather, in growing complexity, one out of the other, mutually contributing to their collective work, which is reality. Processes really apprehended in purified inner experience combine in the dynamic unity of an accomplishment, and the sense, the aim of the accomplishment is being in the whole manifold of its "species," in all the concreteness of its fulfillment.

We explicitly *posit* as real, unreal, possible, etc., that which, at this or that moment, is "at the center of our attention," that with which we are concerned. In the stream of thetic accomplishments there thus arise—in parallel with certain distinctive singularities—singular "acts" in which our advertent I lives. Attention is always turned primarily to particulars or their complexes—the latter on the basis of previous acts of attention to particulars; what I accomplish in actually believing are theses or modalizations of theses concerning things in the world, but I never explicitly have the world. Where, then, is the *world* in my active, onturgic life? Or is the world as described above, after all, an incorrectly grasped phenomenon? Is not this supposedly "original" world a mere secondary image, a mere schematized representation, left over from the empirical sedimentation of countless particular flowing activities?

Even if that were so, we answer, it would not "discredit" the described phenomenon—for the question of the originarity or derivativeness of a phenomenon can be solved only by a constitutive investigation, in no case by objective description. Moreover, there is an important fact of doxic life that should be brought up here along with its consequences. This fact is revealed by *modalization*. Every actual singular thetic activity is subject to possible modalization, possible doubt; each individual reality can be at least tentatively modified: I can always attempt to doubt it; *de omnibus dubitandum* is an evident possibility as long as it is understood as meaning *de omnibus singulariter*. Modalization has, however, a necessary condition. A thesis can be modified only in being *replaced by another thesis*. This implies that *the whole* can never be cast in doubt. But what whole, since we have spoken so far only of particulars and individual activities? Be that as it may, the process of modalization is something that normally takes place in our experience, and precisely in our *advertent* experience. Does not this fact indicate that explicit belief in what is presupposes an inexplicit, preliminary "belief" in the scheme of the normal course of experience concerning things of a given type, along with the possible eventualities of its fulfillment or disappointment? Does it not suggest at the same time that explicit singular belief in a singular existent is possible only on the basis of a general belief in the whole?

An adequate answer to these questions requires that we go deeper than singular activities in our attempt at a subjective description, and that we seek to uncover more fundamental moments of the subjective flow. It is a fact of conscious life that, in addition to the activity in which our advertent I lives explicitly in turning its attention here or there (always toward a determinate particular), there lives in us, too, an activity of a different nature, which does not include this watchful regard of egoity.[18] Limiting ourselves, for the sake of simplicity, to the sphere of perception, we can say that it is part of the essence of perception that its activity is always directed primarily toward a center surrounded by an accumulation of objects belonging to the background of this main subject of our theme. Background objects are also perceived and are thus, so to say secondarily, *en parergō*, thematic; but the main theme, toward which all our conscious productivity is directed and into which it actually leads, is the center of attention. The objects given *en parergō* do not "properly" belong to the central object; they are not what interests us, they could eventually be replaced without this entailing any essential modification of the central theme, but they are nonetheless present and somehow apprehended. At the same time we are somehow aware that we have already had or that we could have these objects in our central, attentive experience; and when the act of attention ceases, its object does not completely disappear for us but rather passes into what could be called the sphere of availability. Beyond the objects *en parergō*, which fill our sense-fields, nothing more is apprehended in a direct, original manner; however, on the basis of "induction," a continuation can be represented either intuitively or in an "empty" (most often purely verbal) manner. The parergic sphere does not end even with the representation of *concreta*, but goes on as the awareness of a certain experiential style, the awareness of a potential continuation *in indefinitum*. Actual consciousness, which engages itself in its central sphere, implies an extensive sphere of *nonactualities*, among which *potentialities*, possibilities of transition and continuation, particularly stand out. Thus, there is consciousness even outside the sphere of the actual *cogito*, though it is inseparably bound up with this *cogito*, so that it is never possible to have a purely "potential" consciousness. It should be strongly stressed that this potential consciousness is not a mere negation, a lack of consciousness, nor the mere actual intention of an indeterminacy. There is a difference between the thematic intending of something indeterminate and its natural occurrence in "parergic" awareness; in the first case, the indeterminate is the center, in the second, the periphery. One can ask what constitutes the specific unity of the concept of consciousness in these two different modalities, whether the unity of the concept of consciousness itself is not abolished here. This objection will help us to specify the concept of parergic awareness. The essence of active consciousness is that our I lives in it, that it concentrates itself so to say into a *determinate* possibility while distancing itself from the others, which are nonetheless retained in varying degrees of force. The unitary core of these two concepts of consciousness would then be their relation to the active, advertent I, which grasps its possibilities or turns away from them. What is important is that the I lives always in the sphere of these potentialities and cannot live otherwise than in such a potential sphere. What we have termed "parergic awareness" is thus no mere *parergon* of the central consciousness but rather its prerequisite. What is truly operative in parergic awareness, at the roots of actual activity, is, so to say, the demarcation of the path, the domain, the sphere of apprehension in which we are actually moving; we say that nonactuality is the *horizon* of actual activity.[19] The horizon within which we live conditions our object orientation; we can live, in presence of "the same things," within different horizons, e.g., the aesthetic, the natural-scientific, or the vital-utilitarian—the horizon is something variable, though not ad infinitum; there are rules for horizon experience, too, an order in which horizons presuppose one another and determine our attention; it may be that one is actualized more than others, but in principle all are always there, somehow available and present. Horizon-intentionality shows just as remarkable a richness of forms as act-intentionality; and only the revealing of all horizon structures can lead to philosophical clarity concerning the function of consciousness.— This introduction has now given us a possibility of phenomenologically grasping the world.

4. The Concept of Horizon prior to Husserl

May we be allowed one more historical remark, which we believe to be not inessential. In the history of ideas, there are phenomena that are long anticipated rather than actually exploited. This can be shown to be the case also with the concept of horizon. Popular speech uses the word "horizon" in a variety of meanings, all of which have a philosophical undertone. It is no wonder that several thinkers have already reflected on this trope of speech. In Kant, we find a consideration using the concept of "the horizon of our cognitions."[20] By "the horizon of our cognitions," Kant is not thinking simply of a *province* of knowledge but rather of "the congruence of the quantity of all cognitions with the capabilities and ends of the subject." What he has in view is the manner in which our individual cognitions are determined by fundamental presuppositions lying in our nature, and he speaks of the horizon as determined logically, aesthetically, or practically; each of these determinations affects in a certain way the tendency and weight of the knowledge concerned. The aesthetically delimited horizon leads to the popularity of cognitions arranged to please; in the practically defined horizon, the subject seeks utility and, in general, the interests of the will; in the logically defined horizon, we move as pure theoreticians. Kant here further distinguishes the "rational" and the historical horizon (in the ancient sense of the term *historia* including also natural history). The rational horizon is narrower; it is an essentially mathematical horizon. Subjectively, Kant distinguishes the absolute, universally human ideal horizon of possible cognitions in general—which the critique of pure reason goes about determining in answer to the question: what can I know?—and the private horizon, which "depends upon various empirical conditions and special considerations" such as age, sex, station, mode of life, etc. Finally, there is also a horizon of common sense and a horizon of science.—All in all, the concept of horizon in Kant is inconsistent, plainly meaning now a simple province of knowledge, now the genuine phenomenon of concrete predelineation, which Kant, in his rigid formalism, regards as purely empirical.—The word "horizon" appears in a somewhat different turn in the historian Droysen,[21] in the context of an account of historical interpretation. The realm of historical method is, according to Droysen, the cosmos of the moral world (i.e., the world of the spirit); the historian considers this cosmos in two different ways: either with regard to the state of the spiritual structures at one given time (presenting thus a static cross-section of a period), or seeking out, within this state, the elements of progress and restlessness. In the first case, he gets the "ethical horizon" in which stood the historical events of the given period and, in connection with this, a gauge for every single process taking place within it. Thus, Droysen understands the horizon of a period as what the historian has to "know" in order to understand the particulars of the period under consideration. It need not be particularly stressed that this concept of horizon is close to the one outlined above, though the problems of historical understanding are, of course, extremely complex and difficult constitutive problems.

5. A Constitutive Sketch of the Genesis of the Naive World

In section 3, we pointed out the differences between the various kinds of activities in which the spontaneously advertent I lives, and what distinguishes these activities from horizonality. The task of a systematic analysis would now be to exactly describe all the basic forms of our conscious experience and, subsequently, to establish, both statically and genetically, how they presuppose one another. This is an immensely complex task, which cannot possibly be fulfilled in the present work, whose aim is merely to give, or rather to sketch an idea of what a constitutive philosophy might be. We shall attempt to outline constitutive problems directly from the genetic viewpoint, providing wherever appropriate a tentative characterization of the given structures. Our problem is to show how both our explicit activity and our horizons throw light upon what we have called "world." To begin with, for the sake of simplicity, we shall leave the whole dimension of empathy out of account and proceed exclusively in the sphere of the constitution of things for the individual.

We start from an assumption which can safely be verified by static analysis: that sense-perception of the things of use which continuously surround us is the fundamental layer of experience, on which all other modes of thetic life repose and to which they refer. A creature living in the world without this basic layer of experience is inconceivable. Perception is an original experience, giving directly the objects of our environment in themselves. Our reflection will be, in the main, an account of what all perception presupposes and how other formations of experience are built on its basis.

In sense-perception, which is an originary lived-experiencing of *objectivities*, not of mere "data," we distinguish *presentation and articulation*. These are phenomena that presuppose one another. Our reason for considering them separately is no sensualist preconception but rather clarity of exposition. Presentation concerns the qualitative filling, while articulation concerns the categorial object units that phrase or "polarize" givenness. How these two functions mutually presuppose each other will appear in the course of our exposition. Yet articulation and presentation are not the whole of perception. What sense-perception gives us are not simply "qualities," nor "synthetic units" and the relations between them, but rather the *life-relation* of objects. What we see at first glance, what constitutes the teleological motive in every perception, is this life-relation: whether objects stand suitably or unsuitably, as a help or a hindrance, in good or decrepit shape, etc. Let us take any literary description of an interior or a landscape: we see that it is composed for the most part of terms designating neither things nor qualities, and yet it is a description of what can be *perceived* in the given environment. When all is said and done, what we perceive in things are the possibilities of action they represent for us, what they make possible or impossible, how they answer our manifold, continuously varying and reshaping needs.[22] The life-relations in which we see things are infinitely differentiated.

Yet despite this far-reaching teleological structure of perception, it must be stated that the presentational component is wholly constitutive for it. In perception, there is always *present* something qualitative. The temporal character of perception is, therefore, the present. This leads us to the question of the relationship of perception and time. Perception takes place in time: what was just present lapses in it into the past, while at the same time an ever new present takes shape. The entire structure of this continuous elapsing can be most simply demonstrated on the presentational component of perception,[23] yet it obtains for all living, throughout. Time is thus the universal condition of being in general, but time in the sense of this original internal elapsing, not in the sense of natural time, *partes extra partes*. The phenomenology of time is one of the most fundamental philosophical disciplines, if not the foundation of all phenomenology. The original flow of time is at the basis of all consciousness and, therefore, of all world-belief, of all theses. Yet we cannot say that transcendental consciousness is *in time*, understood as a homogeneous milieu of instants. Transcendental consciousness *is the flow of time*, it is time. Time is the incessant genesis of a manifold of phases. These phases should not be imagined originally as the points of a continuous line; rather, they are parts of a unitary process of elapsing, which, eternally renewing itself, produces in it all consistent givenness, gives being. The givenness of being (*bytí*) is this *receding*, this *doing and undoing (odbývání)*. Consciousness can have givenness, i.e., can "be," only in receding, and thereby—as we shall see later—things, too, recede. In the very instant of the actual present there begins a process whose result is that the givenness sinks into darkness. Not all at once, nor in such a way as to lose all validity for us; rather, it loses only its validity as actual givenness. The no-longer-given is somehow "retained," it was just there, the I is still reaching out for it, holding on to it; we speak here of retention. Retention starts from the presentational phase and gradually undoes the existent, makes it recede even in its character of actual validity for us: maintaining a weaker and weaker grasp on what has gone by and, finally, abandoning it to obscure indeterminacy. The consciousness of actual givenness, which is itself consciousness of a passing over into nongivenness, thus passes away in the consciousness of a deeper and deeper past. The actual phase with its retentional modifications and the corresponding anticipations—protentions—makes up the concrete present. So the concrete present is not the simple "now"-consciousness, it cannot be said to be a *punctual present*; it has no definite "extension" whatever. The whole of the constitutive process is constantly present in it; in it takes place the creation of reality, and creation is precisely time.[24]

It would be wrong to imagine original time as a series of instants or a qualitative process. It is indeed a process, but of a sort which alone makes possible all worldly becoming. Its function is precisely to constitute a horizon of possible becoming, a horizon of possible qualitative changes. In this accomplishment, all temporal dimensions are equally original; without any one of them, the opening up of such a horizon would not be possible. Time in the original sense is a unitary function of expectation, perception, and retention of what is. In time we are standing, so to say, at the ground of subjectivity. The original present consists in shaping the *actual activity* of subjectivity, the original past in retaining its nonactual activities and the original future in tendencies that characterize subjectivity and constitute what could be called the treasure of its life-possibilities.

Becoming in the proper, worldly sense is possible only within the horizon thus created. Original time is nonthematic; in it, subjectivity with all its interest is engaged in the existent, in its surroundings, and its natural function is to produce succession, world-time in the proper sense. Whereas in original time-consciousness there is a continuous unity of retention, presentation, and protention, all three moments being bound together in one and the same subjective lived-experience, world-time is inseparably linked with processes unfolding *partes extra partes*. When I listen to a melody, my perception of its tones is a unity of retentions and protentions surrounding what is actually presented; yet precisely my retentions make the melody itself into a series of independent events, separate from one another. The unity of original time-consciousness leads to the apprehension of the manifold of becoming. This is its most important accomplishment. In this way arises the first objective time, which is nothing other than a qualitatively manifold becoming, the retained elapsing, or duration, which incessantly, so to say automatically accompanies our entire life as the content of the horizon of the past.

Since our tendencies introduce, into the qualitative manifold that originally makes up our life surroundings, a constantly growing articulative order, there arises for us a world order inseparably linked with the category of the thing of practical use. This order is itself at the same time an order of becoming; as stated above, all normal practical activities have a time of their own, determined by their natural conditions. On the basis of the first objective time, which is the perception of becoming, there then arises a second objective time, articulated according to our needs: the first measured time.[25]

All these constitutive strata are already presupposed when the individual produces his own personal *life*-time, the time of his own life significance, with its scansion according to the principle of his understanding of the world and his own decisions. This time, essentially historical, presupposes the awareness of our own freedom, the comprehension of our life's tasks in a given historical situation; it presupposes, in other words, that the whole process of becoming human is completed, that we have reached a creative level.

The vulgar understanding of time as a line, a series of instants, originates, as Heidegger has shown,[26] in the fact that the time of our needs is determined according to natural processes, most often on the model of distance traveled in space, and that the naive subject tends to forget its original connection with life, which is nonthematic for it. Time is thus assimilated to space—Bergson's well-known thesis—and the mathematical evaluation of time, as carried out by modern science, stands on this basis; time is here conceived as a thing. If we make this concept of time the starting point for subjective analyses, we are in danger of succumbing to the illusion of time as composed of instants, of conceiving its continuity mathematically rather than dynamically, as the triune accomplishment on the basis of which alone a givenness of being becomes possible. If we then apply this schema in reverse to our subjective function, we localize in linear time the very original source of lived-experiencing and are led to false problems. If time were originarily a series of instants, the original lived-experiencing of time would necessarily proliferate into an infinite number of phases, which is a descriptive impossibility; we would end up with paradoxes similar to Zeno's.

From the foregoing sketch, we see that the entire process of constitution is phrased, so to speak, in accordance with the different degrees of the constitution, i.e., of the objectification of time. In describing the general procedure, it is imperative to respect this gradation, indicating the general character of the domain in which constitution is moving at whatever moment. Since we propose in the following, primarily, to arrive at a sketch of the ground on which man's constitutive activity always moves, and since (as stated above) this ground is perception, we shall now turn our attention solely to the first two stages of the process, i.e., the genesis of qualitative diversity and the genesis of things.

Original time is transcendental becoming. If it is to be revealed as such, in this essential character, we must abandon the ground of the world with its manifold theses and its conception of universal time. In the world, time is always at work nonthematically, as a *form*; its own internal becoming is concealed. Nor can it be brought to light by a simple psychological reflection, proceeding already under the sign of world-time, inside which it seeks to localize original time. Time shows itself as what it is only once we suspend all worldly syntheses and thematize the original transcendental process. Such was not only Husserl's but also Bergson's conclusion; in order to thematize time, he found himself obliged to undo all the syntheses of the naive world and rebuild them step by step, from this universal ground up.[27]

In starting from the element of perception that produces qualitative phases, we have shown that all perceiving, insofar as it goes on in time, presupposes horizonal consciousness. Original time-consciousness with its triad of protention, presence, and retention is indeed the genuine ground of all horizonality. This proves fundamentally that sensualism, in deducing the whole range of psychical life from sense-data, is contradictory: the sense-datum itself is possible only on the basis of a temporal horizon and, hence, by virtue of an extrasensual structure. Sensibility is always no more than the center of a larger structure. The actual sensible phase consists primarily in the whole of its immediate retentions and protentions; around this core extends further the sphere of what can still be apprehended as continuously connected with the present and, again beyond that, the largest domain—the domain of the actually undifferentiated. Such is the most general structure of sense-presentation. But we must further study the qualitative differentiation of sense-data. This differentiation is possible only on the basis of the synthetic nature of the original time-flow.

If we are to understand the genesis of the sensible manifold, as it was and is continuously formed in our presentation, we must start from the active (albeit not spontaneously, freely active) nature of our perception, we must understand perception itself as the expression of certain original tendencies. The state of the senses at the beginning of conscious life is certainly not the qualitative diversity we know from our present experience: in order to be able to a certain extent to reconstitute this original state of the senses, we must recall the chaotic impressions we have in the presence of unknown, unexpected, bountiful happenings, where our habitualities have not yet been at work breaking paths and preparing the ground. An adult can never again fully realize such a chaos of impressions, as there are for him, in a radical sense, no new things. Here, the subjective state is not yet differentiated from the objective impressions; there are no stable qualities, no space or time. Nor should we imagine this "chaos" as a *mixture* of all and sundry, from which we would have but to extract in an appropriate way the qualities potentially contained in it; the phenomenon is rather that of a chaoticity per se, an undifferentiated manifold with, here and there, glints of something more determinate that can be set and seized upon by attention and active tendency. In this very impression of chaoticity, there is already something like the germ of a future order; an urge to clarify and work through this qualitative abundance is not long in making itself felt (with quicker success in animals than in humans). Active, practical tendencies come to the fore in *definite* affective dominants, in quest of fulfillment, searching for their way in this undifferentiated embryo of reality.

The tendencies that make themselves felt in this process are primarily the organic, life-tendencies. Yet they could not do the job by themselves without the encouragement of a synthetic tendency, a tendency to qualitative coincidence in the manifold of temporal phases which makes the primal qualities something unitary and firmly outlined, uniting all the subsequently differentiated qualitative nuances under the auspices of a single function; a tendency which gives a constant shape to our organic sensations as well. The need that voices itself in the organic state thus produces, in running its course, a certain melody, a certain qualitative manifold of the temporal process, which in turn presupposes the retentional functions and the tendency toward coinciding. This tendency is then operative not only in temporal continuity but also across gaps in time; in the latter case, it becomes an associative tendency.

The fulfillment of an organic tendency presupposes an important phenomenon: that objectivity is somehow—not freely, but effectively—at our disposal. A tendency can be satisfied only by a subject, through the direct, active contact with its surroundings that is the agency of all our activities. These are our kinestheses, the movements that subsequently provide the ground for the apperception of our own bodiliness. An animal subject is a priori possible only as bodily. From the beginning of life, we live in kinestheses infused with our subjective state of fatigue or freshness, pleasure or pain. If a newborn did not already possess this original kinesthetic function, it could never acquire it by "training." This life in kinestheses, with its necessary connection with global subjective states, is among the most important moments of the constitution of the objective world.

Each of the organic tendencies which originally makes itself felt produces its own qualitative melodies; yet, as life progresses, there are also new tendencies which appear, they, too, in quest of satisfaction and finding before them an already articulated given; the original tendencies then become more precise, enlarge their domain, combine with others. These new tendencies, functioning often on the basis of the prior ones, lead to a differentiation of the hitherto accumulated sensible abundance, catching attention and shattering the framework of the original qualities, as yet but roughly differentiated. The ability to identify and recognize anew certain qualities opens up possibilities of nuances; the differences begin to take on an affective force.

Continuous sequences of such *changes*, retentionally unified, associatively amplified, affectively centered and conditioned, go to make up the original treasure of sensibility. The qualitative melody is, however, originally a series of central values, always set in a background forming its field; what lifts these centers out of their background is affective interest. It should nonetheless be stressed that every quality, and most of all the qualities of the highest senses, is given as a moment lifted out of its surroundings. Associative tendencies lead then to the differentiation of *sense-fields*, i.e., the differentiation of simultaneous qualitative data according to sense-domains, to qualitative kinship. Each qualitative datum presupposes a certain fundamental aspect of which the sense-qualities are variants; everything seen, heard, etc., is in a primary relationship of affinity, established associatively as well as on the basis of the corresponding kinestheses. Each sense-field is, on the one hand, temporally extensive, it stretches into the past, and, on the other hand, it has a contemporaneous dimension; what makes possible articulation within one and the same

domain in contemporaneity is the spatiality peculiar to the domain forming the field. We can distinguish an extensive spatiality, e.g., that of the
visual and tactile domain, and a nonextensive one, e.g., that of the acoustic domain, the articulation of which sometimes calls on metaphors of
extension. The dimension of contemporaneity is thus the foundation of a
rich horizon-structure. We shall now turn to the opening of this horizon.

Within a field one can also, on a kinesthetic basis, yield to the affective tendencies emerging from the background, make a new impulse
the center and let the previous center sink into the background; one
can let one's attention flow freely from one point to another and back
again, and rediscover the structures one started from. In one particular
domain or several at once, there can come about, on a kinesthetic basis,
an experience of the *neutralization of change*. Thus emerges an important
motif: the melody of neutralization. We know now that to be in the center
means the same thing as to affect out of the background; both the one
and the other are modes of givenness of one and the same thing. The
neutralization procedure can then be repeated on any givenness whatsoever; the manner in which it is accomplished kinesthetically remains
the same, leaving us ultimately with a schema of possible neutralization,
relative, of course, to our possibilities of motion, and including, in due
place, qualitative data from different sense-domains. The spatialities peculiar to each particular field thus become so many perspectives within
one and the same space; space constitutively presupposes qualitative becoming, retentionally apprehended as a melodic sequence, and having
kinestheses at our disposal;[28] hence the originally qualitative nature of
space, the nonhomogeneity of its dimensions, as against the intellectual
space of geometry. Space has to do with our orientation, it is originally
an auxiliary in finding our way among things; even as a static form, it essentially presupposes becoming and, consequently, the first world-time,
objective duration.

This all means that space is the proximate condition of the constitution of *things* in the proper sense. Of course, there are a great many
creatures that remain permanently on the level of qualitative melodies;
they know what to do with what is given to them, but these givens are
not things for them, and have no place. These creatures can never have
one and the same in a manifold of aspects; for them, everything is a quality,
either individual or generic. Between such beings and those who perceive
things in space, there must be a fundamental difference in the form of
existence, a difference that keeps the former from operating the neutral-
izing synthesis and helps the latter. It appears to follow from theories of
animal psychology that this difference might consist in that perception in
these lower animals lacks the specific division of the field into center and

background which is characteristic of higher animals and has to do with the phenomenon of attention; in that case, we would have here a unitary structure, incapable of differentiation, without even the germ of an active I.[29] Neither is the life-level on which apperception of space occurs the level of the spontaneous I, relating freely to the world, but rather that of an I governed by affective tendencies and the appertaining external stimuli; nonetheless, there is already a certain preliminary degree of freedom in this apprehension of the explicability of the unexplicated, in the understanding of the background as incessantly repeatable possibilities of progression and transition. For it lies in the very nature of space as horizon that it is infinite; its infinity stems from the *temporal* horizon in which the *process* of orientation is played out.

We abandon now the ground of purely qualitative schemata in the sense-fields and come to an entirely new constitutive level, the level of the constitution of things, occurring to begin with (as it is impossible otherwise, given the essential insight into the synthetic nature of this process) on the basis of tendencies of an exclusively practical nature, inherent in every individual. All these tendencies can be subsumed under two headings, which cover the whole of our practical activity as the principle of the articulation of primary, natural objectivity. There is the tendency to dominate experientially given realities, which can be called the dispositional tendency, and the tendency to coexist and cooperate, which represents the original aspiration to understand and to be understood, and can be called the communicative tendency. Taken together, the dispositional and communicative tendencies form our world; however, these forces do not function identically in all individuals; rather, each one goes different ways in different beings, different subjects, under different social and historical circumstances. Diversity in the articulation of objectivity for us lies in the various ways in which our fundamental tendencies crystallize; this is why different peoples and different professions have different worlds. For the peasant, for example, the dispositional tendency has taken on the form of contact with nature as a condition of life, whereas the craftsman or the factory worker labors in an artificial place, with lifelessly obedient things, instruments, and products. The dispositional interest at the hub of these experiences is different for each one; what is central for one is peripheral for the other, what is home for one is alien for the other, and each one—in connection with his work—sees things differently, with different practical characters.

But let us come back to the initial stages of thing-constitution. The process starts from temporally extensive qualitative schemata, which have a certain life-significance, a certain function with regard to our tendencies. These schemata are now subjected to spatial apperception and localized in space. In kinesthetically effected motion through space, there arise, through partial overlapping of the qualitative aspects of an identical "place," spatial syntheses which give "the same thing" in infinite qualitative variety. The thing is thus constituted on a kinesthetic basis by walking around it, looking at it from different sides; at its root is a typical life-function. As inferred above, things are perceptibilities, but constant perceptibilities, given always only aspectually, along the way of our tendencies. Bergson had this relation clearly in view in writing, in his figurative language: "les corps bruts sont taillés dans l'étoffe de la nature par une *perception* dont les ciseaux suivent . . . le pointillé des lignes sur lesquelles l'*action* passerait."[30] The continuity of space and the continuity of world-time are what makes the wealth of things, with their aspects and the thing-determinations constituted in them, infinite. This is why a thing is but minimally given in mere presentation; presentation must be an element of the whole of a horizon which is no longer that of the surrounding world but rather an inner horizon.[31]

In dealing with things we take possession of reality; our tendencies impose on the qualitative manifold their homogeneous interpretation, the unity of which is that of a life-function, and their anticipations are either confirmed or eliminated in incessant explication and constant contact with concrete things. The tendencies themselves develop, become more and more far-reaching; the dispositional horizon of a child, small and limited to begin with, continually expands in all directions with the acquisition of new kinesthetic possibilities through the use of instruments. The immediate surroundings are increasingly pervaded with a relation of utensility for life—home is something like an enlarged organism.

The constitution of the own body only partially eludes the framework outlined above for the constitution of things. The body is, on the one hand, the milieu of the kinestheses, where we localize all our affections stemming from contact with things; on the other hand, it is itself a thing which is constantly close to us and makes its presence felt at all times. We have, in a way, a twofold experience of the body: the inner experience of having it at our disposal, in both an originary and an acquired manner, and an external experience, for which it is on a level with other innerworldly facts. It lies in our experience of the body that we have *our own* external world, an immediate relation to things as at our disposal, a possibility of holding sway. As this milieu of disposability, that *through which* all our contact with reality comes to pass, corporeality is originally and continually nonthematic; our attention is concerned with the things that occupy us and are available to us, not with availability itself. The same obtains for the enlarged dispositional relation: we pay attention not to the tool or instrument but rather to the work done; only in cases of dysfunction does our attention revert from the end to the means. This is why the center, in our normal experience, is the undertaking we are busy with, the task conceived as a relative end.

This has also to do with the fact that our nearby objective surroundings do not have the same articulation as the more distant environment: the nearby surroundings have a character of preponderantly practical objectivity, allowing the immediate intervention of our action and satisfaction of our tendencies, whereas the distant environment is more coalescent, more global, with a character of possibilities which can be but have not yet been revealed. The nearby is purely practical, the distant often of a more aesthetic nature (though that does not rule out, even here, an originarily practical articulation—e.g., mountains, valleys, roads are units indexed, undoubtedly, as functions of our praxis).

The fact that things have originally and always a life-function also implies that they are originally and always apprehended as elements of an operative connection. For things to have a function means for them to be suitable, fit for accomplishing acts of a certain kind. They are never mere qualitative schemata; rather, they are virtualities of action. This objective agency is not constituted by projecting inner states of the subject into the presented aspects; originally, we see and observe an agency in things themselves: a knife which does not cut and cannot cut in any circumstances is, of course, a knife only in appearance, as it lacks the function which essentially constitutes the thing.

Since all our activities, the whole nexus of our life has a specific order, called for by the operative connection with all its prerequisites, each life-function has a time of its own; the time of things becomes an element of a practical pragmatic connection, time is at our disposal just as other data in our surroundings; in other words, time is measured and action accommodated to this measurement.[32] So world-time, too, becomes a mere element of the unitary pragmatic connection indicated by the dispositional tendency; we come thus to the closure of the originally practical conception of the world, which at this point grows to be universal.

We have seen how, on the basis of the temporal horizon with its two original functions, retention and protention—the one in which being, bursting forth in presentation, is retained, the other forming in its tendencies the articulation of what is presented—there arises a unique and unitary objective reality; on the basis of this original horizonal consciousness, things are realities in *the one world*. We can now attempt to say what the world is, which dimension is fundamental for it. Original time has shown itself to be such a fundamental dimension. The world is not in time; rather, time is the world; already space demands to be explicated on the basis of time, in one of its dimensions. This is what makes "becoming" more original and deeper than all being; not merely in such a way that "being" is regarded as the superficial, static aspect of a deeper becoming, a continuously flowing change, albeit unobserved of earthly eye, but rather because all being is being-in-the-world and the world is not a simple static form but rather, in its most intrinsic essence, a *process*. At the same time it is clear why the world, though continuously functioning in experience, is never the theme of experience: the world is *no being*; rather, it pertains to the function of producing all being and can be discovered, in its pure form, only by subjectively oriented reflection on the basis of the reductive procedure; without reduction, there will always be a risk of reifying the world, of converting it into a "form," into some sort of represented being, no matter how idealized and fluidized.

But all that we have just mentioned still does not do justice to the concrete phenomenon of being-in-the-world, as we have attempted to describe it naively in section 1 of this chapter. In particular, we have yet to get hold of the very most concrete line, associated with the concepts of home and alien. All in all, what we have shown so far in the way of a schema of the constitutive process remains abstract, the bare bones as compared to the concrete structures indicated above. We must, therefore, go deeper still, track down more concretely the production of the universal horizon.

6. Articulation of Experience: The Dispositional and the Communicative Tendencies

The division into home and alien, home and strangeness, which we have seen to be a fundamental feature of the world, is conditioned by the fact that all our tendencies are precisely *ours*: their ultimate goal is our own "satisfaction," they come back, so to say, to their starting point. Home is the part of the universe so thoroughly elaborated by our tendencies that it has become for us, so to say, an enlarged sphere of disposability. We can say that home is the place of normal satisfaction of normal needs, a place where we are safe, the masters (in various modalities), i.e., a place at our disposal. The tendency toward a center of this kind lies in the very essence of all our spontaneous activities; home is originally given in the fact that all our experience is a taking possession of the universe—a taking possession which is successful only within a certain perimeter and which must by nature have a starting point, a kind of encampment amid the mysterious menace of existent immensity.

In a certain, very abstract sense, the entire universe is our home, the whole of it covered by a grid of the very most abstract *familiarity*. Nothing *radically* unfamiliar can ever appear in the context of our experience: it will always be something *recalling* certain facts of previous experience. This lies in the very essence of the sense-fields as qualitative continua and in the fact that the associative tendencies extend to embrace everything that has burst forth as temporally new at its point of origin. True familiarity with an object presupposes, however, the recurrence of *the same*; it is then either individual familiarity (on the basis of spatiotemporal continuity) or typical familiarity (on the basis of a *general* sharing of characteristics, without spatiotemporal continuity), but all these characters of familiarity are established in aiming at a synthetic coincidence. The present *calls out* associatively to the past, drawing attention to previous experiences of a similar object or an object of a similar kind: the familiar is absolutely preponderant over the heterogeneous.

To follow the tracks of these associative calls, to step into the horizon of absence, is to *presentiate*. Presentation can be of two kinds. The first concerns a factually present objectivity which is simply not actual *for me*, and it can then be an adequate presentation, an original reactualization of the experience of the same; this experience does not have to run its course in exactly the same form as previously, since having at my disposal a factually present objectivity implies the possibility to enter its inner as well as its outer horizon. I can, so to speak, *explicate* the object in a new manner, discover new aspects to it in response to new interests, etc.

Secondly, having the past at our disposal is also a kind of presentiation. It is going into the horizon of the past, a sort of quasi-life in the past. The real lived-experiencing of the past cannot be renewed; a quasi-experiencing, a fictive experiencing alone is possible. This fictive lived-experiencing has its specific quasi-present, quasi-past, and quasi-future; it has an entire past world of its own, contrasting with the effectively experienced world, which it can even fully drive out of our attention. As to how far the evidence of memory and, in connection with it, the revivification of the world of the past actually goes, this is a disputed question, difficult to answer one way or the other. The "quasi"-originarity of the lived-experiencing of the past gives itself as a mere *modification* of originary lived-experiencing. There is in reproduction the phenomenon of greater or lesser fidelity (which does not coincide with the greater or lesser *detail* of the reproduction), greater or lesser *approximation* to the original lived-experiential sphere; reproduction is, in fact, real life in a world which is no longer real, and, as real life, it is characterized by its concrete emotional situation which can be closer to or farther removed from the situation reproduced. The minimal degree of reproduction, as against continuous life in the reproduced situation, is merely a cursory and occasional encroachment upon it, touching so to say only the peaks, an awareness of being able to dispose of the past without making full use of this capacity. (Things are similar in the case of the presentification of a purely absent reality.) Thus, associatively mediated, arises the phenomenon of unfulfilled intention, i.e., of a purely significational consciousness; we know where in the horizon our conscious act is aiming, and we know of our capacity to fulfill it, but we do not make use of this capacity, we do not actualize it.[33]

Our consideration of the constitution of objectivity in perception has led us, taking further into account the synthetic tendencies it obeys, to phenomena that transcend actual sensibility and are often designated as the preconditions and first beginnings of thought. This shows that the preliminary stages of thought (and doubtless a large portion of thought itself) are possible without any involvement of sociality. We cannot, however, present further concretizations of the concept of the world, and, in particular, consider the part played here by the great material categories, without introducing the concept of the alter ego and giving an outline of its constitution.

Husserl has described the constitution of the alter ego[34] as a specific mode of presentification on the basis of the presence of an other corporeality and an associative link between the corporeality thus presented and the inner processes that govern it. This particular kind of presentification, which can thus never be the original givenness of the other in his inner being, gives rise to the apperception of other life, and it is on this basis that all our intercourse with others takes place, on this basis that we learn to know them and (as a mirroring of this knowledge and of our social behavior) to know ourselves in the sense of comprehending our own character and other material dispositions. I do not intend here to cast doubt as to whether this presentification and the apperception following from it truly determine the concrete understanding of particular acts in the presentation of a given living being. The question is merely whether this is indeed the ultimate constitutive level for the experience of the other, whether there is not a need for further reflection. We have seen that all presentation is, in its very articulation, necessarily codetermined by the tendencies of our affectivity, and the question is whether the basis of the experience of the other should not also be sought here, in the original *tendencies* manifesting themselves affectively. It is well conceivable that there lie in human nature original tendencies that can be satisfied solely by the full constitution of the other and the experiences given in intercourse with him. Be that as it may, the sympathies and antipathies with which a human being originally turns to the things of the world are not a mere reflection of utility for life but rather contain, already, a germ of reciprocity; we experience originally our surroundings as an *active force*, something that either supports or harms us, and it is in this same context that the experience presentifying (and presenting) the other originally occurs. Indifferent nature, equally uninterested in all its domains, is a complex product of intellectual constitution.

Our entire experience, beginning with the firm constitution of the other in direct intercourse with me, is a co-living, a co-experiencing, a collective wanting and a collective achieving (a co-working); from this constitutive point on, the whole of reality acquires novel aspects, takes on an entirely new coherent stratum of co-experience (in the transcendental sense of co-constitution), as Husserl has finely shown. The *concrete* home, this place of common will and safety where my own will plays an important but only partial role, arises first in mutual help; home is not, as it may perhaps appear on the ground of purely individual constitution, a simple hub of personal satisfaction and security but rather a *shared* center of safety;[35] it not infrequently happens that, when someone very close to us goes away, it ceases to be home and seems all of a sudden empty and strange.

So it is in this modality of co-operation that actual homeliness, actual closeness with something real, true certainty within what-is—the certainty that we understand and are understood (or that we can understand and be understood)—comes to be. The understanding of the other and of myself as members of a community and units of character develops in co-working and co-handling things, in joint or shared occupations, in the subordination and ramification of social functions. All those who belong to a social unit, however ramified, are engaged, in a way, in the same work, from different angles; even conflict is a mode of collaboration, aiming ultimately at the realization of a common will.[36] People understand each other on the basis of these common doings; they originally represent their social function and the manner in which they fulfill it. The alien is then the contrasting phenomenon; it is first of all a relation to doings which are not mine or, better, not ours; a relation to the community of such doings; a relation, in yet another way, to doings I "do not understand," and, finally, to doings that are not my own, and which I do not understand. Circles of strangeness extend into the distance as possibilities, in various factual gradations.

Fellow man is one of the first and most important material categories; the only more original category is perhaps the category of the thing of practical use, constituted as a passive instrument of our action. Fellow man, whether close or strange to us, has a body entirely similar to our own and can always be understood in certain general features. We have the impression that we, too, could do what he does. The doings of an *animal* are—given its different physical possibilities—entirely different; the animal is an intensified strangeness, yet it is an other independent life, helpful or harmful to us. A *plant*, too, is something independent, which asserts itself and goes through clearly defined life periods, but sympathy or antagonism finds no echo in it. Finally, nature in its great strata—nature as the material of our actions and a participant in them, nature as order, and nature as a materially superior, alien, and hostile force—is variously close to us, and variously situated with respect to our home.

These material categories have been a subject of interest to philosophy ever since the beginnings of Western European philosophical reflection. May we be allowed to remark that the Greeks were the first to place at the roots of their theorizing a difference between the *pragmata*, things of human use, which could not exist without man, and the *phusika*, things "grown" out of "nature," which have meaning in themselves,[37] and which they further divided into lifeless and living things, and fellow man. Where *in concreto* the boundaries run between the different groups will vary in various historical and cultural circumstances. In the Western European tradition, the most lasting have been the groups defined by Aristotle. The least reflected upon has been the relation between the *pragmata* and the *phusika*. Even this subdivision has, however, never disappeared from our philosophical tradition, as can be seen, e.g., in the system of categories erected by Dalgarno (1661),[38] the metaphysical titles of which—*concretum mathematicum* (something we have, for fundamental reasons, not yet dealt with), *physicum, artefactum,* and *spirituale*—were adopted by Leibniz in one of his minor logical works.[39] It is perhaps apposite to remark here that Henri Bergson, in revising his at first almost absolute nominalism, also came to the ideas of three aspects of reality, each corresponding to a determinate kind of objective generality: vital, physical, and instrumental.[40] A more detailed interpretation would be necessary in order to show the motivations of all these classifications and their basic agreement.

The types just mentioned—the great material categories—are a priori; they occur in our experience by virtue of the simple fact of our being-in-the-world, and they contain fundamental possibilities of human understanding of reality. They appertain to the world, not to the world's contents. The vast majority of types given in experience are, however, not a priori but rather contingent types, constituted on an associative basis. They are formed by means of an identification cutting, purely automatically, across the manifold of substrates, without the contribution of spontaneity, and they presuppose already the consciousness of individuality and the constitution of individuals, as they are, precisely, unities across the diversity of individuals. Bergson speaks to the effect that generalization is originally nothing else than habit passing from the level of action to the level of thought.[41] Types are the continuously automatically created headings under which our experience is deposited; it is by means of types that our experience is simplified and converted into a substantial abbreviation, that orientation in experience first becomes possible. It can be said that we understand only secondarily in categories; it is not often that we see an "instrument," a "man," or an "animal" in the presented object, not to mention a "thing," a "process," a "quality"; the original mode of understanding is in *types* and individuals.

We have thus brought the transcendental description of our naive experience to the point where a new kind of activity can—and does—set in: free activity, which is not directed in the whole of its course by present affections. This is the first degree of truly personal life, where the subject is, and feels himself to be the real author of his own acts, and where he himself directs his experience. Actual knowledge is possible only in the framework of a personal life; and every systematic form of knowledge presupposes language, which will be considered in the following section.

*   *   *

We can now come back once again to our starting point and state more precisely why we believe that the naive world can never be fully explained by the principles of the world of mathematical natural science with its conception of the universe as the totality of relations.

For the positivist thinker, as we have seen, the world is a totality of facts. A fact is an independent relation, comprehensible in itself, which can to this extent be isolated from the whole. The world, conceived as a totality of facts, contains only realities; the laws governing the occurrence of these realities, for example, are not themselves facts.

The natural world, as we have described it, is neither a fact nor a totality of facts in this sense—if for no other reason, because it is, as universal horizon, the circle of possibilities on the basis of which alone real determinate facts can be apprehended.

A description of the world based on the conceptual means of the modern logic of relations cannot fulfill its task, if only because, in its abstractness, it could show only the most general formal structure of *the* world, but never see how life as such mirrors itself in *our* world, how all its facts are comprehensible only with reference to this foundation. Though lived-experiencing itself is rarely thematic in naive life, the whole of objectivity is nonetheless steeped, so to say, in its atmosphere.

Life itself is then, as follows from the fact that its ultimate essence is concrete time, something unitary, indivisible, nonrelative, in which the whole of the world is continuously present.

4

A Sketch of a Philosophy of Language and Speech

In the preceding chapter, we have attempted to describe the ground on which human life continuously moves. Our starting point was the descriptive fact that our life is always life within a totality which, following linguistic usage, we have called "the world," but which should be distinguished from the universe of things. We have attempted to apprehend this preliminary totality, lying at the basis of all human experience, in three fundamental dimensions: the objective dimension, characterized by the polarity of home and alien, the temporal dimension, and the subjective dimension. Adopting then a reflectively subjective standpoint, we have characterized the givenness of the world as a horizonal givenness; finally we have attempted to penetrate to the very origin of the phenomenon of world in the fundamental functions of subjectivity. These showed themselves to be the fundamental functions of time-consciousness, which thus means for us the original opening up of the horizon within which any thetic activity first becomes possible. We have made clear at the same time how the concretization of this most original world into an ontological schema, encompassing certain fundamental material categories, presupposes the constitution of the other, affectively preconstituted subject, how every objectivity is originally a partner for us and how this relation contains the principle of the "natural" classifications of things. The human universe is already constituted to this extent when theoretical interest and theoretical activity become possible. Man does not live, prior to all self-purposeful theoretical interest, only in predominantly passive functions; on the contrary, he already classifies, explicates, synthesizes, remembers actively as well. The result of all these activities is not, however, the constitution of new layers of reality but rather a mere filling in of detail, a more concrete articulation, and, in general, an appropriation of the one perceived, temporally flowing universe. The fact that man is *capable* not only of perceptions but also of intuitive or "empty" nonoriginary intentions does not yet make for a reconstruction of reality; intentionally, we are still moving here on the level of the one actual reality, identical in different modes of givenness, originary as well as nonoriginary, intuitive and nonintuitive, formed in different domains of sensibility. Continuously ongoing typification, comparison, and observation in our experience produces a more definite orientation in what is given; this takes place originally in the context of our action and, hence, of our affective tendencies. "Better knowledge" thus means, in the first place, a more intimate relationship with the things of our surroundings, not a purely theoretical act, presupposing a tendency toward knowledge for itself. Yet all these activities imply a kind of secondary theoretical regard, which first produces the prerequisite for actual theory—this is the process that we propose to study now. The witness and outcome of this derivatively theoretical process is a peculiar phenomenon—the phenomenon of language. Certainly, language is first of all an instrument of our praxis inasmuch as it serves for the intersubjective exchange of mental contents; at the same time, however, it is already an apprehension of reality which intentionally relates to reality and helps us to find our way about in it, to analyze and elaborate it. In language we have the first degree of every possible theory, what makes theorizing materially possible. If there were not already given, in the treasure of knowledge contained in language, a certain naturally created model of knowing, the idea of a theoretical life, relating to the whole in a disinterested way, could never have emerged. It was then no unimportant motive that made *logos* a primary theme of theoretical reflection at the very beginning of Western European reflection on the self and the world. All theoretical reflection starts from the meaning of words. The discovery of the theoretical power of speech, of *logos*, was the first bar of a movement, the second necessary component of which became a reflection on meaning; the leap into the immensity of the universe has as its correlate a concentrated search for the fixed meaning of the word, the discovery of the cosmos, an *anamnēsis*. As to how far theoretical reflection can ever free itself from its first factual presupposition (language), this is then a complicated question; what is certain is that this liberation—and along with it, the creation of new means of communication—is variously desired and variously realized in different domains of theoretical activity. It has progressed furthest in mathematics, though even here one can still today ask if the emancipation is complete.[1]

1. The Phenomenon of Language

What is language? This is the question that will govern the next stage of constitution, the constitution of an objectivity moving above its own ground. True to the method examined in the foregoing, we must first proceed by description and comparison, prejudging no solution, concentrating our attention on the phenomenon as it occurs in our pretheoretical life. We shall start with a character mentally present to every speaker: what thematically exists for us in conversing is speech (not language), i.e., the means of expression actually used by ourselves or our partner in the dialogical situation. Certain uttered or imagined words and sentences, certain expressions are present to us; we are concerned with them, we act through their agency; the individual faculty of disposing of certain expressions is not itself made thematic in speaking, we do not think about it, our attention is never fixed on it; and even less so on what we call language, as opposed to both actual discourse and the individual habitus of speaking a language. Language is something that works hiddenly; only in special cases, such as the phenomenon of hearing (or perceiving in general) without understanding, can language *announce itself* in our naive experience; e.g., in the phenomenon of a foreign (incomprehensible) tongue.

Linguistic expression and the comprehension of linguistic expression, which is necessarily sensible, are correlative. The understanding of a linguistic expression (nonunderstanding is a mode of understanding) has, however, a twofold orientation; we understand the expression, on the one hand, as a symptom (expressing certain subjective states of mind), on the other hand, as a symbol, a sign for things.[2] Linguistic expression is thus the transmission of objectifying mental acts; it is immediately understood by us as such. At the same time, the expression is a structure in which the albeit important part played by the sensible moment cannot be compared with the role of the sensible in sense-perception: it does not take on the character of an attribute of a substrate; rather, it is something independent, in which the intended objectivity is nonetheless present immediately (and not on the basis of judgment). In the normal course of communication, the sensible as such remains outside the center of attention; attention passes through it, aiming directly at the intended objectivity and its relations; though it does not go unheeded, the sensible is thus taken notice of as a mere stage on the way to communicative understanding. The sensible aspect of language normally plays only this mediating role. This we will have to keep in mind even in analyzing it by itself.

For those who understand the linguistic expression, the intended objectivity is immediately but not really present in it. The understanding of linguistic expressions is not a presentification, the word does not put us in mind of its meaning, it does not set off a process of entrance into the horizon of the past, but neither is it a presentation of objective reality. These two features are common to linguistic expression and *picture* or *image*. A picture, too, may belong to the sphere of actuality (if it is not part of the sphere of the past or that of imagination), but the object of the intention directed at it as a picture is not the reality of the picture but rather its subject, and the reality of the subject in no way coincides with the reality of the picture. The subject is present in the picture thanks to the direct givenness of the picture. The picture itself, the thing entitled "picture," has no overall resemblance to its subject; the relation of the object depicted to the picture is not the simple resemblance of two *things*. The thing "picture" must, however, *contain* certain features generically identical with the features of its subject and be, in these features, interpretable as a quasi-aspect of the depicted thing. This moment must be conspicuous enough to make us ignore the objective synthesis thing-picture; consequently, present reality is disregarded, and what we pay attention to is unreal. But the generic identity of certain features of the picture with an objective aspect is not all there is to the phenomenon; there is also a margin of disparities in which we still recognize the depicted thing, and this interspace is not an inessential feature. Every picture implies a specific degree of fidelity, of likeness, and, hence, an awareness of the distance between the pictorial and the real aspects. The relation of reality to its possible images is a relation of one to infinity.—In all this, linguistic expression resembles picture more strongly than it might seem at first glance; in linguistic expression, too, present reality is disregarded—only an abnormal turn of attention makes it possible to concentrate on the phonic aspect of an expression—in favor of what is in view but not presented by the expression; here, too, the relation of what is expressed to the expression is one of univocity to plurivocity. In fact, a language expression resembles more a picture than a mere sign, symptom, or signal; in the case of a conventional signal, e.g., such as a red light meaning danger or the position of the arm of a semaphore, we are generally, in perceiving these objects, aware of a difference between their presentation and their interpretation; this difference is even more prominent in the indications incessantly given in our experience of things—e.g., a west wind announces rain, the tactile quality of a fabric is a sign that it will wear well, the color and texture of a paper indicate its fitness for writing, etc.; though all these qualitative determinations are given along with, by means of, and in what is presented, they are *anticipations* and have yet to be confirmed or disproved one way or another. I need not momentarily perceive the difference between what is presented and what is anticipated, I can disregard it, the mode of verification nonetheless differs in both cases, and this is necessarily understood in all naive experience. In linguistic expression, on the contrary, there is no distance between what is presented and what is anticipated; linguistic meaning is not *anti*cipated but just as *present* as its sensible bearer; every erroneous perception of a linguistic expression concerns both meaning and bearer, which is not necessarily the case with errors in objective indications.

The understanding of a linguistic expression is inseparably linked with yet another fundamental aspect of our speech consciousness; the phenomenon of speech is at once passive and active. When we take note of relations which draw our attention, there intervenes for us, automatically, an internal linguistic expression; the meaning of the relations is, so to say, fixed and decided for us only from the moment we have a linguistic expression for it, a judgment is made only when it is formulated. This is not said with a view to prejudging the possibility of extralinguistic thought; we simply observe that thought is stabilized and normalized on the level of language, and tends toward it as toward its position of equilibrium. Linguistic expression is thus not indifferent from the viewpoint of pure thought; disregarded in understanding, it is present in reflection as a standard of clarity and definition. A thought in itself is a whole; though there is, in it, the observation of a certain relationship in certain things, the detection of a certain rhythm in a certain domain of reality, a discovery of a way out of the difficulties of a given situation, the thought contains all this merely as the clearest peak of its wave, as its essential center, necessarily presupposing a periphery that extends indefinitely; to analyze a thought in itself would thus mean entering endless horizons. What does the unity of a thought mean, considered in itself? What is one thought? Even in naive life we understand it as something other than one individual judgment, and we speak of developing one and the same thought, of its turnings and variations, alluding thus to a pretheoretical awareness of logical processes having the same internal *telos*. A thought, by itself, has the ability to concentrate within it the entire life and world of the thinker; for this very reason, it is continually in danger of losing its determinacy and escaping us. A thought is something elusive, albeit subjective; it is one thing for it to emerge, and another for it to be grasped and put into effect; in life, we are always in the situation of lagging behind our thoughts, our concrete I with its bygone habits and mental acquisitions must continually grow up to their level. In this context, linguistic expression has a new function and a new character, a character of potentiality: there lies in it the possibility to know where to place our every observation, what to make of our every thought. Before being an instrument of communication, speech is thus already an instrument for grasping thought, and we have, prior to all conscious reflection, a certain awareness of both this and that. Speech is an instrument for us; feeling tells us that it is at our disposal; this feeling of disposing of speech does not mean, however, that we have a mental overview of the entire wealth of linguistic expressions possible for us or, in general, that we can draw explicitly on this pool. The fact of the matter is that in thinking about object relations we experience verbal expressions which come to us automatically and which we either use to our purposes or dismiss, according t) how fitting or unfitting we feel them to be. Our real, truly assimilated, clarified thoughts occur at the level of our actual *linguistic* capacity and not at the level of our ultimate mental faculties and possibilities.

So speech is an instrument which we never really have in hand, of which we never know otherwise than *ex eventu* to what extent it is within our power, an instrument which, in this respect, resembles more our natural bodily organs than it does artificial instruments: it is at our disposal in the same way as the bodily skills which we always simply assume to be in their normal state and as to which only the performance of an act shows how we stand, what is the actual state of our forces which, they too, have their ups and downs, their transitory or definitive failures. There is a yet greater likeness in the fact that disposing of speech is immediate, it happens without any conscious engagement of the body, it is not the availability of something objective, independent. Furthermore, speech is not in us in the form of a certain quantity of expressions "known" to us and used in this or that situation. Speech always aims too—and must necessarily aim—at utter novelty in our life-experience to date; its essence lies in accompanying the whole of experience, endeavoring to master it, testing all possible tasks; emerging automatically yet always with a sense of effort, it is, in short, a force, or, better yet, a process. Speech, our capacity to dispose of linguistic expressions, is in this sense alive, something that cannot be simply objectively observed or determined *per simplicem enumerationem* of what is at our disposal.

If speech is thus experienced as an animate instrument, an *organon*, the next question concerns the manner in which we work with it and the work accomplished by this means. The mode of work is determined by what speech serves, by the end in view, and the end is the work accomplished. The end can be the mere subjective clarification of a thought, the formulation of univocal judgments; we have already partially described this mode of work in the monologue of thought. The accomplishment of this process is the automatic linguistic understanding of things of our environment, an understanding in which we constantly though unconsciously live; it is the fact that reality is for us, as Hegel used to say, a realm of names, that every thing has its name, that we keep a rubric of each one; that an event can be expressed, that for each one there exists already in speech a mode of understanding to which it must willy-nilly submit.[3]

More complex, more important, indeed more fundamental is the social accomplishment of speech. This accomplishment is acting on others by means of the contents of what is expressed, and it has different forms according to the possible modes of action. Nowhere is it so apparent as in language that the entire universe of being is originally understood in a close, personal relationship to ourselves. We do not speak only to our fellow man; rather, we understand our expression as something that concerns at the same time the things said in their own being, as a thing that does not leave this being indifferent. The way we speak of things is not indifferent, there are nuances revealing our personal relationship to them; extreme phenomena, such as when—even with no one to hear—we let off steam by means of a linguistic expression, are possible only on this basis. Relief can also be the end in view in communicating with our fellows; the phenomenon of collective monologue, analyzed by Hermann Ammann,[4] has its place in this context; it is, in fact, normal for conversation to be governed not only by the principle of communication but also by the principle of affective relief. Taken all in all, this principle contributes to the same end as the principle of communication; both can serve the development of indirect experience, though each in a different way. Indirect experience is an experience that the subject does not have, has not had, and cannot have (I, of course, do not mean an analogical or generically identical experience), and which, in his knowledge, is replaced by an experience of foreign experience. The experience of foreign experience is possible only because experience is necessarily translated into an expression. The expression is something involuntary, and the understanding of the expression as well. On the other hand, man also communicates his experience intentionally and interprets what is communicated. The linguistic expression is, in any event, already separate from immediate lived-experiencing. This is precisely why it can also be a sham experience, what makes it possible to tell lies. But the same circumstance also first makes possible communicating independently of the situation in the sense of a narrow present. For this same reason, man has the ability to communicate even what can be understood only from the broader contexts of his life. An animal, in order to communicate, must either bring its partner to share a direct experience with it or concretely signify its demand by mimicking (as chimpanzees do when inviting to play); in any case, there is here either a presented reality or the initiation of a real process, whereas human communication presents nothing besides the phonic manifestation. The function of human communication is not presentation but rather actualization: it causes attention shifts in the addressee, and it is in these transfers that the interpenetration of two experiences, the influencing of the other by the self and of the self by the other, a co-experience with another comes about. Human communication presupposes not merely the narrow present situation, but rather the present situation within the total situation, which is ultimately being-in-the-world; the whole world is presupposed with all its wealth of dimensions, all its categories, and, as its center, living with others concretized in the actual situation. Since this living with others is not a mere indifferent juxtaposition of subjects, but rather is marked by a parallelism or an antagonism of the life paths in which individual subjects seek to assert themselves, and since the action of each individual always involves broader or narrower communities, linguistic communication is a primary instrument of the perpetually renewed social combat. This is why our entire life, all our knowledge and possibilities are concentrated into our disposing of language, into the energy of our speech. Truly human living-together, human co-experience is co-experience in speech and communication.

Having reached this point, we must finally turn a reflective eye on the phenomenon of language itself, while we have thus far considered only the phenomenon of understanding a linguistic expression and the phenomenon of speech as having language individually at one's disposal. While the comprehension of a linguistic expression is always a particular mental act, speech an individual psychic disposition, language is something that is not exclusively peculiar to any one subject, and in this lies also its objectifying force. Whatever is linguistically formulated exists not only for me but de jure for the entire community. Language is to subjective acts of speech and comprehension in the same or different subjects as one is to many. Language is a set of means of expression by which all facts can be formulated (insofar as they are formulable), by which the whole of reality can be described. It comprises a specific sensible aspect, which no linguistic expression is without, and the objectified intentions coordinated to individual formations of this sensibility. However, language should not be imagined after the manner of a mere stock of meanings; it comprises all *possible* expressions, sense-endowed or not, which can result from inserting simple meanings into propositional schemata; the means of expression which are not used de facto but can have a function and come into use some day also have their place here. Thus every language is ultimately coextensive with human faculties of expression in general, but actual language always has a center—usual possibilities of expression, and a periphery—purely virtual possibilities, as yet unused, but attainable on the basis of the laws governing the creation of means of expression within it; the latter are possibilities among which choice is possible, it still remaining (at least partially) undecided whether or not they will become an ordinary component of the language. Thus language is solid being only in part—insofar as it is a reservoir of both simple and syntactically complex objective meanings—and it cannot as a whole be paralleled with finished cultural products. It is true, of course, that any finished cultural product can be so termed only *cum grano salis*; e.g., it is in the nature of a work of the plastic arts that it can be viewed individually, each time with new eyes, just as a musical composition, "identical" in all its performances, allows for a margin of individual "interpretation," as a sort of challenge to the creative spontaneity of the performer; but in all these cases we have to do with a finished, closed whole—language, on the contrary, is not a closed whole. All the less can the being of language be compared with the omnitemporality of an idea or a mathematical proposition. ·

We have voiced the opinion that the limits of every language are those of human possibilities of expression in general.[5] This implies a certain thesis of universal grammar, which is an important philosophical problem: all ideas can in principle be expressed in all languages. We mean thereby all ideas concerning the universe of what is; this ability to express the universe must be mirrored in the very structure of every language. We have seen that the universe in its qualitative variety is articulated, according to our tendencies, into certain agencies, certain processes and certain things, as synthetic qualitative and causal unities; we have further considered typification as consistently carried out articulation. We have seen, in short, how the universe emerges on the basis of the functions of our world. The whole of this process already implies the relational structure of the universe as well. All this must be expressible by language; this then belongs to universal grammar: language must have the capacity of expressing qualities, processes, substrates and their mutual connection, and it must be able to express all this *typically*. This is the concern of universal grammar internally, in respect of meaning; as for expression, universal grammar comprises, as stated above, that language must have a coherent and overseeable sensible material of expression, perfectly masterable from both an active and passive standpoint. The subject must not only understand what he hears but also be able to reproduce it, and this reproduction must be acknowledged by the community.—So much by way of introduction, before entering into a deeper analysis of the functions of language.

2. An Ideal Genesis of Language

The point last raised already provides a transition to the actual analytic procedure whereby we propose to elucidate the relation of language to the world and its position in the whole of our life. Since, according to what has been said above, language is a necessary and lawful result ensuing from the process of communication as its enduring sediment, the constitution of communication must also be the constitution of language; we shall follow it in analyzing step by step (1) the presuppositions of linguistic communication (communication prior to language, the free human person, the birth of active thought), (2) the thought-appropriation of reality and the role of language in it, (3) the sensible aspect of language as the basis of objective meaning, and (4) the forms of thought-synthesis as the basis of linguistic meaning. In brief, we must attempt an ideal genesis of language, having in mind both the origin of language as such and its individual transmission within the community that masters it. It has often been rightly remarked that individual acquisition of language differs profoundly from the original "birth" of speech, inasmuch as a child today comes to understand, discovers language, but does not create it.[6] Yet there is, even in this understanding and discovering, something similar to the original inventive *élan* which is, in present-day man, covered over by reception, and it is our belief that by analyzing the fact of language in its subjective presuppositions we can reach the fundamental stages its genesis must go through—always in connection with the genesis of thought which it furthers and in part explains, as briefly indicated above. The major difference between the origin and the reception of speech consists, admittedly, in the *mode* of invention, not in the fact itself of discovering language, and the origin of language should, as Marty rightly stressed,[7] be imagined without any preliminary intention, but this does not mean that language is not the work of man, a product of our spontaneity. In both cases, the origin of speech implies certain necessary presuppositions, which we would summarize as follows.

The first presupposition of the constitution of language and speech is the apperception of the other, our fellow man. It is this apperception that establishes contact between subjects; the other person in his corporeality is always an expressive phenomenon, I cannot come into contact with him without interpreting his corporeality as a manifestation of his lived-experiencing. We feel the same about *ourselves*; when surrounded by mere things we are alone, whereas the presence of the other acts on us as a specific stimulus, we feel observed, at the mercy of the other's understanding. Prior to any explicit communicative endeavor, we already know something about others, by virtue of our living together with them. Moreover, we have already seen in our analyses of experiencing another being that this experience appears to rest on an original tendency toward coexistence, toward cooperation, toward self-assertion within a community, and the first beginnings of the communicative endeavor, which is an endeavor to actively affect others, to influence them internally in accordance with our own wishes, should be imagined on this same basis.

Communication emerges as an affecting of the other by means of our own expression—as something intentional, but nonetheless directly comprehensible from the situation. A distinction should be made here between signals, on the one hand, and indicated acts, on the other. In both cases, this active making oneself known is a *modus imperativus*: it always somehow commands or at least suggests. Indicated acts, such as a threat or the behavior of chimpanzees when they invite a partner to play—grabbing him by the hands and taking him aside, seeking to somehow involve him in the intended activity—already make use of the fact of natural symbolism which lies at the root of many expressive gestures; they are, so to say, primitive inventions of the communicative effort, directed by an affective impulse. This stage of the active use of signals is also a necessary presupposition of the creation of speech; it is here that the subject gets used to living and actively intervening in close contact with other beings.

But contact and active communication do not suffice to explain the origin of speech, which must be sought in an entirely novel motive. Of all we have thus far been able to say about the formation of reality and our experience of it, there is only one fact that can further serve us as an indication, but only inasmuch as it shows the *possibility* of something like speech, not to be taken as *causa efficiens*. It is the fact that man has an original clarity concerning the whole of being, that he possesses the original world-phenomenon analyzed in the preceding chapter. We have seen there what this original clarity means: it is a function that makes possible the consciousness of reality as a unified whole, forming, in protention, presentation, and retention, the unity of the most multifarious particulars.

At the same time, we have seen that no perception, no qualitative givenness is possible without these original horizonal functions. But perception—and, therefore, the original world function as well—must be presupposed in animals, too, and yet animals do not have language. In what lies then the explanatory value of the fact of world with regard to the phenomenon of speech? This objection would be valid if animals had the same mode of being-in-the-world, i.e., of relating to the world, which is proper to man. The human mode of existence in the world consists in having the world at our disposal (without thematic knowledge of the world); animals, however, do not have the world at their disposal, they do not spontaneously enter into its horizons, so one could say that the world rules the animal, rather than the other way round. Animals, too, have retention, articulation, doubtless also association, typification, and other passive horizonal activities; for animals, too, there are no doubt certain reproductions which passively emerge; yet all these functions do not go beyond what the horizons accomplish so to say automatically, while activity is exclusively concentrated on reacting to stimuli, i.e., focused in the present. As a result of these facts, the animal's universe is poor, it is a universe predominantly taken up with home and the present, where the rest of what is is plunged in darkness. The animal's world is *imposed* on him. Man acts freely with regard to the world; what is imposed on him is *choice.* Man has to actively co-create his life—and, therein, his world. What is given to man in the manifold of his affective tendencies is not a predestined intelligible character but rather a certain possibility of creation, or, at least, of choice. For animals, the "meaning" of life is prescribed in the regular satisfaction of their vital impulses, the periodic succession, demands, and assuaging of which make up their life-form. For man there is no set model of this kind; meaning is something he has to actively acquire, making of himself a true, existent unity, organizing the whole wealth of his tendencies under a single goal. Man is thus something that must by nature make decisions, something that can find or fail life's task. This is why he is free, why freedom is the very ground on which the human relation to the universe of the existent is built; this is what makes the feeling of freedom fundamental for human life. And this too is why man has speech and language: only on the basis of this free disposing which reveals the existent as a universal whole, transcending the present situation, is it requisite and subsequently indispensable to make use of signs which, in their facile and direct disposability, take the place of exis-tent things that we can dispose of only with difficulty and, often, through a long chain of intermediate agencies.

Let us consider a child at the crucial stage of becoming human. He has learned to associate certain sounds with situations; he has learned to produce and dispose with these sounds; now comes the time when his recognition of an object is accompanied by a word—the child has achieved comprehension of the sign and its meaning. What does this achievement presuppose? What kind of mental attitude toward things is expressed in it? The child must be aware, first of all, that the thing named is something determinate, distinct from the other components of his surroundings; furthermore, that it is something constant, independent of our lived-experiencing in general, as of any experience we may have of it; that a certain sign, subjectively at his disposal, can call another's at-tention to the thing in question; that disposable signs are thus a means of intersubjective influence. It is clear that this whole complex structure rests entirely on the possibility of evoking what is not present and on the child's awareness of his ability to have things and his own forces at his disposal; by creating the apperception of a sign, the child already begins to manifest the potential of freedom that lives in him and will show itself subsequently in the creation of objective meaning, then language.

The child, if he is to produce a system of objective signs, must be able to become—at least in a flash—aware of the freedom that charac-terizes him as a human being. This means that he is not blinded by his active tendencies, that presentation does not immediately pass over into action, as in animals. Part of the child's activity is concentrated on dispos-ing with what is not presented, focused precisely on enlarging the region of beings exposed to the light of consciousness; the role of the word also belongs in this context. Recognition accompanied by a word is no longer merely lived recognition, as in animals, a habitual reaction governed by chains of associations; rather it contains already, in the naming, a rudimentary subsumption; old knowledge is actively *used* here to class new knowledge—not only is there a feeling of similarity, the typicality of lived-experiencing at work, but the *meaning* of the word is *constituted* out of this actively apprehended sensation.[8]

The child then plays freely with the thus grasped feeling of familiarity in which meaning takes shape. It is known that meanings in children's speech are at first undifferentiated; some have inferred that they are, therefore, not yet proper meanings, nor the expressions for them real words. It clearly follows, however, from the observations of Stern and Pavlović,[9] who have studied the question, that the use of verbal expressions, though not initially univocal, takes place nonetheless in comprehensible situational contexts; when a child, for example, makes use of the same expression for clothes, a walk, his bonnet, his stroller, all of this is tied to the one situation in which these elements occur. The expression is not used for anything at all, but only in a specific area.[10] Children's playing with meanings and the expressions designating them results subsequently in the discovery that everything has a name, a discovery which Bühler has termed one of the most important for the whole of life.[11]

As for the general mental attitude in this entire process of free play with meaning, several researchers have recently characterized it concurrently as a rudimentary form of the theoretical attitude toward things. Ludwig Landgrebe's study,[12] following in the footsteps of Marty and Ammann, emphasizes in particular the difference between original, affectively guided behavior of children and their behavior in naming, as well as the fact that the child, in naming, does not use expressive sounds but rather formations created in earlier play with his phonic organs, growing out of an imitation of sounds. Landgrebe concludes from his analyses that there is at the basis of the "naming function" (Ammann's term)[13] a conscious distinction between representational and thought-behavior, on the one hand, and emotional behavior on the other. This is, expressed in other words, what we have spoken of as man's becoming aware of his ideal power over the world, of the difference between himself as subject and his tendencies, i.e., of his own freedom.—Maurice Blondel, for his part, in his work on the genesis and development of thought,[14] views the institution of conventional signs as the first act of a purely human, intellectual attitude toward reality, an act which contains already potentially the entire subsequent development of thought. Among psychological facts, Blondel especially stresses observations of retarded mental development in sensibly handicapped individuals, in particular the case of Marie

Heurtin[15] (parallel to the better-known story of Helen Keller); he shows how the institution and comprehension of signs awakens all the fruitful initiative, all the infinite wealth of a mind seemingly condemned to life-long imprisonment, which here breaks its chains.

The birth of language is indeed inseparably linked with the development of thought; thought here is, at first, a naming judgment, i.e., the attribution of a sign to a determinate objectivity, then the analysis of reality by means of language, the beginning of general subsumptive activity. This obtains in the naming stage, when children want to know the name of everything and make this desire unequivocally clear by their behavior, repeating the same process with a great variety of things. Meanings—the types resulting originally from a passive synthesis of coincidence—become *ours*, univocally disposable, only with the emergence of signs which we can have at our disposal; in the naming process, the subject takes possession of the universe and brings clarity into it. The unity of the name embraces, unites a certain region of reality; through systematic linguistic practice the child acquires an idea of the articulation of the whole as shaped by the community in which he is growing up.

This whole process takes place at first openly, not in mere representation, but rather in the effective realization of verbal expressions; thought-development is thereby already integrated into the collective context. Though it can happen that children create their own language, as in the well-known case of Carl Stumpf's son,[16] this is nothing but play, based and modeled on adult speech, presupposing the comprehension of adults and an understanding of their speech; the subjective thought-function of speech never goes without the intersubjective, social function.

It would seem to follow from the very nature of language and its acquisition that the process of language invention in general went through stages of natural signs leading up to the discovery and grasping of meaning, and, finally, as in children, to the understanding of the fact that everything has a name. The affective signal showing recognition of a situation must have become meaning-bearing, and this was made possible only by the rudimentarily intelligent behavior discerned in children as the basis of the naming function and anchored in the incipient actual awareness of human freedom.

3. The Mastering of Passive Experience

Thought begins with our explicit mastering of what has developed in our pre-thought experience practically without our active participation; thinking is the development of spontaneity. No earlier form of experience can explain it—it rests only on freedom as the fundamental form of human existence. At the same time, thought remains originally engaged in the context of our practical ends; provided it is not mere play, it is a strategy for attaining goals. But this is not detrimental to freedom; even so, there lives in thought a tendency toward clarification, toward the active ideal mastering of reality, a tendency that, from the first moment of the apperception of a verbal sign, is continuously accompanied by words.

In pre-thought experience, all synthesis—and without synthesis there is no unified objectivity—comes to pass so to say automatically, with no respect to our I, largely passive. Thought in the sense of judgment is, however, an active synthesis, such that I am aware that it is performed by me; at the same time, in judicative synthesis, relation is thematized and brought to the center of attention. While there are relations present in perception, implied in the categorial formation of what is presented, they are not properly discerned; the purely passively perceived world is a world of qualities, processes, and things. We see colors on things, shades or nuances in colors, we perceive notes as part of a melody, and the like, but none of this is in the proper sense a judgment, the discernment of a relation; rather, it is, as it were, a matter of the automatic functioning of experiential forms. Judgment can arise only where the self-evident functioning of relational consciousness proves insufficient and fails. Original structural awareness functions self-evidently as long as the feeling of freedom, the feeling of an ascendancy over the world and the conscious ambition to master it, remains dormant; but this feeling becomes active very early in man, so that there is in fact no stage at which one can draw a perfect parallel between human and animal behavior. This has been interestingly confirmed by Boutan's[17] and Kellogg's comparative experiments regarding the behavior of infants and animals brought up together;[18] the child is at first at a disadvantage with regard to the animal and its purely empirical and utilitarian method; as long as his own attempts are governed by the principle of trial and error, the animal's better adapted sense-aptitudes and faculties of motricity and association make the child appear considerably handicapped. However, as soon as the child conceives the situation no longer in a purely utilitarian way, from the standpoint of the desired outcome, but rather as play, interesting in itself, as a complex of interesting realities about which he has to obtain clarity, both his behavior and the results achieved show a radical change, leaving animal achievements first slowly then quickly far behind. The child wants to make things clear to himself, to know the hows and whys; in consequence, he actively observes and anticipates, i.e., judges, whereas the animal wants nothing but the result. Judgment thus arises in the context of practical behavior, as a corollary of interest in the mechanism of such behavior, a corollary of striving to actively appropriate it.

A decisive stage in this process of appropriation of the world is the mastering of speech and, first of all, the acquiring of vocabulary in naming judgments; the comprehension of the meaning of a word is indeed a naming judgment, putting into relation a sound formation and an objective intention; the use of the word in recognition is then already a manner of judgment of subsumption; in both cases, a simple verbal expression, a simple name, is in fact a proposition, the expression of a judgment. The mastering of speech presupposes, as an acquired habitus, a long sequence of such judgments which become our possession, as it were, without our awareness. Syntheses then come about on the basis of this possession: what is given shape in the first declarative and attributive judgments, accompanied by a corresponding verbal expression, is in fact the appropriation of prepredicative thing-syntheses.

Thing-syntheses, as performed by judging, take place in forms which, though intersubjectively objective, are not so naturally. The form of a judgment—this specific unification of two meanings in relation to each other—is not simply an object relation but rather a form of synthetic, or, more precisely, of actively synthetic consciousness; the same goes for the form of a collection, i.e., the unification of iteratively added units while at the same time retaining previous ones, or of a disjunction, i.e., going through the parts of a retained whole one by one, with no summative unification. This operation actively grasps object relations which up to then were merely passively produced, such as the relation of whole and part, substrate and determination, substrate and substrate's activity— substrates and determinations are isolated from the represented whole and become components of an actively synthetic rational universe or universe of judgment.

On the basis of the intellectual, judgmental apperception of reality, the perceived universe thus becomes the conceived universe. It need not be stressed further that language plays an important role in this process: language, the primary instrument of analysis of the presented whole, becomes also, *eo ipso*, an instrument of its active synthesis. Both processes, synthesis as well as analysis, are artificial, even when carried out on the basis of the articulation of things themselves; only the actively judging mind can experience the world as a totality of facts, and what is acquired by the process of judging—its knowledge—is a system of actively produced judgments as units of meaning at its disposal.

The *proposition*, as a means of expression of the process of analysis and synthesis the unity of which makes up judgment, or of the thought-processes based on judgments, must develop the results of both the analytic and synthetic procedure; this means that it must have objective, substantial, and syntactic means of expression. Language has to build up means of expression such that the process of object-synthesis can be un-equivocally observed in it. Only thereby can it become an objectification of meaning, fulfill the function noted by so many philosophical observ-ers. Wilhelm von Humboldt saw the essential function of language in that subjectivity here passes over into the object without ceasing to be itself.[19] Hegel expressed the same view with even greater force: "Einbildungskraft ist eine nur leere, Form gebende, bezeichnende, die Form als innerliches setzende, aber die Sprache ist die das Innerliche als Seiendes setzende Kraft."[20] In a similar vein, Julius Stenzel wrote recently that in language "steht der gemeinte Sinn, der innere Gedanke zugleich als eine Realität im Sein da; der Geist steht sich selbst gegenüber."[21]

In order to understand the objectifying character of language, we shall have to inquire into the means of this objectification. These means are of two kinds, sensible and intellectual. They will be dealt with in this order.

4. The Sensible Aspect of Language

We must, then, go back to sensibility, which we have dealt with already in the preceding chapter, and reconsider it from the angle of the sensible aspect of language as means of expression. This, however, makes it first necessary to address once more the question of sensibility in general. In chapter 3, we saw that sensibility is not a set of inanimate atomic data but rather an incessant qualitative creation out of which our affectability and tendency toward coinciding first make something like a firm qualitative datum. Firm qualities are always already an idealization, albeit automati-cally occurring, a unification of the impressional; whether or not there follows a differentiation into ever more subtle nuances depends again on our interests and tendencies, i.e., on affectability. In all sense-domains we thus encounter the manifestation of a sort of contradiction: we have on the one hand a gradual passing of qualitative nuances into one another, a transition which can be refined down to the imperceptible, and on the other hand fundamental discontinuous qualities which divide the qualita-tive continuum, as it were, into zones. The same phenomenon obtains for the intensity of qualities: here, too, we have at once continuous tran-sition and certain well-defined stages which, with more subtle observa-tion, admit additional intermediates (for acoustic intensity, Helmholtz used a scale of ten degrees, Stumpf, originally, a scale of five;[22] a similar scale of intensities is also in use in the theory of colors). From all this it seems to follow that a system of qualities is always the result of the differentiation of originally complex, not easily graspable impressions, analogous, for example, to what we have in listening to and vainly attempting to analyze music which we do not understand, which is beyond the pale of our acoustic habits. This raises the question of the essence of the sensible units: are they something given once and for all, or, rather, are they possible only as the respective members of a system formed in conscious (though passive) genesis? Under the influence of sensualism, sense-data are often held to be, in Locke's words, "the materials of all our knowledge," with a "store" of which the mind is "furnished";[23] on the other hand, it should be stressed that sensibility becomes the important vital function it is for all living creatures only because there constitutes itself for us a system of the fundamental sense-qualities which are at our disposal. Our sense-experiencing is never (once it has reached sufficient differentiation) without a certain scale; the values of this scale are, so to say, "normal," the others are then situated, by their means, as "transitions," "nuances," "impure notes," etc. A scale of this sort is also among the means by which we master reality *idealiter*. Precisely because it is something in internal time-consciousness, a product of its unifying functions, the scale can itself be subject to certain changes; thus, as concerns colors, psychologists admit that a child's scale is at first extremely simple, distinguishing light and dark on the one hand, colorful (as a unitary qualitative determination) on the other. It is also claimed that the color scale of primitive peoples differs from ours and, in some cases, does not distinguish green and blue, blue and violet, red and rose as separate hues.[24] Some maintain that all these phenomena should be explained as an evolution of the evaluation of sense-qualities, and not as the development of sensibility itself.[25] It is clear however that, precisely with the emergence of a qualitative scale, which is, as it were, an automatic result of our tendencies toward coincidence, the very nature of the sense-experience changes, acquiring, in consequence, a different qualitative character. Sensibility itself would thus be, to a certain extent, a historical fact, a fact of creative life. Qualitative scales would have to be analyzed, too, as facts of significance for the lifestyle. Where dark colors are not differentiated, for example, we would have to inquire into the interest which inhibits differentiation. In this connection it should also be mentioned that sensibility can undergo profound *qualitative* modifications by virtue of what it objectively *represents*. This is most obvious with sight and vision. A color has a totally different qualitative character, depending on whether it is apprehended as "free," or as a "surface" or a "volume" color; surface colors offer resistance to the eye in a way that, in free colors (such as the color of the sky, or homogeneous colors viewed through a screen), is out of the question and, in volume colors, gives way to transparency, the eye penetrating into the colored mass.[26] However much this impression may rest upon associative links, it is nonetheless a live qualitative impression, capable of gradation. This is offered in support of the thesis that sensibility cannot be isolated from the context of the objectifying functions, of which it is a live, plastic component—a finding also acknowledged by a number of present-day psychologists. One can cite Jaensch: "Der Farbensinn zeigt . . . jene besondere Einrichtung auf die Erfassung von Gegenständen, die eine Grundeigentümlichkeit aller Erkenntnisvorgänge ist und hier im Gebiete dieser höheren seelischen Funktionen als 'intentionaler Charakter' bezeichnet zu werden pflegt"[27]—and David Katz is in agreement with him on this point. Without this intentional character, of being engaged in the whole of objectification which codetermines its qualitative nature, sensibility could not include phenomena such as the "apparent" and the "genuine" color of an object, color-constancy under changes in illumination and other constancy phenomena. The analytical nature proper to our sense-life, whereby it participates in the forming of independent objectivity for us, would thus seem to be also already, in part, the work of what we have called the free personal standpoint—as opposed to the syncretic character of animal perception, observed by Volkelt and others.[28]—The idea of our sensibility as functionally and hence, in a way, historically conditioned can be illustrated by the acoustic aspect of language. Language as an acoustic phenomenon has, of course, its own sense-*domain* encompassing all the *possible* sounds that can be used for creating words, i.e., produced by our organic apparatus and acoustically differentiated. Linguistic sounds also have the particularity that they are not to be considered as atoms, but that gradual transitions can be established between them. In addition, linguistic sounds can be ordered into continuous series according to their affinities (not into one single series but into several; though that is a fact of secondary importance in the present context). And, as in other sense-domains, we find here too the fact of discontinuity, primary in regard to the supposed continuum. Here, too, a tendency toward coinciding brings about a condensation of qualitative nuances around certain values, so that intermediate sounds are characterized as unsuccessful, inaccurate modifications of the normal ones. This condensation does not take place separately for each "value"; rather, it is governed by certain principles and concerns the whole of the qualitative differences; the sense-domain is the same in different languages, but it is differently structured. The sphere of possible vowels, for example, is illustrated by the familiar triangle of Hellwag, which, for this reason, has been called a "natural vowel system."[29] This "natural system" then contains all the historical systems, "deren jedes für die betreffende Nation und Zeit besondere Stellen des Vokaldreiecks auszeichnet, ähnlich wie bestimmte instrumentale Klangfarben und wie die besonderen Intervalle der verschiedenen gebräuchlichen Leitern, ja auch gewisse absolute Tonhöhen für das Gehör der bezüglichen Nation oder Zeit ausgezeichnet sind. . . . Aber diese Auszeichnungen sind im allgemeinen akustisch zufällig und bedeutungslos . . ."[30] What we hear in listening to speech are formations composed of the values of the scale of a particular language, i.e., phonemes.

In his works on language theory, Karl Bühler seeks to reduce this fact to what he calls "the principle of abstractive relevance," and, hence, to interpret phonemes as conventions.[31] Just as we can conventionally establish flag signals where all that matters is the color and not the size or shape of the signaling surface, a sort of tacit convention selects, according to Bühler, in a phoneme, out of the wealth of characters and nuances susceptible of sense-perception, a limited number of features sufficient for the diacrisis of signs of different values. The other features have no importance for linguistic signifying, we abstract from them, they are irrelevant with respect to the sign function. Perhaps a bit of interpretation is needed here. What convention and what abstraction does Bühler have in mind? Certainly not abstraction in the sense of active observation and isolation of points of agreement in a differentiated qualitative manifold, but rather a nonobservation of disagreements, a differentiation stopped at the right point, so that we do not notice any selection in the proper sense of the word. In short, sounds are not phonemes because they are important for meaning; rather, they are important for meaning because they are phonemes. For the naive consciousness, the phonemes of the mother tongue account for the whole of the sensible aspect of language, all else appears as nuances; in an encounter with another, different language, the naive listener has initially confused sense-impressions, analogous to the "incomprehensible music" mentioned above; these are then followed by an effort to grasp the expressions of the foreign language by means of the listener's own phonological stock, an attempt to penetrate the foreign language by means of familiar principles.[32] Contrasting the phonic values of the foreign language with the mother tongue (which remains the starting point) is a stage which comes later.—Bühler himself draws a parallel between the "constancy of the diacritical itemized description [*Signalement*]" and the constancy of the size of visual objects, of colors under changing illumination, and of sound intensity with change of distance, but he believes nonetheless that the constancy of the diacritical itemized description is a phenomenon of a different kind, since phonemes, in a more precise psychological analysis, are—already in the perception in which we grasp them—closer to conceptual moments than to sense-qualities; however, this is not a truly fundamental difference but only a difference of degree. As to Bühler's opinion that the phoneme is always accompanied by moments irrelevant for meaning (such as timbre, pitch, and other expressive factors in the voice) from which it must be abstractively isolated, the fact is that similar phenomena are to be found in all sense-domains; e.g., in surface colors the qualities are always perceived on a material of a certain structure which can differ while the hue remains the same.

At the same time, it must be made clear that, contrary to the belief of Julius Stenzel,[33] the concept of form is certainly not sufficient to explain linguistic sense-perception. As Bühler has rightly shown, the form principle obtains in language *alongside* the phonological principle; Bühler distinguishes *Klanggesicht*, "sound face," and *Signalement*, "itemized description."[34] Phonemes are not forms but rather analytically elaborated units; they are a matter of the unitary elaboration and penetration of an entire sense-domain by the principle of a unified scale, and it is therefore correct to say that a phoneme is possible only within a system, that it exists by virtue of its relations to other members of the system;[35] and yet phonemes are qualitative impressions, their relations too are given, as it were, as "absolute impressions," with no explicit evocation of the correlative members, just as, e.g., the impression that a tone is high-pitched or weak is given without simultaneous awareness as opposed to what it is so.

The child's finding his footing in the phonological scale is a process of adaptation governed by the end of his making himself understood. It is by no means easy; the active use of the scale, in particular, begins with rough approximations, which only later slowly make way for more accurate achievements.[36] Correct pronunciation is the result of a long-term effort; psychologists have observed that it often comes after grammatical proficiency and the acquisition of a considerable vocabulary.[37] On the other hand, language cannot function without at least a rudimentarily adapted sensibility. The process of language acquisition forms a whole in which sensibility and meaning are mutually helpful allies.

5. Language as Objective Meaning

A unified phonological scale is a prerequisite of language as objective meaning. In order for language to acquire the faculty of representation, in order for us to be able to see in a linguistic utterance more than the mere acoustic phenomenon, there are, however, further conditions to be fulfilled. The associative theory, with its claim that each individual word calls up a certain idea, is insufficient; understanding a language would then be a series of discrete acts, in Bühler's words, like "a veritable inner machine-gun fire,"[38] which is far removed from the actual phenomenon of linguistic understanding. We would do better to consider Wittgenstein, in whose ingenious theory understanding new meaning on the basis of already known signs is possible inasmuch as the proposition is a logical picture of a fact,[39] and language a logical picture of the world. Along the lines of Wittgenstein's conception, it would be possible to understand that the meaning of *propositions* is immediately present to us in the perceiving, just as the object depicted is present in a painting: interpretation of an overpowering suggestion based on a similarity of aspect. The individual word would then have meaning from the moment it is understood that it can appear in propositions, or sentences, as a representative sign.

Analyzing the relationship between fact and proposition, we discover however, in between, a third element that does not fully come into its own in Wittgenstein: the thought of, or judgment on the fact. Wittgenstein presupposes a priori that the thought is essentially the same thing as the proposition, i.e., the logical picture of a fact.[40] He presupposes, consequently, the theory of the receptive, nonproductive nature of thought, from which follow further consequences of his theory, such as the nonexistence of logical "objects,"[41] etc. In keeping with our subjective method, we must, on the contrary, track down the judging activity in order to achieve clarity on these questions. We have characterized judging as the active effecting of a synthesis in the grasping of relations between things. The original theme of judging is thus a fact, something real (or supposedly real); the fact (as an isolated unit) is constituted in judging. At the same time, however, the judgment is *pre*constituted as a nonreal, purely thinkable entity, susceptible of apprehension as the object of a higher-order judicative act, but originally nonthematic in judging as such.[42] Without going any further, this fact alone shows the process of thought as creative, a creation not of reality but of ideal formations. We must now follow in greater detail the creation of these ideal formations, which are units for thought and, in this sense, have a kind of "existence" that we know, of course, to be dependent on our subjective activity.

Let us take the attributive judgment "S is p." It can be said of this judgment that it represents an objective relation of attribution, since the thing here is represented as an independent moment, the property as a dependent one. If thought were indeed a mere depiction, it could never think the members of this relationship differently, in other forms. In actual fact, it is capable of rendering the dependent moment ideally independent, making it into a kind of secondary substrate without losing sight of the fact that what is thought thereby objectively is exactly the same as was previously thought in attribute form; it is capable of making the entire fact "S is p" into a secondary substrate, while remaining aware that the fact itself is the same in this new form.[43] This process is indeed of great practical value: if not for it, systematic reflection—which requires a series of judgments, Descartes's famous chain of deductions of which all links can be held, so to say, in one mental gaze[44]—would be impossible.

Having thus seen that a formal discrepancy between thought and fact is possible, that *the same* can be thought not only in a variety of subjective modalities of clarity and belief but also in different objective thought-forms, we must ask to what the character of depiction observed in linguistic expression actually refers: is it *primo loco* a depicting of thought-formations, or rather of objective facts? This is a variant of the older question whether names are the names of ideas or rather of things, often debated especially in British philosophy.[45] Here, too, what is ultimately in question is whether language is, originally and consistently, a picture of things or of ideas, and whether it should be (in consequence) intellectually or objectively oriented. Who is right: Leibniz, for whom language is a "mirror of reason" (*Spiegel des Verstandes*), or Wittgenstein, who sees it as a "mirror of the world" (*speculum universi*)? Should we, accepting Wittgenstein's thesis, seek then to purge language of all that does not correspond to his objectivist ideal, all that is a product of thought itself, of its synthetic and formative activities, reflexively turned toward the producing thought itself? We believe the postulate of a critique of language to be fulfilled in precisely distinguishing the two sorts of "being," reality and ideal formations, admitting an insurmountable distance between the two, and subjecting the process of forming the ideal, categorial being to close investigation. Putting the properly signifying function of language into relation with facts alone, and not with thought-formations, would mean, however, to fail to appreciate the fact that the fundamental function of language is intersubjective contact, internal communication.

The problem of the objective presentation of linguistic meaning must therefore be elaborated on the basis of the fundamental schemata of the synthetic function of thought. Understanding a language, as Karl Bühler rightly stressed, is not a matter of the successive correlation of meanings, nor, as we have seen, of the sentential expression univocally representing the structure of a fact. It resides in introducing objective signs into certain forms, certain general thought schemes, of which we have at our disposal a certain number that we can then connect in a lawful manner. The starting point here is a twofold fundamental schema: the judgment expressing an attribution, the assigning of certain determinations to a substrate considered with no regard to possible changes, and the judgment expressing a process. The analysis of this twofold schema brings us to three essential moments: the concept of substrate, a concept for determinations, and the concept of a synthetic relationship between the two. Consequently, it is impossible for language to be composed solely of object-expressions; in other words, language must contain names for substrates, names for processes, names for (object- or processual) determinations, and a means of indicating the unity of the synthetic meaning, syntactic signs. We presuppose here that a process cannot be conceived of as the property of a substrate; to say of something that it moves or changes does not mean to select, out of the totality (so to say) of object-determinations, one that is assigned to the thing; rather, it means to consider the thing (or, at least, the determination that changes and must then be made into a secondary substrate) as a whole, to observe what is happening as a process engaging the whole of the thematized thing or object-moment. A verbal, processual determination cannot be simply converted to an attribution; this is confirmed, among others, by the fact that all languages know the difference between nouns and verbs.[46] We are here in the presence of one of the facts common to pure logical grammar and to general grammar, if we understand by pure logical grammar (in Husserl's sense) the theory of possible forms of thought, and by universal grammar (in Meillet's sense) a comparative empirical theory of the grammatical facts common to all languages of the world. Language must have certain means whereby these fundamental categories are differentiated; in addition, it must have means for expressing their belonging together in meaning, and it is a historical fact, too, that there are no languages without grammatical auxiliaries—at once a fact and a law, which Bühler has termed "the dogma of lexicon and syntax."[47] This is tied up with the fact that a linguistic proposition is rooted in a judgment, and the judgment is understood as a synthetic whole in which the different parts require one another; speaking and listening live in a continuous process of anticipation and fulfillment of intention aiming at wholes the schema of which is always somehow outlined for us from the very beginning of the proposition; the intention needs to be guided in a certain way, and this is the role of the syntactic grammatical auxiliaries.

Thought is, in general, something like the movement of intentionality, which takes place in certain forms and dimensions (disregarding the one universal and various more particular horizons in which it always moves). This will become clearer in presenting a few basic findings of the theory of intentionality. A judgment is the result of a series of intentional acts (judging) which can either possess their object (thing and objective relation) fully, in the original (a statement of fact, e.g., a perceptual judgment or any judgment performed with evidence), or be merely empty, unfulfilled intentions of which we know only the *meaning*, what they are aiming at, but not what is their actual import. A judgment is a whole of meaning that can be understood even without the evidence of the originary givenness of its object, without this verification; verification and meaning do not coincide, as some contemporary philosophers would have it—their claim is belied by a simple reflective glance. Nonetheless, mere consciousness of the meaning of a judgment spontaneously tends toward verification: it demands, so to speak, a veritative synthesis. We would say that such a judgment is a saturated but unfulfilled intention. On the other hand, an individual term, insofar as the whole sentence is not grasped, awakens an unsaturated intention: a consciousness of the need for completion in a whole, represented according to one of the possible thought-schemes. The intention of a predicative synthesis is thus to be distinguished from the intention of a veritative synthesis on which Husserl first demonstrated the dynamic character of intentionality, though this is no less proper to the predicative dimension.

The distinction between the saturated and unsaturated intentions awakened by certain linguistic expressions is destined to replace the theory of categorematic and syncategorematic expressions that is traditionally part of general grammar. Anton Marty, who elaborated this theory particularly thoroughly on the basis of Brentano's psychology, replaced these names with the terms "autosemantics" and "synsemantics," defining autosemantics as means of expression capable by themselves of evoking an independently communicable psychical phenomenon, which is not the case with synsemantics.[48] The division of terms according to this principle is an age-old practice; it originated with the Stoics, was extensively theorized by the medievals, who knew it from Priscian, and later taken up by Leibniz; it is noteworthy that it was never used by the science of language, that linguistics manifestly never felt the need for this doctrine. It is moreover not easy, according to Marty, to understand how synsemantics differ from mere meaningless syllables; a recent interpreter of Marty admits, regarding synsemantics, the consciousness of a certain syntactic function even outside the context of speech.[49] Does this not mean, however, that synsemantics too have a certain meaning? A preposition, for example, evokes the idea of a two-argument relation; only the intention of isolated synsemantics is necessarily unsaturated, the intention of a syntactic whole with empty spaces. As to the possible objection that a syllable too is linked with a kind of unsaturated consciousness, one can reply that there is a fundamental difference between mere protention toward a complete word and unsaturated consciousness. Protentional consciousness intends in conversation a certain word, it anticipates a well-defined linguistic reality, and this intention is capable of fulfillment or failure; if the anticipation becomes effective, the complete word, which of course has a meaning, is in fact already present. Unsaturated consciousness, however, is meaningful even without the filling of the arguments.—Auto-semantics, on the other hand, are representatives of saturated intentions. This whole discussion is of interest to us inasmuch as it illustrates the global character of the process of speech comprehension; this process is impossible without a dynamic unity of which the individual expressions are moments and which, in anticipated thought schemes, is present *prior to* the parts into which linguistic expression breaks it down.

We regard as logico-grammatical categories the concepts of sub-strate, substrate-determination, and process term; concrete grammatical categories, on the other hand, understood with Henri Delacroix as "tout procédé morphologique isolable et qui correspond à une notion,"[50] are tied to the specific conditions of concrete languages. Grammatical categories are not logical categories. But neither are logical categories always used, in languages, in an objectively correct way; a verb does not always express a process (or its modality, a state), nor a noun a substrate, yet we understand from the objective context what the intention concerns. This is why judgments expressing a process can be converted to attributions, after the manner of the whole of traditional logic, though we cannot help sensing a certain forcibleness in the procedure; the attributive form is then used simply as a transitional stage of the intention, and we resort, so to say, to an improper mode of synthesis. *In concreto*, of course, such a linguistic expression can also manifest a particular way of viewing objective relations; the Indo-European verbal sentence is thus rooted in a specific, active, and even personal conception of objective relationships, which is carried over onto purely attributive relations (*der Himmel blaut*—"the sky blues"). So it is at times difficult to tell where the boundary between the mere inner form of language, which does not involve the thought itself, and the true form of significational intention actually lies. But such considerations should not lead us to conclude, as some do,[51] that logical grammar is impossible, for even mere inner form, from which all proper meaning has already evaporated, still refers to a process of expression *proprio modo*, whose structure has an objective basis.

A full account of the functioning of language in thought and com-munication would now presuppose further description of the develop-ment of the syntactic forms through which the subject asserts control over reality. Having anticipated thought schemes at our disposal is indeed what lays the foundation for the mastery of the world through thought; this, along with thinking in language, first makes possible an extensive development of thinking in empty intentions, so important and charac-teristic for the praxis of human life; through this we first acquire, to the broadest extent, the actual faculty of analysis of reality. Speaking—be it subjective, i.e., linguistic thinking, or objective, i.e., intersubjective contact in language—presupposes of course the immense, continuously creative and infinitely rich world process; and the unitarily qualitative nature of this ultimate process, in which all is retained, and novelty integrated and anticipated in a unified manner, forms the true *ineffabile* of life which is not to be bound by any analytic law; in its ultimate essence, life cannot be grasped, but only manifested through expression. Thinking in syntactic forms ventures into this universal horizon and seeks to assert its control over all beings appearing within it; the meaning of all active intentional thought-syntheses lies ultimately in this appropriation of the world. The relationship between reality and judging, mirrored in the relationship between reality and language, is an unending task. We can differentiate and express ever subtler distinctions, give expression to ever more complex relations through increasingly complex syntactic schemes; the field of meanings and schemes at our disposal in thought and language can grow continually larger—there will never be an adequacy between the two.

The process of disposing with language, a direct consequence of the tendency toward holding things ideally at our disposal, toward clarity about them, toward truth, begins thus with the mastering of the most obvious and crudest articulations of experience and their insertion into elementary syntactic schemes; it unfolds under the influence of the conceptual and intellectual wealth contained in the objectively attained level of linguistic development, and culminates in independent linguistic creativity on this basis: every creative activity has its own special language, growing, of course, out of a common, universal fund. Let it suffice to indicate that this entire process of mastering the world, this entire, specifically human tendency toward life in truth, must be reflected in the means used by man for broadening, sharpening, and deepening his faculties of expression; connected with this tendency is the fact that language necessarily comprises the phenomenon of inner form, which so strikingly shows it to be something continually informed and transformed, a form remolded ever and again in a living process. The artificial "language" of mathematics has no need of an inner form, since reality has to submit to it, whereas real language seeks to follow the articulation of reality.

As is clear from the preceding, our problem here was not to study all the functions of language and speech (the expressive aspect, e.g., has been almost totally left aside). We have confined ourselves to a single task: to show how language rests on human freedom (as determining the human life-form) and how it is to be explained from the principle of free activity. For us, to live a truly human life means to live always in language and, through it, to come to terms with the world and our fellow men.

5

Conclusion

While the human world is historically variable, as we have seen above, there is something else—of fundamental importance for our problem— which does not change in history: the relationship between receptivity and spontaneity in the constitution of objectivity. Free, active thought, the constitution of categorial entities such as concepts, judgments, sets, numbers, mathematical theorems, is possible only on the basis of passive constitution, the constitution of sensibility in internal time-consciousness, followed by the constitution of the sensibly given object in the manifold of presented data. As we have seen, language is an important stage of this categorial constitution, a prerequisite for its higher levels. It is only on the basis of the fact of language as objective meaning that there can arise a purely theoretical tendency, seeking to find out what everything is, abstracting as much as possible from direct usefulness and, more generally, from integration in the contexts of human life. Language is indeed the means that every more or less extensive analysis of reality has to use to fix and order its results. Every *thaumazein* wonders perforce at an already articulated world, every problem presupposes already formed concepts which serve it as terms; in addition, language alone is capable of objectifying subjective thought processes and thus of bringing the processes of categorial constitution to higher clarity and supraindividual validity. Language is at our disposal, a living storehouse of categorial constitutes which the theoretical tendency seizes upon from the first, though it is not immediately able to clearly distinguish in them objective validity from mere instrumental value.

If it can be said that science was born on the day when the first evident demonstration was carried out, there follows an important consequence for our thesis. Demonstrations are operations with judgments, judgments are categorial constitutes which, even if they refer to extrajudgmental objectivity, are "entities" of their own kind, omnitemporal units. Science thus arises and moves on the plane of categorial constitution, which has been shown to presuppose, prior to it, the constitution of the naive, sensible world. *It follows that the results of the sciences should not be taken as starting point for analyzing the world, if only because they are high-order constitutes.* This does not mean to say that science has no noetic value, that it apprehends no objective laws; on the contrary, without a doubt, but the essential of the scientific process is to produce concepts and judgments which serve to articulate, to grasp, and to master the given naive world in a new way. It is thus, for example, that the introduction of appropriate concepts (such as the concept of mathematical law) in physics gave birth to the modern conception of *nature* as the object of mathematical natural science; this breakthrough of mathematics into a sphere once governed by a totally different approach then leads to the increasing exclusion of certain categories (e.g., substance, causality) and their substitution by mathematical analogues (function, functional relationships). Yet this reforming of the principles of understanding things, this reformation of our world constitutively presupposes the naive world, more fundamental, more important, primary by nature, and built by other constitutive means—the world of our everyday praxis, which forces itself upon us in perception and asserts itself as judge and arbiter in questions of reality and unreality. And we can say more than that. In its struggle against anthropomorphism, this reformation, which constitutively presupposes the naive world, does not and cannot draw the radical consequences, it cannot totally abstract from everything relative to man, and this for a very essential reason: the tendency toward the dehumanization of the world, as it was called in chapter 1,[1] is itself indexed by an eminently practical human tendency, namely, the tendency toward as complete as possible control over reality. This tendency is satisfied by the conception of being as mathematical (obeying mathematical laws) infinitely more so than by the naively biomorphic, the anthropomorphic, or the theological conception. The idea of technical control is at the very root of the modern conception of nature, and modern philosophers and scientists as well are under its influence even when they believe themselves engaged in purest theory. The history of the development of modern science has yet to be written from this point of view, investigating how this tendency made itself felt in the outstanding founders of modern mechanism; the significance here of Leonardo the engineer, Bacon the insatiable political practitioner and visionary, Descartes the mechanistic physician, etc., has yet to be made clear; and even in Galileo himself, opposition to the "imprecise" Aristotelian world can be shown to be connected with the ambition of total (both intellectual and practical) control over reality, an ambition gratified to the utmost by the mathematization of the universe.[2]—Since this entire conception of the *rational controllability* of the world is relative to a tendency proper to man, a tendency which comes into play in history with now greater and now lesser energy, we can say that, though it may be a way to eliminate anthropomorphism in particulars, such will not be the case in the overall understanding of being, which remains relative to our vital necessities and endeavors. It thus becomes manifest once again that the hypostatization of natural science is a false metaphysics which, believing that it has its starting point in objective laws and explains both the objective and the subjective universe on their basis, fails to realize that the meaning of the objects it starts from presupposes subjective tendencies, and that these are what actually gives its proceedings their criteria and shows it the way.

Metaphysics in the proper sense of the word, genuine philosophy, is rather the theory of constitution. A field of rigorous scientific investigation opens up here for philosophy, but the orientation of this inquiry is not what objectivist ontology takes it to be. Its task is not to overcome the subject, understood as an obstacle to the perfect knowledge of the world, but rather to seek in the subject itself the law of experience which gives rise to reality in all its forms, in the entire manifold of its phenomena. This is one (the ideal) task of philosophy: to carry out first of all a detailed analysis of all human experience, to seek to clarify the immanent laws of experience and perform all the operations of variation made possible by these laws or structures. A second task, closer in style to traditional "metaphysics," is that of universal history. Universal history is for us a whole, which comprises the history not only of mankind but of all creatures; we envisage it as an *interpretation* of the whole world process on the basis of the fundamental structures of possible subjectivity, as brought to light by constitutive analysis. The task of such a historization of the universe could be termed creative evolution.[3] The creative evolution that the whole universe goes through in the activity of constitution, up through the highest accomplishments of conscious creation in human history, is of course a superhuman task, presupposing above all much more intensive progress in the sciences and much more intensive philosophical analysis—only jointly will the two be able to manage the task of interpreting all existence from the inner sources of life itself. There is, however, a much less demanding task that must first be taken up, the closely analytical task of elaborating structures that could barely be suggested in the philosophical impetus to date, thereby preparing, in an unpretentious yet creative manner, the future unity of science and philosophy. This task can be undertaken all the more willingly since the very idea of constitution—this profound, key metaphysical idea—guarantees the unity of the life process in all its most varied manifestations and products, and teaches us to turn to the forces of inwardness where there are problems to be solved and acts to be accomplished.

"The Natural World" Remeditated Thirty-Three Years Later

I

Looking back on our first philosophical work after so many years gone by, we are struck by the lack of system and the unfinished conceptual analysis of the questions dealt with. We did not even succeed in clearly stating the question, to say nothing of proving that the solution we had in mind was the only satisfactory one, if only for the time being.—When we say that modern man lives, on the one hand, in a naturally given environment, and, on the other hand, in a world created for him by mathematical natural science, the idea comes naturally that the contradiction in which he is continually obliged to live—the contradiction opposing the purely objective necessity of mathematically conceived nature and all being for which this objectivity serves as a model to lived-experienced life—is the work of a certain *metaphysics*, namely, the method of direct and indirect quantification, *hypostatized into the primal, original reality*, the very substance of the world, determining the essential character of all its attributes, components, and aspects, of everything that depends upon it. We did not, however, succeed in precisely formulating the definition of this contradiction, nor did we clearly draw all the major consequences that follow from it: the impersonalization of subjective experiencing, the forgetfulness of the intentional nature of lived-experience, the disregard for the twofold sense of body and corporeality, the crossing-out of the objectivity of qualities . . . Here throughout a tendency toward "scientization" is making headway, and scientization is understood primarily as objectification, carried by the spirit and the means of both indirect and direct mathematization. In their own domain, mathematization and objectification are eminently legitimate methodical procedures. The question is, however, whether they can cope with the problem of the *world*, whose comprehension implies that a certain part of being relates to being *as a whole*. Here, mere objectivity, endowed with mathematical exactness, pervaded with geometrical regularity and governed by causal laws, can give no explanation. Nor will it suffice to introduce the concept of subject as a necessary complement. The "subject," too, can be conceived of in such a way as to acquire the mode of being of a mere thing. The whole complex of the original givenness of the world will have to be submitted to a new, principled analysis, not only bringing to light its various components and aspects but inquiring into their originally given mode of being—only thus can we come closer to a solution.

But what does it mean to inquire into the mode of being? Basically, nothing other than to inquire, for such and such a component of being, into the temporal character peculiar to it, to ascertain where it belongs with respect to the various levels and dimensions of time and temporality. Abstract objectivities are characterized by timelessness: localization at a determinate place of the one objective time has no meaning for them. Object realities are situated in the objective time common to all things, though measurable always only from the standpoint of a certain system. The objects of the natural world, its practical objectivities, are in a time that can be designated as "time for . . .": time for work, for rest, for play. One could say that our lived life itself takes place at various levels of time, the most original of which cannot be called being in time, but rather the being of original time itself.

Why is time an indispensable component of the definition of the being of existent things? Temporal levels and horizons are various internally coherent modes both of the separation from the whole that means individuation and of the synthesis, the combining that first defines and determines the existent *for us*. A finite creature, in its encounters with the existent, is dependent on synthesis, on the unification of what it has lived through, and, finally, on its own temporality. Time (space is one of its dimensions) is that without which neither the being of particulars in the world nor our clarity concerning the existent, our comprehension, our comprehending behavior and action, and, finally, knowledge would be possible.

What comes of thus acknowledging temporality in the characterization of being? A twofold thesis: on the one hand, the existent cannot be understood without a relation to being, and, on the other hand, the being of things cannot be ascertained without a relation to the openness for what can be understood, for the *meaning* without which our experience would be unthinkable. The philosophical doctrine traditionally called "metaphysics" has focused since ancient times on the being of what exists *without this relationship*. The problem of the natural world, understood in depth as a restitution of the original character of the being of the world and its components, is thus connected with the question of a revision of metaphysics.

Modern science, especially natural science, is metaphysical insofar as it fails to inquire into the mode of being of its objects, insofar as it simply posits their reality without investigating the meaning of this reality; this means that metaphysics, in its natural-scientific version, ignores the problem of meaning in general. "Meaning" is consigned to explicit conscious human activities, to language, logic, and science; and even here, it is regarded as a mere "picture" of the facts.

The description and ontological characterization of the natural world is, on the contrary, in its entirety a study of sense and meaning. But meaning is always meaning for someone, there is no meaning in general. Objects, things do not have meaning; rather, their being has meaning for us, makes sense to us, and *this is precisely why* we can encounter them in experience.

Since meaning is always *meaning for . . .* , the study of the natural world will necessarily be a *study in reflection.* Study in reflection makes it possible to place the study of the natural world on its natural ground, to accomplish it, not in a speculative manner, but rather by analyzing given structures in search of the presuppositions of all meaning contained within them. Unlike objective perception, reflection does not transcend into things outside us, but remains at first attached to our own existence. We say that it is immanent, whereas external perception is, as to its type of being, transcendent.

A philosophical consideration meant to grasp what, in all experience, is the primal ground of all meaning, cannot do without reflection. Reflection, self-apprehension, is its element. The scope, the nature, the meaning, and the possibility of reflection remain, however, problematic.

The scope: what can we embrace, what can we grasp of ourselves in reflection? As we all know, the *communis opinio* answers, starting with Augustine and Descartes: the self-certainty of our existence. But the self-certainty of existence does not include the apprehension of its *contents*, of its *structure*, and, most importantly, of its essential *nature*.

Reflection does not relate to contents—not in the absolute, but as a whole. This is because the content of my internal life is extended in time and stretches beyond the domain of what I remember of myself—I forget myself, my lived-experiences, just as I forget other events. But, if reflection does not grasp the entire scope of my experiencing, is it not at least possible to distinguish a sphere that it does indubitably grasp from that which is not apprehended in it? Is not my living presence such a sphere of absolute immanence, where reflection is entirely free, at home, on absolutely certain and evident ground? Is it not possible, then, to define precisely this *sphere of my own immanence* and to reduce the task of philosophy to what is observed within it: so that the conditions of possibility of all my experiences would lie here at hand, unnoticed but graspable?

But, apart from the question whether absolute immanence is indeed possible, is it truly the goal of all reflection? What is reflection? Under what conditions do we accomplish it? What makes it in principle, ontologically, possible? Can we assume with Descartes that reflection is something like turning the eye to an object, not this time to an object that continually eludes us, like the external object, but rather to one that simply offers itself up, since it is analyzed solely in living presence?

Modern Cartesians, like Husserl in a good many of his works, assume that (1) reflection has no "mundane" stimulus and motive, it can be accomplished in the purity of a sheerly theoretical interest in experience as such, an interest anchored in nothing pretheoretical implying the thesis of the world; (2) reflection apprehends an object which is clear in itself, and apprehends it, not in its mere "appearance," but rather in its absolute being, which is in no way modified by this apprehension; (3) the evidence of the *cogito* guarantees the grasping of the reflective object in the original, and this object is the stream of lived-experience, the stream of consciousness, which can be apprehended by reflection in its very essence, in its essential specificity.

But is reflection truly something purely theoretical? Is it indeed the realization of a totally pure, disinterested view? Is reflection in its genuine essence a transformation of the bond that ties me to my own existence? Does it really—in consequence—give access to a totally new ego, the absolute transcendental subject, the stream of lived-experiences that "constitutes" all objectivity? Is this experiential stream, in which each lived-experiencing has its own type, its own essence, and its own essential relationship to other experiences, truly the essence of my being? Is not such a conception a fundamental misunderstanding of the being of my own ego, of my own being? Is not the essential nature of my—or anyone's—own life wholly "practical"? Is not the discovery of the self, of our ownmost existence, essentially different from what can be ascertained by *mere* view? In reducing the question of the essence of the ego to the question of its lived-experiences are we not eschewing its true nature?

We believe, on the contrary, that reflection, however radical, even that which performs an *epochē* with respect to all preconceptions, is a *countermove* against the automatic tendency of life not to see itself as it is, to look away from itself, from its essential uncertainty concerning itself and its possibilities—against our tendency to turn elsewhere or take refuge in illusions and false tranquility, blinding ourselves to our own sight which would expose us and paralyze our myopic security regarding the pitfalls of human existence. Reflection is a countermove against the *interestedness* of naive life.

True, the *origin* of all clarity lies in a certain kind of interestedness, since clarity is possible only because there exists a being that must *accomplish* its being as something that is not simply there, but rather as a "charge" laid upon it, so that this being is necessarily concerned with its mode of being. Interestedness is, however, ambivalent: it can be an interest in uncovering our being or, also, in covering it up and leaving it in concealment. We must therefore make a distinction between the fundamental interestedness in being, which lies at the root of all that is human, and bad interestedness, interest in an average, comfortable, nonproblematic, nondisquieting mode of subsisting. The being and existence of things is uncovered solely *by virtue* of an interest, but not *in keeping* with interests. Interest in our own being gives the *possibility*, but not the *reality*, of truth.

This is why we can say that interest (and, naturally, first and foremost, interest in ourselves, in our own being) *discloses* being in its being, but that is not to say that it *opens* it. Disclosure—the possibility of actively acquiring truth about what is—does not yet mean the reality of truth which, on the contrary, remains to be conquered from interestedness.

While disclosing the world, interestedness also maintains its closure, since it expresses itself originally and primarily as a factical being in thrall to shallow, subsidiary interests. It produces a factical tendency to see things, and ourselves, not as they are, but rather as we wish, as we "need" them to be.

Reflection appears as an indispensable counterfactor to this tendency, the countermove we must necessarily deploy if we are not to become its helpless victims. And the being which deploys this countermove—unnecessary in animals—is precisely the being to which the world is disclosed, a being which lives in an abundance of possibilities in which it understands innerworldly beings. An animal is entirely what it is, its possibilities are also its realities. In it, every possibility is simultaneously actualized, and it has, therefore, no need of a world, of anything beyond the surroundings that are at any time at its reach. On the other hand, a being having knowledge of the world and of itself, but which sees itself and the world, not as they are, but as it wishes or needs them to be, would necessarily get lost in this entanglement in itself; it would return— paradoxically—by dint of clarity and disclosure to unclarity and closure.

The countermove of reflection belongs first to the connection of the countermove proper to freedom which, though made possible by disclosedness, is not one with it—freedom in the most various senses, from the freedom of any act of initiative to the freedom of moral autonomy. This means however that reflection, the self-apprehension in which I grasp myself precisely as I am in my mind's eye, insofar as it is capable of apprehending my presence, necessarily implicitly includes the world. In taking interest, not in the *world* of experience, in what is posited for experience, but rather simply in the internal structure and form of experience as such, I, who reflect and carry out a principled reform of my interest, am nonetheless, precisely inasmuch as I thus reform myself, a worldly being, a being which, in freeing itself from shallow interestedness, does not acquire a *ground outside the world* but merely the purified ground of the world in which it already lives—purified from self-preoccupation.

The condition of possibility for reflection is precisely that we have a pretheoretical understanding of the danger of shallow interestedness, which, despite all our disclosing, does not allow us to truly open up to things.

The onlooker who heeds the manner in which life gains access to itself and to things is thus not an *entirely* disinterested onlooker, but rather someone *struggling against* the fractioning of interest in his being into a multitude of factical interests; he is interested in disinterestedness, in truth—and, in this will to freedom from preoccupation with his own factical self and its interests, he remains worldly, though not explicitly *positing the world*: originally, the world is not at all the object of a positing, it is neither a *thesis* nor an attitude that one could take up or abandon and replace with another; on the contrary, the world is the *condition of possibility for all clarity and consciousness in general.*

Lived life does not originally take place in a relation to "objects" but rather in our understanding of practical things and, within this framework, of ourselves as well, as that for the sake of which praxis, doing, handling, comportment exists. And this means (since the busyness we live in and which constitutes our primary understanding is never simply present but always temporally extended in stages of possible realization) that what we are busy with can never be *given* in the mode of immanent givenness in the sense of the self-presence of an absolute being; hence, a dilemma: either we understand the concept of reflection as such an absolute self-givenness (but then reflection will really and truly be a leap into a mode of being radically different from the being of prereflective life), or we have to *divest* the concept of reflection of its character of accessing a being of absolute immanence, a being that does not "give itself in adumbrations" (i.e., in perspectives).

The reflection in question here cannot be a simply mirroring reflection, the immanent intuition of an absolute being, so much is beyond dispute. Of course, reflection is meant to *see*, as present, what tends to elude us. Hence, its meaning does include the *givenness*, the presence of the seen. It would be inaccurate, however, to reduce reflection to the mere givenness, the mere certainty of that which is seen. The givenness of what we are and must see ourselves as in order to pass over from our factical possibilities to our true possibility (where we are not in thrall to our contingent factical interests—to our preoccupations) implies a *responsibility* for what we have been so far and what we intend to become. Even our present, what we can observe regarding ourselves, does not escape this law of temporal tension, which has its source in what we essentially are, in our existence as *living in possibilities.*

It is thus impossible to discover even the essential *structures* of our own life, impossible to understand what our own self is, if we do not take into account its essential historicity, its essential *possibility* and *responsibility*, and if we reduce it to a pure object. The whole of Cartesianism is, however, just such a reduction to the object of a certain grasping. Cartesianism is fascinated by the problem of the knowledge of the objective world as knowledge from absolutely indubitable principles. It is for this reason that it views reflection as a mere starting point, guaranteeing the solution of this question.

As a result, instead of grasping our self in its selfhood, it *transforms* it into a "subject," a stream of *cogitationes* each of which carries its own meaning, its *cogitatum*, in itself, while the question of their significance in my life history never arises apart from the problem of the foundation of scientific certainty.

This also gives us the answer to our third question. Immanent reflection in present self-givenness does not by any means necessarily present, *eo ipso*, the intrinsic determination, the essence of a thing, if by essence we understand that which *makes* the object of reflection what it is.

What then makes the object of reflection what it is? What is the being of the reflected being? Nothing other than its interest in being-in-the-world, its interest in its own being, which is not indifferent to it: it does not "stand apart" from its being, on the contrary, it brings it *along with it* into its seeing. Now, this being is essentially not given in the present, neither wholly nor aspectually. It cannot be *given* at all, but only *acquired*, conquered, discovered—in struggling against something that originally conceals it, covers it up, and falsifies it. That of ourselves which *gives*, offers, shows itself to us, can here provide a pretext for drawing our attention away from the proper task of *first opening* our own self. Socrates already knew that the main obstacle on the road to knowledge, which begins with the discovery of the question, is the false opinion that we already know.

Absolute reflection, on the other hand, takes no interest in my being-in-the-world, which is essentially incapable of distancing, separating itself from its anchoring in things, from its merging with the twilight of the rest of being out of which it arises and into which it sinks, from its limitation, its finitude, its suffering, etc., in the face of which it seeks and finds itself. Absolute reflection is interested *solely in the givenness* of this being-in-the-world. It has left anxiety and struggle behind it and stands on firm ground, on the ground of the absolute from which all meaning stems—its own, as well as that of everything else. This is not a stage in the self-discovery of a finite being but rather its transcending into something totally different. Reflection as absolute is an act that means that, for the self, taken in its essence, the whole struggle is meaningless, since truth begins only where all this has been left behind. It means that "salvation," real self-discovery, can never be attained in the world, but only by transcending it. That self-discovery in the world is always purely apparent and preliminary, while true "existence" is the contemplation of the extratemporal source of time contained in the "living presence."

Absolute reflection as revealing the absolute would thus be utterly exclusive of, and opposed to, the reflection of existence, reflection in the framework of existence as finite. The solution would not consist in infinite interest, in intensifying interest in our own existence, but rather in total *disengagement*. In eliminating the engagement in finitude which is the stuff of life, we would be left, not with *nothing*, but with true being, eternal life.

But is not absolute reflection—the revealing of the meaning of the countermove to engagement in finite being, i.e., the releasing of the infinite from the finite, the awakening of the self-forgotten infinite to itself—shown here precisely in its attachment to the finite? Is not the infinite revealing itself here tied, *by the countermove*, to that from which it looses itself? Can it, by its meaning, free itself from the finite, or does this meaning presuppose its prior existence as an absolute in self-forgetfulness? Its coming-to-itself would then mean that this forgetfulness was not mere nothingness, that there was behind it the interest unconsciously at stake in life; it would thus presuppose the structure proper to worldly self-seeking: self-blindness, self-forgetfulness, self-discovery.

Of course, a philosopher of absolute reflection can always be expected to declare this a false problem and to regard our questioning as the projection of a finite human structure into the absolute. But do we not see here, on the contrary, that the supposedly absolute reflection is merely a distorted stylization of motivated reflection? Being in self-forgetfulness, the self-identification of the absolute with a finite being as a mere fact which would ultimately provide the necessary starting point for all understanding, for all ultimate explication of all being—this sounds absurd: what kind of an absolute is this, if it knows nothing of itself? Can the reflective knowledge of the absolute proposed by methodical philosophy be its true, full knowledge? Does not the term "self-forgetfulness" hide a mystery which philosophy seeks in vain to unravel? In fact, the correlation between self-forgetfulness and motivation suggests itself to us so forcefully that we are more or less obliged to say: there must be here some deep motive, essentially inaccessible to us. "The crux of all these idealistic dreams is, however, that they cannot make evident any motive explaining why the infinite dons the mask of finitude, why the primal One should split up into obscure quantity, why the Idea should abandon the pure ether of self-equality and descend into becoming—why Spirit, being with itself, goes out of itself. Nor did Husserl present any phenomenological grounds for the self-constitution of human finitude."[1]

At first glance, we might find a third solution tempting in its transparent rationality. It tells us to go neither the way of absolute reflection nor the way of existential commitment in the finite. Both ways attempt to solve the problem of life, the problem of spirit, the problem of existence once and for all—metaphysically. They put the question of essence without taking into account that essence has to be somehow accessed, and that the *way of access* can be illuminated without ever gaining a definitive grasp of the object as such. The way of access can be grasped reflectively: we thus obtain reflective philosophy as a method regressing from objects to their conditions of possibility. But we obtain neither an absolute of consciousness nor an absolute of existence.

Phenomenology, reflective philosophy, will be a science concerned with the founding of the special sciences, a problem it can manage; it will be not only *philosophia* but also *scientia prima*. But it will take care not to lapse into a search for the essence, the being of consciousness, etc., since nothing of the kind is within its possibilities of thematization. Phenomenology, for reasons of *method*, can inquire only after that which can be given in reflection. By nature, it can be nothing other than a method leading to the conditions of possibility for objects to be *given*, not to their being as such.

This objection is easily formulated *in abstracto*, as long as we do not concretely analyze the object of reflection, i.e., experience. But once we do go into such a concrete analysis, once we begin to analyze, in particular, the primordial foundations of science, we come to see—as did Husserl in his analyses of the original founding of geometry—that the intention of science is anchored in the intention of life, aiming at an originally existential, practical truth, which subsequently, through idealizations, is understood as an aspect, a phenomenon of truth in itself.

The intention of truth in itself grows out of original truth relative to life; the former presupposes the latter. Truth relative to life then presupposes in turn, without any doubt, the truth of a life that somehow "knows" about itself, albeit in a way which has nothing to do with objective or reflective knowledge but is rather a praxis having some sort of "understanding" of itself. In concretely performing the task of reflective self-elucidation, we are thus quickly brought back to the question: does reflection originally belong to the context of pretheoretical life as an internal praxis, a means of its illumination, bent on not falling prey to its own interestedness, or is it something fundamentally different? And if it is different, how do we then avoid the consequence that it really and truly is the gateway to the absolute? The meaning of relativity that is not relativity with regard to some particular idea (e.g., the world in itself, knowledge in itself = absolute truth) is not transparent. If we understand the task of clarification as relative to the idea of absolute self-givenness, which cannot, as such, be clarity in the world, we arrive at the standpoint of absolute reflection. If we understand it as relative to the idea of true existence, existence in truth, which does not avoid itself but, on the contrary, wants to see itself as it is, our position is that, not merely of methodical, but of essential finitude.

Reflection thus means, in all that makes sense of it, beginning to philosophize in contact with a being that illuminates itself, that is "disclosed," though this is not to say, by any means, that it is, to its whole extent, a lighted being, a being of clarity. A disclosed being is simply one that requires clarity in order to exist, but this means only clarity concerning the fact *that* it is, not *what*, or *how* it is. And this, in turn, in no way means that it is nothing more than this "that." On the contrary, a being illuminating itself presupposes, in all its meaning, that it is not without unclarity, insofar as it is not an object for itself, as it "accomplishes" its clarity without representing it, by the mere fact of projecting a "for-the-sake-of"; just as it accomplishes its clarity, it can also produce unclarity concerning itself and its situation: this realization of possibilities as such means either a diversion, so as not to see myself, or a concentration on what I essentially can be.

Husserl's transcendentalism focused all its attention on the relation between two kinds of being: the being of consciousness in its streaming experience of the world and the being of objective nature. Husserl transcends from nature considered as the world, autonomous and founded in itself, to a world of spiritual experience which this transcending shows also to be entirely autonomous in its meaning. Nature endures in progressive objectification as the identical ground which in our objective experiences, originally embedded in subjectivity, appears in an infinite approximation. This way of bringing transparency into our experience of nature obtains under the condition that experience itself can be integrally grasped in its autonomous meaning, constructed purely from within as the unity of an act whose teleological result is precisely the unified world, a world of objects valid for all subjects of experience. Husserl believes that he can thus, at the same time, lay foundations for both the natural and human sciences.

The human sciences, too, or sciences of the spirit, have, however, their own *problem* of appearance; they cannot be founded on a consciousness immediately self-given in pure reflective intuition.

There is here a contradiction, a sort of paradox: only *if the spirit can become* completely transparent to itself can we exorcize *once and for all* the ghost of naturalism and justify the objectivity of exact scientific knowledge. And only if the spirit *is not* transparent in its entire essence can we proceed to the task of founding and constructing the human sciences, meant not so much to discover an enduring essence appearing in aspects, but rather to uncover the contradictions and illusions which barricade or stand in for reality, and are more a veiling than a manifestation of it—contradictions and illusions which are thus incompatible with the unveiling of reality: seeing-through does not mean *relativizing* but rather *doing away with them.*

Only if the nature of the spirit is, in itself, contradictory, ambivalent—if the spirit is also a being which is not completely transparent to itself, which, for this very reason, naturally strives after transparent, i.e., objective meaning—will it, perhaps, be possible to combine the two objectives and reach a solution. This means that the phenomenological method will have to be given an essentially different meaning from that assigned it by its inventor; it cannot consist in a pure intuitive grasping of phenomena without interest in the thesis of the world appearing in them, since the phenomena themselves, as well as the life to which the world appears, need to be *not simply observed* but *conquered* from that which, in them, obscures their meaning and, thereby, conceals them. Reality in appearance is not a problem exclusively with regard to the one objective nature, but also with regard to ourselves, to our own bodily-instinctive substrate, with which we have to come to terms, and to the others whose reality we have to master both inwardly and outwardly. We are not only a consciousness which retains and anticipates, but also which represses, is forgotten, recollects, protests and resigns itself, deceives both itself and others. (The relation to the world of objective appearances, too, is part and parcel of this struggle with ourselves for ourselves, for our internal purity, for a clearly mastering view. The possible meaningfulness of Bacon's description of human "Idols,"[2] precisely in relation to the knowledge of nature, would otherwise be incomprehensible, and no less so the "psychoanalysis of science" postulated and carried out by Gaston Bachelard.)[3]

Reflection is essentially dialectical. This means that in order to reach a standpoint raised *above* nature, it cannot put itself into a position of pure *separation*, of pure self-consistency in a realm of pure immanence. For the spirit, there is no standing above the world without at the same time standing in the world. The world is always already contained in the spirit itself; the spirit cannot define itself by itself, it becomes what it is only by relating to the world, to its essential partial structures, only by embodying itself in them and grasping its own possibilities thus created: the path of the spirit is a path through the world to itself.

Phenomenology and dialectics must go hand in hand. Phenomenology resists in vain its dialecticizing. Its deepest reflective discoveries show the spirit in its dialectical character. Thus, the intentionality of consciousness = a consciousness which is eccentric, which has originally no knowledge of itself, does not grasp itself, and yet is there; how?—in ignoring itself, not seeing itself, (tacitly) denying itself. The aspectuality of perception—the nonperceiving of what is given, of what I see. The horizonal openness—givenness of the nongiven, presence of the non-present, etc.

The dialectical interpretation of phenomenology has both the same starting point and the same goal as the Cartesian one. The starting point is the ontology of the natural world: we cannot regress beyond the fundamental features of human being-in-the-world if we do not want to fall into contradictions which present the spirit, in one and the same respect, as the condition and the conditioned, an innerworldly fact and something which conditions the world. The fundamental structure: myself and the others in a world which is common to us, a collection of the same natural things, is unsurpassable and cannot be modified but merely detailed, more clearly understood as to the relation of its various components, the teleology of its structure. This is neither positivism nor skepticism, though it shares with skepticism a subjective starting point and a subjective method: there is no other way of legitimizing the primal fact than its radical elucidation. At the other extreme, it shares with Cartesian phenomenology a common goal: the autonomy of the spirit which must have the possibility to attain truth and, in this sense, to stand above realities, not to be a dependent component of them—it must have *freedom for truth.* For this to be so, there is however no need to jump head first into absolute reflection, to sever at once all bonds tying the reflecting I to the world—radical reflection is itself *motivated,* it is a *critical* reflection, its prejudice is true freedom from prejudice, since it is a negation of the *bad prejudice* of the mundane I, a negation of the interestedness that is not only theoretical but also practical, so that radical reflection must itself be motivated out of our forever *future* dimension: it does not stand by itself, it is not an absolute which all of a sudden wakes up from forgetfulness to consciousness; it is, rather, a countermove against that which would make our I forever lose sight of itself—it is part of the search for one's own self.

The primacy of reflection over a purely objective approach to the "things themselves" does not lie in the self-certainty of consciousness, and even less in the supposed absoluteness of the inner being, but rather in the fact that only a being which understands itself, i.e., a being interested in its own being, in *authenticity*, can also understand other things in their being and in their being as they are.

For these reasons, we can no longer identify with the conception of phenomenological reflection that we held to in the original version of our *Natural World*. We can no longer accept the interpretation of the "phenomenological reduction" as the gateway to the absolute. We do not accept absolute reflection. Reflection lies in self-understanding. This includes, as one of its essential aspects, self-presence, the view of the self from within. It can be artificially made independent for epistemological purposes: such was the original task of the phenomenological reduction. But the theory of objective knowledge has, of course, repercussions on the character of being of that on which it is founded—on the character of the "transcendental subject."

The method of reflection we hold to at present cannot be that of the uncovering of hidden intentionalities by means of objective clues. It stems from an understanding of the three fundamental ecstases of temporality and of the movements of existence anchored in them. The concept of movement applied here implies, of course, an entire ontology, but one that can prove of value in the understanding, in the hermeneutics of the fundamental phenomena of human life. The phenomena that it seeks to elucidate by analysis have the same claim to general accessibility and demonstrability as Husserl's intentional structures.

That being the case, how should the problem of the natural world be redefined? It is a problem concerning not only objective, but also subjective being. The problem of the object as a unified, mathematically objectified system of nature, and the problem of the naturalization of the spirit inserted in this system. In the face of this understanding of what is, in the face of this vision of being, the problem of the natural world is about finding a conception of the relation between man and objective being which would make it possible to understand the original, independent character of both (undistorted by preconceived, albeit successful and efficacious models, such as the model of natural science), as well as the relatedness which goes along with this essential originality and autonomy. The natural world—in which pragmatically useful as well as natural, and human as well as animal beings, the works of man as an individual as well as those of history are given *in the original*—is a phenomenon whose originality must first be described and analyzed and only then interpreted, in such a way that the phenomenon does not vanish with the interpretation. In this process, it will appear that the naturalization of the spirit, which was at the beginning of the whole problematic, is but one of the two great perils guarding the entrance to it: the other is the hypostatizing, the absolutizing of the subject when its naturalization is brought to light and the ensuing danger obviated, yet without grasping in its full originality the essential character of the "natural world" as a whole.

II

Our present views on the prehistory and history of the problem of the natural world, in accordance with the foregoing, can be outlined roughly as follows:

1. Descartes

Modern philosophy takes from Scholasticism the concept of an absolute being, correlate of absolute truth. This absolute being is, however, envisaged differently: as the correlate of a mathematical, deductive system, guaranteeing equal distinctness and certainty in the entire complex of knowledge. This presupposes a new mathematics, capable of mastering continua and carrying out the indirect mathematization of qualities, processes, causal relations. Descartes formulates the ideal of one science as a chain of reasons. The metaphysical principles—the soul and God—are given: the former in immediate reflection, the latter by an eminently simple proof. The third principle, nature as *res extensa*, is based on the other two. The philosopher's whole attention is concentrated on the *res extensa*, from which follow all the consequences that go to make up the actual usefulness of the one science: medicine, mechanics, and true morals (the mastering of the passions of the soul). In Descartes, reality is thus mathematically objectified, truth is absolutized, but the spirit is not yet completely naturalized, since knowledge of the world is wholly and absolutely free, and the mind in interaction with the body, i.e., natural causality is not completely mathematized. In two respects, however, naturalization has made great headway: (1) the soul is united with the mechanism of the body, and the meaning of prescientific experience is biological finality, adapted to this bodily mechanics; (2) though the *cogitatio* itself is conceived of as intentional (the *cogitatio* has various ideas as objects), the idea is taken, not as a thing as such, but rather as an *image* of external things, i.e., it is understood under a model of causal action inherited from tradition. In Descartes there thus begins (1) the dissolution of the intentional structure of consciousness as discovered by him (the self-certain structures of the form *ego cogito cogitatum*), (2) the repression of the phenomenon of subjective corporeality, which was also his discovery (the "union" of the soul and the body in a single substance).

2. Spinoza and Leibniz

Universal mechanism excludes any causal intervention whatsoever from without. This consequence of mechanism, i.e., the mathematization of causal action, makes nature into one autonomous, closed whole. In Descartes, this stage has not yet been reached, but it is clearly defined in Spinoza and Leibniz. Nonetheless, even in these two thinkers, the spirit is not yet completely naturalized as a *component* of nature, but only as something that can be coordinated with it, something that must, consequently, have a somehow analogical structure: *ordo et connexio*. Both Leibniz and Spinoza state explicitly that there is no causal connection between the spirit and nature. They preserve thus the possibility for the spirit to gain access to truth. "Ideas" become, however, by dint of "coordination," real parts of the subject, and the world breaks up into a plurality of private worlds with nothing to justify why they are all phenomena of the one true world.

3. Locke and Berkeley

Locke naturalizes consciousness by means of the oldest of all mechanistic schemata—space and "letters," elements, *stoicheia*. This is a consequence of the conception of ideas as real representatives of things, things in miniature, which Descartes already inherited from tradition, but which does not play an important part in his thought, since he accords no significance to sense-ideas, considering them, as confused ideas, not to involve truth. Once empiricism shifts emphasis to the senses, the result is, however, that the spirit becomes extended and divisible as a *res extensa*.

On the other hand, the two constructions on the same principle of building from elements—the objective and the subjective—differ in one fundamental respect. The objective construction is a direct, integral, necessary mathematical law, of which our subjective image is a mere approximate appearance. The elements here are the components, the arguments of mathematical functions. The subjective image does not have this necessary character; the elements here appear as atoms given in advance and bonded with the mortar of a *subjective* connection.

Since access to the objective world is through the subjective, this leads to a *critique* of the objective connections which earlier philosophy regarded as the genuine guarantee of the truthfulness of thought. Such connections are contained in the concepts of substance, causality, the unitary I, or, again, in the notions of mathematical idealities. All this now becomes problematic, whereas the world as given in sense-"ideas" is rehabilitated. Hence Berkeley's return from the world of modern "materialistic" natural science to what is reputed original. The fact that spirit *itself* is naturalized here goes unnoticed: the spirit is seen as intrinsically composed of parts united, if not by real causality, at least by some sort of analogical correlations.

4. Kant

Kant, as is well known, accomplished an essential turn, leading philosophy away from the direct viewing of, and inquiry into, what nature and the spirit are to a fundamentally different investigation, inquiring after the conditions of possibility of the knowledge of what thus is. Thereby, nature as an object of natural-scientific knowledge came to be seen from a totally novel and hitherto unsuspected standpoint, "subjective," yet distinct from the empirically psychological standpoint of the mere facts of inner experience. The problem of *validity* made it necessary to view the objectivity of natural science as the result of a constitution, as a meaningful formation erected in a consistently logical manner, taking into account the unity of experience. This presupposes, without further analysis, that sense-objects—nature as it appears to the natural scientist—have the same mode of being and givenness as constructed objectivity. Given Kant's way of stating the question, there is thus no room for a difference between the natural and the constructed world. Kant's philosophical turn is nonetheless of essential importance for our problem, inasmuch as his transcendentalism, though substantially different in terms of method, is a preliminary to Husserl's, in which the problem of the natural world is first clearly articulated.

If our problem has no place in Kant's theoretical philosophy, this does not mean, however, that it is wholly absent from his thinking. On the contrary. In the difference between Kant's theoretical and practical philosophy, between a philosophy of thoroughgoing necessity, inserting even man as a phenomenon into one single connection, and a philosophy of freedom, postulating the intelligible realm of morality as thing in itself, there asserts itself, in an original, philosophically radical interpretation, a difference between two domains of meaning—the mathematical idealization of natural science, on the one hand, and, on the other, the originally given meaning of life which can neither be interpolated into the former domain nor rationalized away by it. If moral freedom is an element brought into the problematic from the naturally given reality of prescientific life, this motif of the natural world is of greater ontological consequence than the world of mathematical natural science, which remains, on the whole, a mere phenomenon. The primacy of praxis and freedom, thus explicitly realized for the first time in philosophy, would then be originally drawn, here already, from the opposition, albeit unelucidated and constructively covered over, between the two worlds.

Kant's contributions to the problem at hand also include the endeavor, manifest in the *Opus Postumum*, to obtain for *corporeality* the status of an a priori condition of thinking consciousness. This extraordinarily important idea, anticipating some of the most modern themes of present-day phenomenology, is, however, not thought through to its conclusion in Kant: it would probably have led him away from the empiristic residues in his theory of sensory receptivity as ultimate, atomic data.

Very insightful progress was made in this respect by Maine de Biran, a thinker Bergson spoke of as "the French Kant."[4] According to one of his most sagacious contemporary interpreters, it was Maine de Biran who discovered the phenomenon of the "subjective body." "By tearing away, not the idea, but the very being and reality of movement from the sphere of transcendent being, [he] defines the real body, and not the idea of the body, as a subjective and transcendental being."[5] What Maine de Biran is getting at here is one of the major features of our original experience in the natural world: the localization of lived-experiencing in the body, which is something immediately given, prior to all perceptive experience. Action in the body is not given by individual impressions; rather, it precedes them, and consciousness of it is a necessary condition for the experience of particulars.

5. Hegel

Another important element of our problem, though not one easily dealt with, is the contribution of what could be termed the first life-philosophy, at the turn of the nineteenth century. Hamann, Herder, and their romantic followers emphasized some significant aspects of the natural world, e.g., the original givenness of the other as against the conception of the isolated subject, familiar to modern thought since Descartes. Goethe attempted to apprehend and preserve in their originality, against Newton's physicalism, the natural visual qualities, regarded as a natural correlate of our visual relation to the world. Hans Lipps, in his essay on Goethe's theory of colors,[6] has shown Goethe's natural science to be a specific type of conscious understanding of nature which has nothing in common with the intention of mathematical natural science and turns a new page, developing the original intuitive experience which stems from a prescientific perspective. Goethe's natural science is governed neither by the idea of a mathematical reconstruction of given nature nor by the notion of teleological factors presupposing natural-scientific mechanism; rather, it is based on an intuited type and its modification as it presents itself to the senses seeking without prejudice intuitive meaningfulness.—The romantics, too, Novalis and others, go back to the givenness of nature as the correlate of an intuiting, immediately comprehending life, and the problematic of "enlivening"—the starting point of Hegel's theological-speculative juvenilia, insofar as their central theme is life and love—belongs undoubtedly to the same context. Here, all solipsism of the isolated subject is surmounted, and "life senses life";[7] here, with much greater originality than later in Feuerbach, emphasis is put on the primacy of the experience of the other in love, on the original miracle in which we are at once identical with the beloved and apart from him—a miracle in which life itself manifests itself as self-division and unity across this division.

In Hegel's philosophy of subjective spirit, the entire "life-philosophy" of his time is doubtless contained as at once preserved and overcome. The "process of evolution," from which the philosophy of subjective spirit starts, means that the natural base moving toward its goal is constantly preserved in its overcoming, that spirit, even in its highest form, as free activity, remains preserved as soul, i.e., as bodily nature gathered together, integrated into unity, into the life of an organism, the primary ideality of nature. Nature wakes to spirit as to its truth, i.e., to what it is, envisaged not individually and unilaterally, but as a comprehensive totality. This awakening of nature is the soul, and awakening is not simply a metaphor, but rather a real free judgment of self-differentiation from pure exteriority. The soul is the *assertion* that this exteriority is an untruth which cancels itself—so that the truth of nature is simple, total ideality. The soul is not simply a private ideality, an immateriality for itself; on the contrary, it is the "*universal* immateriality of nature"[8]—the soul integrally contains the entire immaterial aspect of nature, the soul "is in a way all things."[9] The existing soul, the feeling soul, the actual or acting soul are the three modes of this original unity with nature, with a corporeality that should not itself be comprehended as the coarse, external, "material" corporeity of pure matter; there is also a total, connecting, unifying face to nature, with which the soul is in harmony and sympathy, rather than being bound to it by an external relation. This is why the relation of body and soul is far more a unity than a causal relation in the usual sense, the relation of two substances—here there is in actual fact *one* substance, i.e., nature in its progressive sublimation and integration. We can and should understand the activity of the senses at once on the basis of this sympathy with the immaterial aspect of nature and as proof and phenomenon of this immateriality; just as, conversely, the embodiment of the soul must be posited as counterpoint to the spiritualization of nature. (Harris believes this "embodiment" to refer to the phenomenon of the "body schema";[10] I regard it rather as a reference to the body in general as the subjective faculty of *acting*, the active body, lived-experienced as activity.) The soul is, in itself, the totality of nature, just as the individual soul is a monad, though by no means a windowless monad; rather, it is the *existent concept*, the existence, the manifestation of the speculative, i.e., the unity of the self and the other, the unity of unity and non-unity.

There is no doubt that this conception is extremely close to the natural worldview—sensibility as sympathy, the immediate relation between the spiritual agency and corporeality, sensible qualities as consonance with the immaterial aspect of nature and, at the same time, evidence of life in the objective world, the unity of the world in the plurality of monads—though Hegel grounds all this in his general philosophical conception, he does so essentially without reconstruction, without doing violence to the originality of these data and structures, seen here, not as mere phenomena of a "true," i.e., mathematically construed nature, but rather as worldly reality itself in its immediate form.

Thus, Hegel does not philosophically devalue the natural world, he does not degrade it to a mere preliminary of mathematically conceived nature; it is devalued only from the viewpoint of his philosophy of spirit, as a level of immediacy which has not yet succeeded in elevating itself to the freedom of the absolute spirit. Nature and the world as we see them immediately in our sense-data and life praxis are, of course, not true reality, but no more so is the world of the pure object, of ideal mathematical objectification—the immediate world is, on the contrary, closer to the "spirit"; it is unjustified, as would be any stance of finitude, only in claiming to be the whole of reality.

6. Feuerbach

The Young Hegelians effect a return to finitude which, through its emphasis on sensibility, would seem to lead even closer to the natural world, more precisely in the form represented by Feuerbach's defense of the ontological import of sensibility.

If sensibility—or, as Feuerbach says, the heart—is the true approach to being, it follows that true reality is the sensible world, by virtue of its contents of both things and living beings, especially fellow men. The world of natural science, essentially mediated, will thus not be reality— Feuerbach views Descartes and Cartesianism coldly—but rather the unmediated world of affectivity and sensible contact. Feuerbach admits that sense-data too can be mediated; their specific advantage is nonetheless the immediacy with which they bring us face to face with real being, with existence.

The important question then becomes what kind of being is it face to face with which, and in which, our senses place us. There are statements in Feuerbach that appear to attest to an endeavor to go beyond the limits of traditional ontology, moving in the circle of essence and existence. His polemic against Scholasticism in both ancient and modern metaphysical philosophy inspires hope for something better. His remarks concerning the interestedness in being which is part of man's character seem indeed to fall under the heading of a philosophy of life. "Before you think the quality, you *feel* the quality. The *suffering* precedes the thinking."[11] "As the reality of the sensation is the quality and, in turn, the sensation is the reality of the quality, so also is being the reality of the consciousness. But likewise in turn the consciousness is the reality of the being. Consciousness is alone the actual being" (65).—What is meant by "actual" being? We would be tempted to answer: being as act, accomplished being = life.—"True speculation or philosophy is nothing but true and universal empiricism" (63).—That sounds phenomenological.—"Only the needy being is a necessary being. Existence without need is unnecessary existence. What is generally free of needs also has no need of existence. Whether it is or is not, is indifferent—indifferent to itself, indifferent to others" (66).—Here, too, we would expect the statement to be turned around: life is a mode of being whose being is not indifferent, whose being matters to it—more or less Heidegger's definition of existence.— "A being with no need is a being with no basis. Only what can suffer deserves to exist" (67).—Here, however, existence has clearly taken on the meaning "to occur, to be a fact."—"A being without suffering is a being without being. A being without suffering is nothing other than a being devoid of sensibility, devoid of matter" (67).—How evident it would be to go from here to the temporal character of life! But this Feuerbach does not appear to see.—"Where words cease, life begins and being reveals its secret. If, therefore, non-verbality is the same as irrationality, then all existence is irrational because it is always and forever only *this* existence. But irrational it is not. Existence has meaning and reason in itself, without being verbalized" (135).—This sounds almost like understanding that would not be rationally objectifying knowledge.

In reality, however, what Feuerbach presents as a critique of Hegelian Scholasticism is a return to authentic Scholasticism, to a faded echo of pseudo-Aristotelian ontology. In showing that thought being is not real being, that the ineffable "this-here" is precisely true being = existence, that this being is given by the senses, that speculative philosophy confuses the subject and the predicate, etc., Feuerbach merely renews commonplaces of Scholastic ontology. At the same time it becomes clear that "suffering" is conceived as causality (in an unspecified sense: the object appears to us because it exerts a causal influence on us, i.e., on our sensibility). "The mystery of their interaction [the action of the body on the spirit and vice versa—J. P.] can be solved only by sensuousness. Only sensuous beings act upon one another. I am I—for myself—and at the same time You—for others. But this I am only insofar as I am a sensuous being" (145). I originally understand everything that affects me as a freely and arbitrarily acting being; such is the case in childhood (144). The other is thus simply another being acting on my senses, as I act on his. Love is a passion, *passio*, suffering, this is why it gives being. "Being as the object of being—and *this* alone is truly, and deserves the name of, being—is the being involved in sense-perception, feeling, and love. Or in other words, being is a *secret* underlying sense-perception, feeling, and love" (145).—What being? The being of a particular being, its existence as opposed to its essence, its *positing*, being as opposed to non-being.—"Pain is a loud protest against identifying the subjective with the objective. The pain of love means that what is in the mind is not given in reality. The subjective is here the objective, the concept itself the object. But this is precisely what ought *not* to be, what is a contradiction, an untruth, a misfortune—hence, the desire for that true state of affairs in which the subjective and the objective are not identical" (146). See also (133): "Being is wherein essence posits itself. That which is my essence is my being." Though Feuerbach is aware of man's interestedness in his own being, he interprets being as *esse existentiae*, as the being of given things, "objects." Hence, the forced explanation of hunger: the walls of the stomach grind against each other, calling for an "object," something to be put inside them. Desire is desire for the object = for an external object exerting a causal action, the accomplishment of which = a thesis, a positing.

Under these circumstances, it is no wonder that Feuerbach imagines that his philosophy of sensibility, suffering, and objectivity could combine with natural science, replacing the previous misalliance between philosophy and theology (78). The ontology that he represents does not in fact depart from that of natural science: particular objects have an existence which does not really differ in them from what they are, they act causally on one another, and our life takes place in a stream of such interactions.

The end result of Feuerbach's critique of Hegel's philosophy is thus a materialistic positivism. As a matter of fact, his conception of theology as alienated anthropology (anthropomorphism), of metaphysics as theology in the stage of abstraction, and of the anthropological philosophy of his time as a return from alienation, shows an analogy with Comte's law of the three stages. Feuerbach's positivism is, however, materialistic because he believes in material substance and causality. It is thereby conducive to natural-scientifically oriented materialism in general. Feuerbach's rehabilitation of sensibility thus results in the exact *opposite* of the natural world.

7. Mach and Avenarius

Feuerbach and materialistically oriented neo-Hegelianism have led us back to the concept of a unitary material nature in itself, the object of natural science as a unified continent of rationality, and a true "being in itself," to which our sense-experience, with its historically "outdated" theoretical interpretations, relates as a plurality of phenomena through which this unity passes as a single pole in infinite approximations.

This concept is now accepted with none of the mitigating reservations that tradition still offered to thinkers of the sixteenth to the eighteenth century. There is no longer any theological-metaphysical screen to tone down the sharp impact of this image of "true reality" on the reality of our lives. The importance of this period lies in the fact that the project of Galileo and Descartes, coined three hundred years earlier, is only now worked out in its existential as well as theoretical consequences. Philosophically, the project has won the day. Philosophy itself has, therefore, nothing more to accomplish and is no longer taken seriously. The one and only competent authority in matters of knowledge is special *science*, positive, applied, and efficient.

In the framework of this coherent but philosophically unelucidated conception (unelucidated inasmuch as there is no explicit reflection either on the concept of phenomenon or on the relation of the phenomenon to the natural world, or again on the relation of the phenomenon to what appears in it as one reality, all these issues requiring *philosophy*, which has been given up to the boundless contempt of the "practitioners of positive science"), the duality of positivism and materialism as a twofold *interpretation* of this one situation is an inevitable reflex and result of the lack of clarity.

Materialism stresses the standpoint of the natural-scientifically conceived thing in itself, i.e., the *res extensa*: that which appears, in its objectivity, as opposed to appearance; and consequently, in addition, the standpoint of *explanation* as the meaning of scientific work; the concepts of substance and causality serve here not only as methodical guidelines but, at the same time, as the metaphysical groundwork for the whole objective construction. Positivism, on the other hand, stresses the standpoint of the phenomenon as such; explanation is considered nothing more than a means of orientation within appearance, but it has a provisional character; its importance lies in the discovery of the lawfulness of the phenomenon and its further, deeper dimensions, its meaning is a function of its "fruitfulness."

As two different conceptions of naturalistic physicalism, materialism and positivism share a *passive understanding* of phenomenon. The phenomenon is seen through the eyes of empiricism which, as we have already shown, understands the "ideas" of sensation as really intrinsic parts of the spirit, and the spirit, consequently, on the model of the *res extensa*; this spiritual *res extensa* is then dealt with in accordance with the most ancient mechanical concept—that of the *stoicheia*, the atoms, and their composite, collective syntheses, whether mechanical or "chemical" (where the "sum" is more than the juxtaposed parts).

In the framework of this particular question (whether the synthesis is mechanical or of another kind) positivism has the merit of inquiring into *the phenomenon as phenomenon*, a question that materialism does not consider of primary importance. And this is the question that leads, by virtue of its inner logic, to the discovery of the problem of the natural world as the "subjective" basis upon which the search for objectivity and progressive objectification first becomes meaningful.

In this context we should mention Mach's concept of the "analysis of sensations":[12] what is originally given to us are not really intrinsic parts of the mind as such, but rather syntheses, things. Sensations as elements must first be attained. This analysis promises important scientific results, as it will be made clear that the traditional conception, taking as elements the data of the five senses, is a prejudice, and that the data are considerably more abundant. Mach is among those who, in the course of this inquiry, discover the qualities of the form, or Gestalt. The discovery of the phenomena of constancy, brought to the fore by Ewald Hering,[13] is part of the same context. The notion of neutral monism, so attractive to thinkers at the turn of the twentieth century, lies then in the idea of the composition of two great orders of experience: (a) a purely objective order, in the relation of the elements to one another, and (b) an order of "prehension" (to use the term coined by Whitehead, who later transformed this concept), i.e., the surroundings of the organisms in relation to their nervous system.

We must, however, allow to Richard Avenarius the merit of formulating anew, on the basis of the notion of neutral monism, the problem of the world as a phenomenon endowed with a stable, constant structure, constituting firm ground beyond which philosophical analysis cannot go.

Avenarius's attempt to purify experience from the all too many metaphysical admixtures to be found not only in philosophy, but also, mainly, in natural science, leads him away from the study of the *content* of experience (the concern of the special sciences) to observing that an inquiry into its *form* brings us shortly to an invariant structure which has in part a purely immediate, descriptive character, and in part contains a mediation, a hypothesis, but a hypothesis that can be neither omitted nor replaced by another without doing violence to the experience. In taking note of our environment and of ourselves as an element of this structure, we also make the hypothesis that the statements of others mediate an experience of *the same* environment. We thus obtain the primal form of all experience, the human concept of the world,[14] including: the self → the environment ⇄ the experience of others, whose statements and non-statements also go to make up the immediate environment. (The others, as an element of my environment, are given immediately; their experience is mediated.)

It is impossible to go beyond this fundamental structure, to regress in greater depth. Every other "world-concept" presupposes it and is a modification of it. The basic formula of this "natural world" is: the self, the other, the common environment. In dealing with the meaning of the utterances of others, the purpose is not to *explain* or interpret these utterances or my own experience, but rather to give a *general description* of the tenor (*das Wesen*) of my experience, so as to be able to apply the same to others.

This natural or human world is modified when, instead of simply describing our experience and observing its lawful correlation with a certain objective phenomenon of the environment (called C, the central nervous system), we *project* it *inside* objective processes and understand this projection as the *cause* of our experience. By virtue of this "introjection," the outside, the surrounding world, becomes inside, while the cause is now the true outside, the "thing in itself," as can be seen in animism, theology, and metaphysics. Introjection is thus the true motive for relinquishing the natural world-concept.

Avenarius was the first to grasp the necessity of describing the natural world. He also understood that no causally explicative substruction could ever enable us to go beyond this world. On the other hand, his own description, which avoids personal concepts (the "self" is merely a name for a "bundle of ideas"), and knows nothing of the original localization in the body, nothing of the body as not only experienced but also experiencing, a description which sharply opposes my own environment, as given, to the statements of others, as hypothetically mediating, is undoubtedly itself evidence of a fundamental naturalization of lived-experiencing; it is, therefore, a failure.

Nonetheless, in observing that we all have a *common world* to which we relate, that we must take this fact as our starting point and that science must somehow come to terms with it, however much it may appear to offend common notions, Avenarius became, in point of fact, the starting point of a new ontology of the natural world. He did not himself present it—though he discovered the a priori which every conception of nature must obey if it is to be experienceable—he immediately naturalized it, conceiving the a priori relativistically as a result (and, of course, a causal result) of the adaptation of human organisms to natural circumstances in a millenary process of accommodation. Thereby, he ended up contradicting his own key thesis concerning the originality, the inexplicability, the primacy of the fundamental structure of the natural world.

8. Brentano, Uphues, Schwarz, Bergson

In the 1880s and 1890s, one of the traditional elements, a very ancient theme of the complex of the natural world (or problem of "naive realism," as some call it) separated from it and acquired a new focus—the problem of the objectivity of qualities.

The question of the qualitative plenum of the universe goes far back, and it can and should be brought into the complex of the natural world as a nonautonomous component. Mathematization, as a method of objectification, carries with it the question of the relations of quantities to the more original and more primarily given qualitative contents. (Hegel's logic, too, bears the mark of the primacy of quality, the mediacy of quantity.) What leads now to a reformulation of the problem is, however, the question of the concrete scientific realization of the conception of the one mathematical nature as true transphenomenal reality.

The fundamental contradiction arrived at here, and which compels a revision of the whole problem of quality, is the contradiction of perception, or sensation. The natural-scientific worldview is forced to regard sensation as a state of mind caused by the action of the outside world, and, hence, as a really intrinsic component of mental reality. That being the case, it proves difficult to explain its character of objectivity (as opposed to emotions and other states considered as lived-experiencing itself, and not as its object).

In the 1870s, Franz Brentano attempted to demonstrate the scientific character of philosophy using the positivist method. Philosophy reaches the positive stage of its development with the scientization of psychology, its fundamental discipline. Scientific psychology will, however, have to start by defining the mental as opposed to the physical phenomenon. To this purpose Brentano makes use of two traditional motifs, one Cartesian, the other classical, modified by Scholasticism. The Cartesian theme is formulated as follows: the mental phenomenon evidently guarantees its own existence, the physical phenomenon does not. The classical theme is then: the mental phenomenon is characterized by the intentional "in-existence" of an object.[15]

Physical phenomena are, for example, a sound, the color red, the spatial extension of a form, etc. Physical phenomena are thus precisely what the physicalist view regards as the influence of physical processes on the spirit, on the mind—i.e., from this standpoint, as subjective. Brentano does not directly attribute an objective, absolute existence to them, but he does sharply distinguish them from mental phenomena in the proper sense, and thus imposes the question of their ontological status: how, where and under what conditions are they supposed to exist?

In the 1880s, this question was put in very clear terms by Goswin Uphues.[16] Brentano thought it sufficient to declare that there must objectively exist something analogous to qualities in the usual sense, not the qualities as such. Uphues, along with others, showed that this circumspect concession is equivalent to admitting the objectivity of qualities. He forcefully underlined the objective character of sense-data. On the other hand, he did not venture to identify the qualities with the things themselves: rather he saw them as an effect of things, a result of the mutual interaction of the thing in itself behind our organs and those standing behind the qualitative image of things.

Uphues's solution goes only halfway, taking the view of mathematical natural science and splitting it between the unknown causes of phenomena and their phenomenal effects—an unnecessary complication if the objectivity of quantities can somehow be combined with the objectivity of qualities, as was shown by Hermann Schwarz in his *Problem of Perception*, published in 1892. Schwarz does not directly prove the objectivity of qualities. He regards it, as a metaphysical thesis, as *proprio sensu* unprovable, but he believes it to be maximally compatible with the viewpoint of naive realism, whereas the acceptance of some sort of imperceptible things in themselves would needlessly complicate the matter. At the end of his analyses Schwarz comes to a conclusion close to Avenarius's positivism but which goes beyond it. "At no point in the problem of perception does it seem necessary to admit, in general, things in themselves. If we want nonetheless to bring into our considerations the concept of thing in itself, the only logical way is Uphues's. . . . We would do even better to abstain from any precise hypotheses concerning the origin of sense-data. It can suffice to depict the lawfulness of the given sensible world, on both subjectivist and realist ground, by admitting a parallel congruity of the various perceived and unperceived sense-processes; this parallelism reaches as far as scientific explanation; we have no motive to suppose its reaching beyond, though there is on the other hand nothing to make this logically impossible."[17]

Schwarz presents a kind of analysis of "naive realism," which he sees as having a methodological and a metaphysical component. The methodological component consists in the ordering of sense-impressions, the metaphysical component in assertions concerning their existence outside the domain of givenness. The methodological dogmas of naive realism interpret sense-data according to the tripartite schema of "thing/property/causality." Tactile data, as enduring, lacking all oppositions of perspective, and affectively marked, are the basis for the objectification of the *thing*, the common data of the other senses (under normal circumstances) the basis for the objective *properties*; all other events registered by the senses (those that are fixed neither in the thing nor in the property) are attributed to the action of *causes*.

Schwarz's theory of naive realism is, of course, a *theory*. And this is its weak point: instead of beginning with describing and analyzing the state of affairs, in order to acquire the essence and forms of sensibility as a phenomenon, it starts from a ready-made view, which is taken for granted. The objectification observed in the above-mentioned three stages presupposes a certain atomism, inasmuch as it attributes to sense-data the character of purely objective elements, as in Mach and Avenarius. In actual fact, our sense-experiencing should be considered in a number of respects: (a) in relation to our affective-volitive and motive life, i.e., in a bodily context; (b) in relation to our personal situation and to our insertion in it; and (c) as an aspect of the objective environment, in the context of objectification. It is significant and characteristic of our natural intuition that its "dogmas" are neither reflected nor put into words, and are, in fact, the work of those who formulate them: objectification progresses along these lines, but does not conform to them programmatically. The naive view has no *positive* hypotheses, it proceeds in a negative manner: it holds that a thing or property remains unchanged where there is no reason to acknowledge change, and such a reason occurs where we *see* a change, where we immediately observe it. This does not mean that, for the naive view, the perceived world is a collection of things and their properties—the things with their properties *are in the world*, rather than the world being made up of them; things stand out in, rise out of the perceived world, but the world is an infinite wealth, whereas the thing and its properties are merely centers of crystallization within it.

Be that as it may, the "dogmas of naive realism" as formulated by Schwarz show the *discrepancy* between the natural view and the scientific attitude. Schwarz is the first to point out both the *continuity* and, at the same time, the *variance* between the methodological principles of common sense and those applied in natural science. Whereas Kant sees here an identity, e.g., between natural (sensible) and scientific causality, Schwarz observes a difference in the sensible conception, insofar as sensible intuition knows no interaction, no link between action and reaction, and is full of anthropomorphic ideas borrowed from the sphere of psychophysical activity. But this itself presupposes that the relation to our own body as something over which we hold sway is one of the fundamental factors of the natural view.

Schwarz also expresses a healthy skepticism about the then current idea of the tactile qualities hard/soft, rough/smooth, and recognizes only one fundamental tactile datum, i.e., the contact of extended materiality. (Concerning this contact, one could further doubt whether it is at all thinkable in sheer isolation, without any connection to the actively passive aspect of the mobile body.)

The "naive realism" of authors like Schwarz and those he regards as authorities (Riehl, Helmholtz) is thus not the natural worldview but, at the most, only one of its components, its emphasis on *things* and their privileged reality as compared to qualities and processes—it is a "natural worldview" which has undergone a certain degree of reflection: approximately at the stage in which it is taken up and made conscious by thinkers such as Aristotle and, mainly, the Aristotelians.

Important are Schwarz's demonstrations that the precedence granted in naive realism to tactile data over the data of the other senses has purely subjective and practical reasons, which cannot stand up against scientific objectivity. There is no reason why the world should not be just as well described in acoustic, or visual, as in tactile terms. If we are to be consistent, we cannot privilege any one sense: either all data are objective or all are subjective, and we have the choice between integral sensible realism and a no less uncompromising subjective idealism. Natural science shows correctly that tactile data, like all others, are simply one of the manners in which the outside world announces itself to us, that all sense-data are equally signs of the world, but it does not draw the right conclusions. Physics, too, prefers a tactile, i.e., a mechanical explanation of all other manifestations of reality. Once again, however, this preference is purely practical. There is no reason why we should not be able to comprehend a lawful connection of acoustic or visual data just as well as the usual mechanical laws. And there is no reason why we should not envisage an overall lawful correlation of mechanical, optical, and acoustical data even outside our perception. We must, of course, admit that our sense-data are apprehended as given in the activity of our nerve organs, and by no means as they may exist in themselves in the extraphysiological world. Nonetheless, it would go against common sense to imagine that the qualitative aspect of the world is due exclusively to the activity of the nerve organs, since physiology, too, knows only physical-mechanical explanatory principles. In connection with this, the idea of specific sense-energies, taking this non sequitur as the starting point of a whole branch of research, is false not only philosophically but also with regard to physical methodology. Natural-scientific research is not qualified to answer the question of the subjectivity or objectivity of qualities, no more than that of the true significance of the parallelism between mechanical (tactile) processes and processes pertaining to other qualitative domains; the only question within the competence of science is how the mechanical processes which accompany secondary (acoustic, visual, etc.) sense-data in our sensory organs are dependent on these organs. Science here decides for the affirmative, showing, e.g., that our sensory and, in particular, nerve organs are also objective structures localized in the mechanical domain (and doubtless also, in parallel, in certain qualitative domains) like other facts of nature, and that it would therefore be absurd to adopt for them a different set of basic natural laws, even if certain specifically conjoined causes do produce specific effects.

From a methodological viewpoint, it can be noted that Schwarz's concept neglects the specific feature of the tactile-mechanical domain that makes it the starting point for *mathematical idealizations.* The primacy of the mechanical sphere for the objectification of the world would seem to be originally linked with this feature, as Husserl later attempts to show (and as was already intended by the neo-Kantians, especially of the Marburg school). This circumstance is, however, not decisive for the methodological question of the objective scope and meaning of secondary qualitative data. In this respect, the critique expressed by Schwarz and the authors he refers to remains valid. The question of the objectivity of qualities is a philosophical issue, which sciences such as physics, chemistry, physiology are not competent to solve, since they themselves always already move on the ground of a certain solution of it: on the ground of uncritically accepted assumptions. This is not true only of what Schwarz terms the "postulates of naive realism." "Naive realism," as Schwarz himself states, is based on the tripartite schema of thing/property/causality, on a certain conception of being, and, therefore, a certain understanding of what is. The same goes for the philosophical theories that do not share the one-sidednesses of naive realist methodology, integral realism and subjective idealism: the world is, for them, a collection of things, either substances or qualitative and quantitative structures, the unity of which is given by relationships of mutual functional *coordination.* All have in principle the same mode of being, for all "to be" means the same thing: to be objectively present, the possible object of a present *thesis*. But what if precisely this basic stock of philosophical instruments is inadequate for solving such problems as the *reaching over* from the domain of one mode of being to another, the *encounter* of being with being which makes up understanding in its various modalities—including, without a doubt, perception?

In any case, the critical inquiry into the results of natural-scientific metaphysics accomplished by Schwarz and his contemporaries meant not only a distancing from this metaphysics, but also, for many, an important impulse to a renewal of the qualitative worldview. The renewal established itself primarily in the *philosophy of life*, a domain which mechanism, methodically excluding the qualitatively creative component from its field of vision, is incapable of mastering.

Bergson's *Matter and Memory*,[18] published in the late 1890s, stands at the source of this vitalist orientation. Though *Matter and Memory* contains no analysis of the natural world and, in general, knows nothing of this problem, the point of view is that of the primary givenness of qualities and their absolute objectivity. The work touches on a whole array of important phenomena (only touches, without for the most part even beginning a methodical description or analysis). The specifically human spatiality as *oriented* (the fact that things surround us in accordance with our possibilities of acting upon them), or again perception defined as *virtual action* (this implying also the relation between perception and anticipation) are, for instance, mentioned and taken into account in extensive contexts, though not analyzed. Avenarius's conception of two orders in which the same elements ("images") occur is implicit here in the question of how one and the same image can become part of two systems, one of which means that it is modified with respect to the real influence of neighboring images, the other that it is modified solely with respect to the image of the body and to its possible action. Bergson then focuses on explaining that perception is not the *creation* of images but rather a *choice* with regard to the possibilities of action of a living being, capable of using things from its environment to its own purposes and in view of its own possibilities.

Though our problem is never formulated in so many words in Bergson, he and his conception of "pure perception" (i.e., perception containing no element of memory) represent a very important stage on the way to it. Bergson tries to find a *metaphysical* answer to questions that need first to be developed on the level of descriptive analysis. His attempt at explaining the act of conscious perception, though quite ingenious, does not go beyond the sphere of ontic metaphors: the figure of total reflection, the idea of real action as passing through and virtual action as thrown back are hardly more than images. That there must here be creatures capable of understanding their own possibilities and uncovering things in connection with them is something he presupposes, but does not analyze. That the uncovering of things needs to be mediated by something in which things are first *uncovered* things, i.e., what they are, but not solely in themselves—this is concealed by Bergson's ontic images. On the other hand, his endeavor brings to light the one-sidednesses of both realism and idealism, and he sees with remarkable perspicacity the necessity, not for a subjective, but rather for a cosmic solution.

Bergson's rehabilitation of the qualitative worldview had immense influence on thinkers of his time and subsequent years, an influence we cannot follow in detail here. Its impulse is echoed in Whitehead and the Anglo-Saxon neorealists, in Alexander's[19] and other metaphysical ventures. Max Scheler combined the idea of perception as active choice with certain principles of Husserl's phenomenology.[20]

9. Husserl

Husserl conceives the task of describing the natural world as a transcendental problem which he attempts to solve on the basis of the concept of intentionality resulting from the adaptation of Brentano's "intentional in-existence" to a novel purpose. He thus revives, by new means, Kant's transcendental question. But now the difference between the natural world, our life-world, and the world of science—which presupposes the initial, natural world and submits it to methodical exactification and to "idealizations," thus remodeling it into a new form—comes explicitly into play already in the sphere of experience itself.

In Husserl, we find a description of the "natural attitude" and the "natural world-concept" in the lectures entitled *Grundprobleme der Phänomenologie* (winter semester 1910–11), pp. 2–29.[21] With some reservations and corrections, this description clearly links up with Avenarius's 1891 work, *Der menschliche Weltbegriff*, of which Husserl undoubtedly made a close study, as is borne witness to by the marginal notes and underlining in his personal copy. In Avenarius, the schema of the natural world-concept is M–R–T, the individual/the environment/the others; in Husserl, the starting point is the I with its acts and experiences, existing in a body which is continually present and in which the stream of lived-experiences is localized in a specific way, incommensurable with the localization of properties in things; the others with the particular "idea" of the reciprocal exchangeability of experiences, of perspectives on the same time and space; and, finally, things in the one space and the one time to which the I and the others belong as well. The description of the localization of lived-experiences in the body is particularly stressed, perhaps because it makes Avenarius's theory of introjection impossible from the outset: localization in the lived body is an original fact of the *I*-experience, something that does not come only from the projection of my standpoint "into" a foreign body. Husserl notes in conclusion to his first rough sketch: "Here, we break off. Clearly, these initial descriptions could be continued according to the given delineations and could be much enriched by new lines of thought. It could also be shown that *philosophical interests of the highest dignity* [my emphasis—J. P.] require a complete and encompassing description of the so-called *natural concept of the world*, i.e., that of the natural attitude. On the other hand, it also could be shown that an exact and profound description of this kind is in no way something that can be accomplished easily but rather requires extraordinarily difficult reflections."[22]

Husserl does not say what "philosophical interests of the highest dignity" he means, but it is clear from what follows that the matter has to do with the very foundation of all systematics, with the ontological characterization of the world, with transcendentalism and its specific character, peculiar to phenomenology.

After roughly outlining the basic features of the natural world in their singular factualness, Husserl addresses the a priori attitude, which does not thematize facts but rather their essential, noncontingent correlate, the *eidos*. In the eidetic or a priori attitude, what we thematize is not reality but objects having no existence, no being here and now, i.e., ideas. Thus, in contraposition to nature, there is the idea of nature. The sciences concerned with the ideas constitutive of the idea of nature are, for example, geometry (as the theory of spatial figures, not abstract geometry in the modern formal sense), the pure theory of time, of space, of the possible deformations of things, etc.—taken together, they will make up the ontology of nature. The theory of causal connections, the "pure science of nature," is also relevant here.

Husserl then submits his description of the natural world to the procedure of ideation and brings it into the a priori sphere. Accordingly, the description no longer grasps mere fact, as in Avenarius, but rather the a priori structure. This structure has an evidence peculiar to itself, in accordance with which all experiential knowledge is bound to the sense, or meaning, contained within it. This meaning is then the object of the ontology of nature, and factual natural science is tied not only to concepts such as thing, property, change, cause, effect, space, time, but also to the notions of person, experience, act, appearing, disposition, etc.

All natural science thus presupposes the thesis of the natural world-perspective, investigates being in this framework, and is bound up with the *ontology of the real*. This "real ontology" is an a priori discipline, which develops the pure sense (or "givenness") of the natural attitude. The question whether the *belief in the existence* of this idea may be further justified, and how, is a subject apart. The same goes for the empirical genesis of the idea. The idea itself is, however, valid a priori. So the natural worldview is not simply what every human factually brings into the world as a result of the legacy of collective experience; rather, it is an *idea* to which all meaningful discourse concerning the world is bound. It is thus incorrect to assume either that men, animals, etc., could develop another concept of the world, or that the natural concept could be modified in experience, through the influence of some experiential motivation, as Avenarius's school believed to be the case.

Only after this critique of Avenarius does Husserl address the most important problem, the meaning of the thesis of the existence of the world. The thesis, as an act of the subject, presupposes of course the thematization of subjective lived-experiencing. Husserl now distinguishes subjectivity in the sense of psychology, including rational, eidetic psychology, from phenomenological subjectivity, acquired by suspending both the belief in the factual world and the orientation on the essence, the idea of nature. He operates here at first with the "*distinctio phaenomenologica*" between the essence of man (as part of spatial nature) and the essence of lived-experience, a distinction wholly analogous to that by means of which Descartes proves the "immateriality" of the soul. There follows, known from the *Ideas*, the exposition of the primacy of phenomenological, immanent perception as against the empirically transcendent (to lived-experience): phenomenological perception grasps its object in the original without unilaterality, though perhaps incompletely, it does not refer to further complementary experiences. And the text goes on to show how, in the sphere of the reduced lived-experiences, there is also, nonetheless, a certain transcendence, an occasion to pass on to experiences other than the actual one; retention, recollection, anticipation are also possible, in addition to perception, and one can acquire by means of all this a continuous phenomenological stream of consciousness, the stream whose accomplishment is experience. Further, it is shown how the reduced objectivities forming the poles of experience are "immanently transcendent" indexes of courses of experience; the experience of the other is analyzed, as well as the possibility of other phenomenological experiences, reduced nature as what binds together the phenomenologically reduced lived-experiences of the universe of monads. In short, Husserl shows that individual as well as eidetically transformed phenomenological experience, studied as truly pure experience in the phenomenological attitude, is essentially independent of the thesis of nature, of being, of the world—that the experience of the world, of things, is thus, by essence and nature, independent of things, that it has its own a priori laws, its own structure that remains valid, whether the world exists or not.

The 1910–11 lecture course is one of Husserl's most important works, a text containing a blueprint of his entire philosophical problematic. Without these lectures, it would perhaps be quite impossible to embrace this whole in one view. Though many of the later eminently important concepts with which "transcendental phenomenology" operates are lacking here (the opposition noesis/noema, the concept of constitution, the concepts of static and genetic analysis, etc.), on the other hand, the fundamental line of thought, passing over from one attitude to the other under the dominance of the natural worldview, is clearer than anywhere else. This concept remains dominant in Husserl up through his last work. Under the title of "life-world," the natural view serves as the systematic axis of the *Krisis*, too—though, of course, the *Krisis* remains unfinished.

The line is as follows: (a) the fundamental description of the natural world in an empirically unique attitude; (b) the unveiling of these main features as a priori structure of the world in the eidetic attitude (implying: the outside world is not something to be *proved*, being-in-the-world is an a priori of our life); (c) this a priori is studied by phenomenology in a new attitude, which does not imply the thesis of the existence of the world and is, therefore, wholly independent of the world's facticity; (d) hereto pertains not only the study of the momentary individual givenness of the self, but that of the entire stream, of the entire monad, as well as of all the other monads.

Another very essential contribution to the problem of the natural world is the characterization of the world as the horizon of all horizons. The concept of horizon has to do with the fact that experience does not take place exclusively in the actuality of what is really present; rather, what is really, "originally" given acquires meaning only from potential connections. "Every lived-experience has a *horizon*, which changes with the alteration of the nexus of consciousness to which it belongs and with its own alteration from phase to phase of its flow—an intentional horizon of reference to potentialities of consciousness that belong to the lived-experience itself."[23] "Ultimately, only *the uncovering of the horizons of experience clarifies the actuality of the world* [my emphasis—J. P.] and its *transcendence*, at the same time showing the world to be inseparable from transcendental subjectivity, which constitutes actuality of being and sense. The reference to harmonious infinities of further possible experience, starting from each world-experience . . . manifestly signifies that an actual object belonging to a world or, all the more so, a world itself, is an infinite idea, related to infinities of harmoniously combinable experiences—*an idea that is the correlate of the idea of a perfect experiential evidence*, a complete synthesis of possible experiences."[24] The idea of the world, the world as an idea are understandable only if we conceive the world as a totality, not of real data, but of data in their lawful relation to the inexhaustible, unrealizable potentialities—horizons—which are a priori open to us and give meaning to each singular actual experience. (One could say, in other words, that each thing carries with it a sphere of demonstrability, a sphere of that in which it shows itself to be what it is—its own sphere of phenomenality; the world as the horizon of all horizons would then be what makes it possible for each singular thing to show itself.)

Yet other complementary themes are subsequently adjoined to the problematic of the natural world, in particular the emphasis placed (1) on the genetic component of transcendental phenomenology, (2) on the traditionality of the experience of the world, and (3) on the emergence of a universal science, of its idea of absolute truth, pole of endless approximations, and of true nature, which is one in all these approximations as in its manifestations.

Rather than systematically describing the natural world, now called *Lebenswelt*, life-world, or world of our life, Husserl in this later period presents important separate fragments toward such a characterization. He points out the fundamentally different idea of truth—a practical idea, never rising above the situation—peculiar to the prescientific view; the indeterminacy or, rather, incomplete determinacy of the objective typicality characteristic of it; and its essential "subjectivity" (in the sense, not of lived-experiencing, but of the experienced!). Several passages of the *Krisis*, in particular in the lecture "Die Krisis des europäischen Menschentums,"[25] refer also to the world of primitive humanity as partaking of a different mode of being than the world of scientific nature, universally valid as an absolute existent in endless phenomenal approximations.

True, it is not sure what Husserl's final picture of the original, naturally given world would have looked like, but the sketches toward it that he does present are manifestly oriented on the problem of idealization, of objectification, of the origin of natural science; even in the world of naive natural life, notice is thus taken primarily of those features which provide the significational groundwork of objectification and the subsequent process of naturalization.

The major shortcoming of Husserl's conception is the failure to completely overcome Cartesianism in the conception of consciousness as a being *quae nulla re indiget ad existendum*.[26] This position does, of course, make it possible to surmount psychologism in logic as well as in the theory of the knowledge of nature. Since consciousness, in transcendental phenomenology, is thematized as independent of the thesis of objective existence, it shows itself to be in principle independent of natural interaction and, thereby, autonomous in its own essence as against objective reality. This conception also carries with it the possibility of understanding the natural life-world as an aspect of the "true" being of nature, independent of the contingent historical environment. But it does not in itself make it possible to grasp these historical aspects, historically subjective reality in its own nature, though Husserl does ask at one point: "is it not obviously a good and necessary guiding notion that one seek to ground an investigation of factual spirits in their historicity upon an essential knowledge of the spirit (and of the community in which spirits live) and that one proceed from these to create 'exact concepts' and exact, unconditionally valid truths as ideal poles for all spiritual factuality?"[27] It is, however, a question whether the concept of consciousness as intentionality, as Husserl himself defines it as graspable in reflection with absolute evidence, is indeed a suitable starting point for the sciences of the spirit, and whether it is really capable of solving their problems. The fact is that, no less than the natural sciences, the "humanistic" sciences, too, distinguish between "being-in-itself" and "mere appearance." But the relationship between appearance and the "true world" is not the same here. The appearances that the natural scientist "objectifies" are themselves, in a certain sense, already objective; they are not a lived-experiencing but rather that which is experienced. Consequently, the appearance as appearance does not vanish or change with its explanation, but remains unaffected in its phenomenal nature.—In the human sciences, on the other hand, we have to do with appearances of a different kind, appearances in which we live and which are not, for us, appearances as long as we live within them. The appearances of this kind must first be objectified in order to become appearances. We objectify them in various ways: in uncovering their presence through a change of attitude; in focusing on the neuralgic points which life automatically turns away from and discerning in them its *interest* in not seeing; in developing this attitude into a systematic method for unveiling prejudices. Only in this distancing attitude do we acquire the insights that make possible a deeper understanding, beyond the run-of-the-mill, automatically functioning comprehension of human affairs, and there is here a dividing point similar to that which differentiates natural science from the instinctive mastery of the corporeal world. Just as natural science successfully accomplishes its objectification only then, when it interprets objective qualitative data as approximations to mathematical ideals (from that moment on, its image of the world and, most of all, its impact on the world, its control of the world is incomparably more accurate and deeper than in common praxis), the humanistic sciences begin to control man by first compelling him to appear, to emerge from concealment in the unapparent, automatically unwinding sequence of everyday phenomena.

10. Heidegger

Heidegger's breaking through the subject concept in his conception of existence as, in its being, concerned with being as such, understanding being both in totality and in its different orders, represents, from the viewpoint of our problem, a new and essential contribution. Only if man in his self-understanding does not originally see himself as he is does the question of the *motives* of this self-understanding arise, a question that is not in search of mere *causal* connections but is precisely a question of *motivation*, i.e., a matter not of external causation but rather of the internal structure of life itself.

This significance for the transcendental foundation of the humanities and the social sciences is not, however, the major importance of Heidegger's novel approach to the problem of the natural world. The major importance lies in his wholly new way of putting the question of the mode of being of the beings of this world. This is no longer mere "presence here and now," but rather *existence* (being-there) and *coexistence* (being-with), as far as man is concerned, and "*handiness*," or "*readiness-to-hand*," in the case of both pragmatic and natural things, both combined in "being-in-the-world" as the essential character of human existence.

Heidegger's new question of the original mode of givenness, prior to "objectivity = presence here and now," shows above all that we cannot make do with Husserl's conception of truth as self-givenness, derived as it is from the equation being = objectivity = presence here and now. The philosophical regression toward original givenness as the source of all meaning must therefore go beyond self-givenness, not that self-givenness is denied, but it is deemed insufficient: self-givenness can still be a derived mode of givenness. The same being can appear in different ways, originally or in diversely derived manners. Phenomenology thus finds itself in a new situation. Husserl, in defining truth as self-givenness, approached the problem *from the viewpoint of language*, from the basic linguistic situation in which a signification is maintained as identical without taking into account the mode of givenness of what is meant. In his exclusively epistemological orientation, he did not however realize that the mode of givenness goes deeper than the opposition "presence/absence."

This complicates the task of phenomenology. The opposition "presence/absence" allows for the development of the *method of clues*. The object as an identical pole of experiential manifolds provides a clue for unveiling the intentional structures correlative to objects of a certain essential character. The task of phenomenology is basically fulfilled when this correlativity is unveiled, in reflective self-certitude, in the whole of its foundational structure. Of course, the primacy and predominance of the dynamic, temporal structures over the static structures becomes clear in time, making, here too, the *tendency toward originarity* appear as the major and, perhaps, ultimate sense of phenomenology. But Husserl's understanding of originarity remains oriented toward the idea of objectivity, toward the primal institution of the ideals and idealizations that make possible total objectification. Here, too, practical behavior is uncovered as a more original level of the approach to things, practical truth as the prime, "subjective" form of truth, as opposed to the truth of the theoretical attitude. Nonetheless, this new orientation never goes so far as to problematize the *being of the subject* in the same way as being whose original approach to itself would not be reflection, self-apprehension in an objectifying, donating *view*.

While Heidegger's approach to the self is also a reflective view, this is a view which is not guided primarily by the idea of registering given presence but rather of being referred to oneself in the accomplishment of one's being, in taking over one's comprehended and apprehended possibilities, in a self-realization which is not the making, the manipulating of the self but rather the original discovery of, and seizing upon, the *proper* possibility of a being which relates to itself in such a way that its being matters to it, that it is not "indifferent" to its being (i.e., indifference is even then a mode of being possible only to such being, *taedium vitae* is possible solely in man, whose being is a self-relation). For this reason, the primordial form of this relation is not the direct orientation on an object but rather the practical seizing of a possibility, an identification with a "for-the-sake-of-which," which does not mean the *representation* of this "for-the-sake-of." The fact that Heidegger grasps these phenomena again in reflection is by no means contradictory to what he has in view—his reflection is, of course, guided by the idea of a being which *is* wholly *its praxis*, so that what it grasps in its (in a certain sense, objectifying) reflection will be precisely non-objectifying phenomena, phenomena which do *not* make objectivity an explicit object, do *not* make it the accomplishment of a synthesis, etc. The existential analysis does not exclude a reflective grasping, conceived of, however, not as mere internal intuition, but as an *understanding* of Dasein's[28] own being which exhausts itself in its accomplishment, so that its features are not "moments" or qualities of an object but rather modes of its being, modes of its comportment, modes of its relating to its own being.

One could ask here whether this is not a dogmatic approach which in actual fact presupposes self-certain reflection.[29] I would say that reflective self-apprehension is indeed a starting point, but one that is insufficient, just as the thematization of external objects remains possible but is a nonoriginal approach to things. Reflective self-apprehension, in which we do not always live, has its origin and its ground; existential phenomenology is capable of explaining the origin of objective from nonobjective clarity, whereas the opposite is not possible.

On the other hand, it does seem that Heidegger's analytics make his ontology of existence excessively formal; though praxis is the original form of clarity, he never takes into consideration the fact that the original praxis is necessarily and in principle the activity of a *bodily* subject, that embodiment must therefore have an ontological status which cannot be identical with the body's being come across as present here and now. The illumination that characterizes existence is the illumination of a bodily being. This does not and cannot mean the reintroduction of a substance-substrate, which would compromise the whole ontological status of existence; of this there is no doubt. Substantial corporeality is, in terms of cognition, the result of a secondary thematization, but there must be a primary existential status of corporeality that makes possible localization among things, as well as acting upon and receiving action from them. And if corporeality has not merely an ontic but an ontological status, it follows that the drama of authenticity, the drama of the truth of existence, will have to be enacted with respect to this dimension of life.

The body and embodiment belong essentially not only to what is revealed, uncovered by the illuminated, disclosed being in its being-in-the-world, but to the ontological status of existence as such. In what way is a question that cannot be answered simply by reference to facticity, since facticity, determined as in Heidegger by *attunement,* is once again nothing explicitly bodily. The body belongs not only to the problem of one's own spatiality but also to the sphere of one's own possibilities. The body is existentially the totality of possibilities that we do not choose but into which we are inserted, those for which we are not free, those *we have to be.* This does not mean that these possibilities lack the character of existence, i.e., of something set to me in its unicity as a task that I must take upon myself and accomplish. But it is only on their basis that the "free" possibilities are opened.

Another remark concerns what is one of Heidegger's major contributions to our problem of the natural world—the problematizing and differentiation of the very concept of world, traditionally understood for the most part as the universe, the sum total of existing things. Heidegger, as we know, distinguishes two ontic and two ontological concepts of world: (1) the totality of what-is in the mode of given presence; (2) the regional concept of the possible objects of a given domain; (3) that "in which" a factical Dasein lives; and (4) world-liness, the ontological character appertaining to the world in this third meaning.[30] It is important that Heidegger ties his analyses and his definition of the world-liness of the world to the relation between Dasein (the disclosed being concerned with its being) and the innerworldly beings to which Dasein is referred. The analysis has shown that innerworldly being does not have the mode of given presence (*Vorhandenheit*); rather, as *pragma* (*Zeug*),[31] it is referred to our possibilities and to how things stand with it in this or that respect (the *Bewandtnis*). In other words, innerworldly beings are uncovered in their *handiness* for praxis (*Zuhandenheit*). Heidegger then pursues the foundation of the innerworldly mode of being in the being of Dasein and arrives at these conclusions: (1) the being of Dasein—for its own sake—founds a certain praxis (a certain "what-for"); (2) the praxis—the "what-for"—founds a certain respect in which innerworldly beings appear *as what* appears; and (3) this "as what" shows the being to which the entire structure is referred. In connection with this, the world-liness of the world is then defined as "the wherein of referential understanding as that in regard to which Dasein lets beings be encountered in the essential character of 'how things stand with them in this or that respect.'"[32] We see thus that the world is determined with respect to the *pragmata* and to the uncovering of the *pragmata* in a certain regard. Though Heidegger goes on to develop the concept of world also as concerns being-with, he does not further define the world in its world-liness. Notwithstanding, it would be of the utmost importance to ascertain in what ontological feature of Dasein lies the possibility of encountering the other as a sui generis *innerworldly* being; there is obviously a gap here, due once again to the fact that Heidegger ignores or minimizes the problem of corporeality. The other as other must be in a certain way "uncovered" and in a certain way "disclosed," both must somehow be connected, the possibility of *uncovering disclosed foreign being* must be included as a fundamental possibility in being-in-the-world, in the world-liness of the world.

The emergence of an inauthentic self, the self in the mode of the "One," shows then Dasein's avoidance of itself, its flight into the world, away from the unease of its authentic being. The question is now *into what world*, into what dimension of world-liness Dasein flees in its flight from itself. It is clear that this flight is above all toward the dimension of being-with, and only in special cases (dullness due to work, to busyness) toward the dimension of *pragmata*. Thus alienated, Dasein has "fallen prey to the world," "fallen unto the world"—but this metaphor means in actual fact an entanglement *in itself*, in a certain manner of relating to oneself in the mode of avoidance, of not-seeing. What Heidegger calls fallenness into the world, and regards as our first and most frequent mode of existence, is in actual fact an entanglement in ourselves and a flight from our own disclosedness no less than from the uncovering of things in their thing-ness, in that which they truly are.

This leads still further. Heidegger speaks as if the *possibilities* that lie in our "for-the-sake-of" (I exist for the sake of my being; my being, my life, is dependent on my "leading" it, on my carrying it out in the possi-bilities with which I identify in accomplishing = realizing them) were un-covered to me directly by my "being for the sake of." In actual fact, what I *want* to accomplish "for the sake of my being" is always codetermined by what I *have to* accomplish in order to be able to do or accomplish anything at all. My possibilities are possibilities of existing in the world, possibili-ties of moving about, of protecting myself, of dwelling, etc., possibilities of feeding, of providing for myself and my family, of reproducing . . . , and they all have a certain historically changing, yet *given* form, through which I first search for my own possibility and my own path. The obscure concept of "possibility," i.e., of a certain task which, as existence, I can and must take upon myself, implies not only the original "for-the-sake-of-myself" but also, already, the *world*. I am originally disclosed to myself not only as existence, but already as *existence in the world*, as *bodily* exis-tence, and corporeality here has an ontological, not an ontic meaning. No doubt, everything I accomplish is enacted for the sake of my being, but at the same time there is a *fundamental* possibility that must be open to me, a possibility without which all the others merely float in the air, baseless, senseless, and unrealizable. This, the primordial, is thus no con-tingent thing, nothing ontic; rather, *as first possibility*, its ontological status is that of a basis for all existence. This is not just one possibility among others. It is a privileged possibility which then codetermines the whole of existence in its meaning. This ontological basis is corporeality *as the possibility of movement.*

What makes the link between the "for-the-sake-of" and what follows from it as our concrete task is left unsolved in Heidegger's schema. I be-lieve the link resides in life's embodiment—what I can do is given by what makes it possible for me to do anything at all, and that is my corporeality, which I *must take over* prior to all free possibilities. My "for-the-sake-of" dis-closes to me these original possibilities of action (bodily worldly, pertain-ing to my being as being-of-the-world), which then, in turn, disclose in-nerworldly things as their correlates, as what can be understood from the possibilities of action. Action acquires thereby the concrete form of con-cern in a certain factical historical context in which then appear the pos-sibilities of my *proper* task, freely glimpsed and chosen. Since possibilities occur, however, in two forms: on the one hand, as taken over, and, on the other hand, as chosen, the world too, in our "being-in-the-world" in the ontological sense, is necessarily represented twice, as is expressed in Heidegger's speaking of the "thrown project" of the world.

This bodily character of existence, the body and holding sway in the body as an original, wholly irreplaceable component of existence and the true source of all its possibilities, is particularly forcefully stressed by Merleau-Ponty, following up Husserl's analyses of the "wielding of the body" in the line of the French tradition stemming from Maine de Biran. Merleau's contribution to the phenomenology of the natural world understood as the perceived world is, for this reason, exceptionally important and forms one of the bridges between the phenomenology and the metaphysics of the natural world.

11. Summary

Heidegger's philosophy was not intended as an analysis of the "natural world"; its aim is a "fundamental ontology" of human Dasein which, in turn, was meant to serve as the starting point for a renewal of ontology in general, a new way of putting the question of the essence of being, which had fallen silent since the tradition running from antiquity through the Middle Ages had been exhausted.

Its contribution to the problem of the natural world is incidental. It has been of help in elucidating, in *Sein und Zeit*, the question of the mode of being peculiar to original innerworldly, extrahuman thingness, in which it unveils "pragmat-icality" and "handiness," rather than the "objectivity" still seen by Husserl (despite isolated insights into the initial imprecision and situatedness of the original concept of truth pertaining to the objectivity of the primordial, natural world). The world that we call natural is in Heidegger the world of *pragmata* ready to hand along with that of human taking care in mutual understanding, with- and against-one-another. Though this world is as a foundation to the world of science, its discovery presupposes a radical *change in the meaning of being* of those things which originally appear in the natural world—appear, that is to say: *are*. Hence, *appearance—being as the manifestation of beings*—shows itself to be essentially, not a supratemporal structure of the transcendental subject constitutive of being, but rather the fundamental "event" which makes being possible.

Heidegger's attempts at a new ontology have made it necessary to go into the problem of truth in greater depth. Husserl showed that the truth of judgment presupposes, as a deeper level to which it relates, truth in the sense of *self-showing* in the original, that this is the criterion governing the truth of judgment. The truth of self-showing, however, refers further to the sphere of the practical comportment in which our life plays itself out, to the sphere of self-understanding through the actualization of our own possibilities. It is thus this praxis which is the original sphere of truth, of the unconcealedness of things. But the unconcealedness of things has also a necessary presupposition *in things themselves*. Things are not merely "objects," they are not mere presentations to which our intentionality appends its own meaning, drawn from the depths of the subject, from its personal transcendental history. Things are, on the one hand, "in themselves," which is of course to say closed in themselves and inaccessible; in order to show themselves in what they are, they must step out of themselves and show themselves in something else. This other, in which things show themselves, in which they become phenomena, is not *another thing*, an other reality; if it can be said to "be," then only *cum grano salis*; but precisely the fact that it *is* no thing allows for it to be the being of appearing things. Of course, in order for the *pragmata* and handinesses to be able to show themselves in what they are, there must be here yet another reality, i.e., a human being who understands his possibilities; but the world, the nexus of understanding that makes it possible for this or that instrument, utensil, or other *pragma* to *appear* in relation to our praxis, is neither my reality nor a thinglike reality; rather, it is an interval, the space of being of the thing in question. Being and the world, the light in which things appear, in which they emerge, cannot be understood from the existent things themselves; on the contrary, these presuppose being and the world in order to appear. We can, therefore, never proceed so as to explain being from beings, from existents; on the contrary, beings are what they are in the light of being. To interpret the world as a subjective horizon, for example, after the manner of Husserl, is a metaphysics of subjectivism, reducing being to a particular being, to the subject of cognition as a privileged type of objectivity, as object par excellence.

It can, of course, be said that Husserl's phenomenology, with its conception of the reduction and its defining of a sphere of pure phenomena, *quae nulla re indigent ad existendem*, contributed in more than one respect to this ontology of being in its difference from the beings whose being it is. The reduction, showing the sphere of appearing to be autonomous, or, as Husserl sometimes said, "pre-existing," opens undoubtedly the understanding of being, especially in the noematic sphere, as distinct from the appearing beings as such. But Heidegger's ontology presupposes at once this understanding and the annulling of the reduction as reduction, as transformation into a reality of the noetic, subjective sphere. Heidegger turns the situation around: the event of being, the opening up of the phenomenal sphere, the "temporalization" of time and the clearing of the world (world = light),[33] is what makes possible humanity, the birth of man. Inexplicable yet shedding light on all and everything, the event of being is contemporaneous with the "birth" of man. Being is not the human being, nor does it rest on human beings; being is neither our perception, nor our thought, our affectivity, etc.; on the contrary, being human—human being is possible solely because our thinking, our perceiving, our feeling takes place always in the light of the world, in the light of being.

But, if this is so, then the original natural world is the encounter of being enclosed in itself with man, who by virtue of his conscious finitude exists always in the totality of what is—and perhaps also, ultimately, with the vaguely sensed being which surpasses all finite existents—in the revealing but, at the same time, always concealing event of being. It is indeed always only in part that beings are uncovered to us, only in a particular situation, from a particular perspective, and in a particular aspect of being, never as a whole; concealedness goes hand in hand with uncovering; no less than being, which at once reveals and conceals it, the whole of what-is is essentially a mystery.—Such a "natural world" would of course not be an object of phenomenological description; the analysis of its structures would lead only to already existing results, independently of the original event of being which makes them possible and conditions them through and through—the original world could be grasped only in the cipher of a mythical narrative of the marriage of earth and heaven, of the assembly of earthly and celestial beings, of the here below and the beyond.

Eugen Fink, thinker of a yet more unrepentantly speculative bent, asks then: Is there not here still too much of an anthropological cast? Is there not still an excessive emphasis on what is close to humanity, is not the event of being itself still understood too much from the standpoint of human phenomena, from the standpoint of meaning, of *logos*, of meaningful discourse? Is not the world still seen solely as the totality of those potentialities that we know how to *decipher*, that we are capable of reading out of its actualities, from what is uncovered? Does not this conception still excessively ignore the original closure of what is into itself, the primordial nonindividuation, the dark night of existence? Does this not lead, on the other hand, to a tendency to put all being in the proximity of the human, to assimilate it to human creativity? But what if what-is generates already other existents—the existence of individuation as such— simply by coming forth from out of itself, through the agency of being? Are not things in their existence, in their individual determinacy, always a being for another, are they not always, as *determinate* individuals, *outside of themselves*, in a certain environment, i.e., always already something that has come forth? Is not the world as universal environment, as space-time containing and mediating all and everything, at the same time the universal being which lets individual existents communicate, come forth out of themselves as the condition for them to be what they are?

Will it not be possible, in this way, to receive into an ontological context the world in the strong sense of the word, the independently existing world? Will this not be a rehabilitation of the ancient, age-old *phusis* as *archē*, holding sway in all particulars? What the being of what-is is for us (the ground on which we stand, on which alone we are what we are as beings whose being lies in understanding), space-time is for things: the unindividuated, antecedent, global framework of all individuation. Itself indivisible, it divides and at the same time unites all and everything; it is a whole which is not made up of parts, at once incommensurable with every part and wholly contained in each one. It is not an existent thing, and it can be thematized only in the relations provided by objects within it. The appearing of things, which it makes possible, is not an appearing for a subject, but rather appearing as coming forth into individuality, as coming to be. It is an appearing to which the singularized things themselves are inwardly indifferent, an appearing that is not apparent for itself, an appearing plunged in the night and shadow of primal beings and primal being.

Things would then be what they are by virtue not of the secondarily human opening but already of the primordial, "physical" opening of what-is by being. Their first coming forth from out of themselves, out of the mere closure equivalent to dark night and, in this sense, to nonbeing— Hegel's word, "being and nothing are the same,"[34] applies precisely to this nonappearing existent, limited to itself—would make them participate in the qualitative wealth of determinations which the natural worldview brings with it. At the same time, however, they would be made to participate directly in the infinite wealth of relations and relational systems and possibilities in which modern natural science sees physical being in its elementary composition and its potentialities of action, in the immensities of its both potential and really developed forces.

Our own individuation, too, would belong to this universe of primordial individuation, encompassing everything which originally appears in its mere befalling, unfolding, coming to be and passing away, with no inner participation or interest in being. We ourselves, with the particular manner in which we single ourselves out from the world through *inwardly relating* to it, would participate in this primitive individuation. As in all other things, our being, too, would be a movement between coming to be and passing away, from its own beginning to its own end. *Our* specific movement would, however, be characterized by a non-indifference to being, an interest in our own being and, in connection with it, in the being of what is in general, and this on the basis of a *new manner* in which being conditions what is—not merely in its coming to be and passing away, but rather as a clarity which makes possible an encounter *within, inside* the universe, a clarity which reveals the universe in its connection with life. Such would be, ultimately, the meaning of the attempt to understand existence as movement—movement would be here the middle term between the two fundamental ways in which being uncovers existents and thereby shows itself to be their origin and ruling principle, *archē*.

III

The fundamental difference between our present standpoint and that developed in 1936 is as follows: we no longer understand the world as a totality of objects constituted in pure consciousness, the correlates of all kinds of intentionalities; rather, we now view the world, in the sense of the totality of what is, as the correlate of life in a "world" in the sense of a comprehensible context, the key to which resides in something else again. Consequently, the original gateway to the natural world is not contemplative reflection but rather reflection as an integral part of our praxis, a component of our inner action and comportment. We do not turn to the natural world in mere theoretical curiosity, in order to examine the structure of existents as correlates of the structures of experiential flows; we turn toward it because we are searching for life in its originarity, seeking to make sense of things and of ourselves. (This intention was of course already present in the original text of our *Natural World*, but we had not yet understood that the method advocated there does not lead to concrete human life *in the world*, in society and in history. For, though the phenomenological reduction as gateway to absolute reflection does indeed offer a solution to life's questions, it leads *beyond the world* and shows concrete life to be meaningful only, or above all, insofar as it is the life of science and philosophy.)

We believe that we thereby remain faithful to the original intention of phenomenology, which was to bring phenomena to light as opposed to mere speculation in the pejorative sense (genuine speculation is nothing other than the showing, the monstration of what appears and reveals itself). We attempt, in addition, to take advantage of Heidegger's radicalization of the phenomenology of intentionality in his phenomenology of life as existence and of Fink's idea of the ontological analysis of life as being necessarily, in each and every moment, *an analysis of the world* with its fundamental moments of time, space, and motion. The ontology of life can be broadened into an ontology of the world if we understand life as movement in the original sense of the word—what Aristotle was on the track of with his notion of actualized *dunamis*. Aristotle's *dunamis*, viewed as substrate and forced out of spatiotemporality, back into the enduring, present framework of substance, could not fully develop its ontological import. On the other hand, *human life as dunamis*, as possibility being realized, is capable of restoring their original ontological meaning to the concepts of space, time, and motion.

There is a modern conception of motion as a structure of interrelated continuous quantitative parameters, distance traveled, time, speed, acceleration, etc. This conception is the result of an objectifying idealization of the original movement; it has in the proper sense nothing to do with mobility; its specificity as a quantitative structure lies in making real movement predictable and controllable.

Among modern thinkers, Bergson brought to bear against this conception a notion of "inner" movement, lived-experienced consciously, from within. Where the quantitative conception sees diversity and an infinite plurality, movement viewed thus from within is one, a single act. The unity of the act is the unity of duration. Duration is an indivisible unity, every stage of which contains all previous stages; for this reason, it is necessarily individual and original.—The shortcoming of this conception lies in that it is psychological, based on a nonelucidated concept of consciousness, and lays exclusive emphasis on the past, on passive memory, or, as Husserl would say, on the *retentional* aspect.

Aristotle's conception, with its emphasis on the *realization of dunamis*, puts forward the aspect of protentionality, futurity. Potency is, however, localized in a substrate, which makes change possible by enduring unchanged, by lasting in change. Movement is thus thrust back into the sheer present, into time as a series of instants forming a linear continuum.

We can get further only by *radicalizing* Aristotle's conception and understanding movement as the original life which does not receive its unity from an enduring substrate but rather generates itself its own unity as well as that of the thing in movement. Only movement thus understood is the *original* movement.

Our radicalization of Aristotle lies in answering fundamentally in the affirmative his question whether, and how, *genesis-phthora*, coming to be and passing away, can be conceived as movement, and in *seeking to find our way to the essence of movement precisely from the "movement of substance,"* the movement of coming to be and passing away of what is—movement thus no longer presupposes constituted being but rather constitutes it, first makes this or that being *apparent*, causes it to manifest itself in its own original manner. Movement is that by virtue of which *it appears* that the world has, for a certain time, a certain place for a particular reality among other particular realities.

Aristotle's solution, defining movement as a change in a subject, or substrate, made possible by the changelessness of the substrate, is unsatisfactory, since the substrate itself *endures*, i.e., undergoes change of its temporal determinations. But duration is not a mere change of temporal arguments in something atemporal. Both duration and change are in time, time must be a factor of their formation. Time can therefore never be a mere external framework, a mere number added to the thing itself in comparing it with the changes of other things; time must itself be what makes possible both the elapsing and the enduring of things.

Only life as movement represents moreover a substantial contribution to the problem of *praxis* as the fundamental element of human life and history which, implicitly or explicitly, has been a major object of the strivings of the whole last great period of modern philosophy since Kant. Earlier philosophy, while promoting practicality and stressing practical, effective knowledge, knows only such effective knowledge as stems from statements of fact, from theory. Kant in the practical sphere finds access to the whole realm of "true" being, and shows the precedence of synthetic activity, an element related to praxis, over contemplation in theory. The speculative idealists then raise this activity to the absolute, make it, so to speak, into a praxis of the absolute, conceiving the absolute not as mere substance but rather as free activity. In the post-Hegelian return to finitude, the praxical view holds its ground, and with added emphasis—speculative philosophy is criticized precisely for its character of consecutive understanding, justification, and reconciliation. The late Schelling, Cieszkowski, Feuerbach, Marx, speak, each in his own way, of praxis, Kierkegaard of inner action. All their attempts and initiatives lack a coherent philosophical basis which would, insofar as possible, give them unity and justify both the primacy of praxis and, therein, its—ever and again alleged, but never proved—potential for creating meaning and truth.

Praxis remains ontologically indeterminate as long as its proponents emphasize simply the being that precedes thought, without specifying the *character* of such be-ing. Every existent is practical and active, each and every one enters into "causal" connections, every actual reality is an act, a manifestation. But only a reality which not only is not indifferent to itself but can realize itself only insofar as it is not indifferent to the fact *that* it is and *how* it is—only a reality capable of understanding its own being (and this means at the same time understanding being in general, being as a whole, understanding the *world*)—is active in the eminent sense, i.e., in such a way that its action does not concern only existents in their reality, that their being too must be opened in it, that the inner richness of what is, its tenor, its fullness, its meaning is opened up in and through this action. The action of such a being is something that exceeds its own framework; despite its minuteness and insignificance (measured by the dimensions of the cosmos), such a being is in all it does an internalization of what is, an action for and in place of others, it is a great objectiveness— insofar as it shows itself capable of letting existents unfold in what they are, in their inner essence, without falsifying or deforming them (though this, too, lies in its nature as a possibility).

All human action is thus "open" (for existents and their being). It is open precisely as *action*, i.e., as a self-responsible movement, one that I take upon myself as an act. Movement is the realization of possibilities. To realize one's own possibilities means to realize that which, by nature, man alone can be not only for himself but also *for things*.

Existence as movement means further: existence is *essentially bodily*. The corporeality of existence is not only part of its *situatedness*, part and parcel of the situation in which we always find ourselves; all our activity and creativity as well, our affectivity and our comportment are bodily. This corporeality is manifest already in the metaphor of human "transcendence." Lived and living corporeality is, however, essentially something psychical, if not spiritual. Lived corporeality is soulful, it is the unity of what, in other regards, is *partes extra partes*, it is the possibility of action which precedes and opens every fact and experience of action. It is on the basis of corporeality that our action is always a movement *from somewhere to somewhere*, that it always has a starting point and a goal. It is by virtue of corporeality that our existence is, as regards its action too, fully occupied with bodily needs, with the repetition, the restitution, and the extension of its own corporeality. The circle of existence—existing for the sake of oneself, for the sake of one's being—always somehow includes the circle of life, carrying out vital functions in order for life to return to and into itself, to be the goal of all its particular operations. (Existence is a modification of life that passes from instinctual univocity to practical plurivocity and is no longer concerned only with itself as existent but rather with its *mode* of being, with the manner in which it *realizes* its existence.) By virtue of its corporeality, existence as movement is related to the great *powers* which shape the naturality of nature prior to all singular objects, first and foremost to the earth as the first immobile referent of all movement and as the power holding sway over all things bodily. A *power* is something other than a mere force: whereas a force is by nature referred in its action to a counterforce which reacts upon it, a power is the ruling determination of an entire sphere of being which has no counterpart (or where the counterpart is phenomenally negligible).

In our view, existence cannot be grasped simply by the concept of temporality in the sense of the trinity of anticipation, presentation, and retention. Heidegger is right in insisting that temporality "temporalizes itself" differently in different moments of existence. We could perhaps attempt now to show that the temporalization of temporality leads directly to three different movements, depending on which moment of temporality is stressed, though temporality as anticipatively retaining presentation, i.e., the unity of all three moments, is present in each one of them. The emphasis laid now on the past (on what we passively accept as given), now on the present (which we actively modify), and now on the future (in regard to which the modifying takes place) is what gives each of the three movements its distinct sense. When the accent falls on the "already," the future, too, is purely awaited and, hence, passively accepted as a coming which, already present, merely repeats and activates an already given potential. Here, the whole of temporality is temporalized from the past. In the movement emphasizing present things and tasks, this passivity is abolished, ready-made potentials are put to use in order to alter the present, but what holds sway over us in this present is, once again, an alien, autonomous, and already existent power. The second movement, though oriented differently, beyond itself, toward things, is thus once more under the rule of the past—a hidden rule, no longer immediate but mediated by things. The accent on the future requires, on the contrary, that the *already* existent cease to be regarded as the decisive instance of possibilities, that the possibility of not-being come to the fore and sharpen our eyes for that to which alone we can, and must, *give ourselves up*.

From this triple sense of time arise then *three movements*, which are, of course, not all on the same plane. All three are movements, since there is a fundamental human possibility realized in each one, and the definition of movement is a possibility being realized.

A distinction should be made between *overall* and partial or singular movements. Overall movements are linked to the fact that our life *is* a movement, that our existence in the world is an ongoing *journey*. The overall movements can be defined by their meaning and the resulting line drawn by them. Partial and singular movements are individual, intermediary kinestheses, acts, and actions, which provide, at a given moment, the locus, focus, and vehicle for an overall movement, without its being possible to compose the overall movement out of partial and singular ones.

The corporeality of all motion thus does not mean here, as in the classical Aristotelian concept, that the body is the common *hupokeimenon* of changes occurring upon it. The corporeality in question here is not objective, material corporeity, the corporeality of something that persists unchanged as substrate of all changes, but rather living and lived embodiment which is, at the same time, a real action, sinking the roots of existence in the world of effectivity in general. It is not a changeless substrate but rather a chunk of lived-experiencing, which, like all experience, is itself a train of changes.

Nonetheless, the corporeality of all motion keeps before our eyes the fact that, insofar as we move, take action, and in so acting understand at once ourselves and things, we are part of nature, *phusis*, the all-embracing world. When interested and occupied above all with human relations and social functions, living in and for work, organization, struggle and competition, we tend to forget this natural aspect and, at the same time, our relationship to the all-embracing *phusis*. The first of our fundamental, overall movements, *the movement of anchoring or sinking roots*, which grounds the other two, is, however, most suitable to remind us of this supremacy of *phusis* in the whole of our life. In fact, *all* our actions, including precisely work and struggle, take place solely on the basis of this instinctive-affective prime motion, which constitutes so to say the ostinato of life's polyphony.

1. The Movement of Anchoring

The meaning of the movement of anchoring is to explicate the given situation, to appropriate what is given in it. Not the transformation of what we come across, already there, but rather an acceptance, first and foremost our own acceptance by that into which we are placed. Only insofar as we are so accepted can we develop our own possibilities, those which are given with us and can only be taken over, since they are not our creation but, rather, co-original with us.

Naturally, we are accepted in more than one sense, acceptance itself is ambiguous. We are accepted by that into which we are born—accepted by the world "wherein," by birth, we are. In being born, we have singled ourselves out from the world, from the context of its processes, we have become something for ourselves. But we are at the same time accepted only if we are ourselves an uncovered object, if we are discovered as something that is for itself—our acceptance, the objectness of our being, conditions our independence and is contemporaneous with it. Of course, the world does not accept us in its immensity but rather in its human exponents: in the human microcommunity, in human coming together, the world has thrown a span marking off something like an outer inwardness which screens the true figure of exteriority (which it fundamentally is), protecting the inside contents from the overwhelming force of the outside. Of course, the glacial outside remains indirectly present in this shelter and safety, betrayed by silent hints.

We make ourselves accepted by showing ourselves in our dependence and by bonding. Dependence is the situation of something singled out, something existing for itself, and an independently existing being is at its most dependent when all the contact with the outside required by its needs, the necessary replenishing from its surroundings, has to be mediated by others. The accepted being is initially a mediated being; the world, for it, is its parents, those who take care of it; it itself needs at first only to radiate its dependence, its helplessness and neediness, at the same time *bonding* with the utmost intensity to those on whom it depends— bonding ecstatically, in such a way that all separation and isolation is thereby actively surmounted. This active fusion is a pleasure, a bliss in which the magnetism of acceptance is no lesser than in the radiating of neediness.

The radiation of neediness and the bliss of bonding, satisfaction, and fulfillment: such is the understanding, or rather the understanding comportment that reveals the first being to address us in and out of the world. The alternate succession of displeasure and bliss, implying in both cases rudimentary control of the body and openness for how the world sees us, is also an implicit expression of the nonautonomous autonomy of life, its bondage at once to the other and to itself. Everything we do, our each and every function leads back and opens into life: every coming out of ourselves shows the way back, life's movement is a closed curve, and the blissful bonding which assimilates the outside without which we could not live is, in a way, a triumph over the incompleteness of individuation, over our sensed neediness. Instead of the totality of the world, which is the nonindividuated prerequisite of individuation but has no being for itself, there is here, for the first time, a relation to the whole which makes this totality live, appear, become a phenomenon. True, bliss leads to sleep and is never so full as in sleep; this, however, enhances rather than cancels its ecstatic character.

The unveiling of the being to which life originally bonds, the understanding of its expression, is necessarily accompanied by a concealing of all the rest of what is. Concealment has here the peculiar form of screening, shelter, safety. It is, of course, a relative screening, a relative protection, depending on the circumstances and on the possibilities realized by the protectors in their unprotected adult life. The darkness, the un-truth, the non-manifestness of the original golden age lies in this necessary shading.

The safety of this mediating and protecting world is then the milieu in which we acquire the possibilities with which life in the big world, the world of work and struggle, later operates as something taken for granted. The face of someone close becomes, with its expression, the face of the world, the gaze turned to us by things, the way appearing things "look" at us. The body, whose activity at first went no farther than the appeal radiating its helplessness, acquires control over itself in maturing and through a playful discovery of itself and its surroundings, an activity in which it no longer just lets itself be moved, fed, satisfied, but acquires autonomy in one function after the other—a progressive ingress into the world of working and actively coming to terms with the big world.

The progressive acquiring and attaining of what we are, of what is *already* there, the acquisition of both bodily potentialities and relations to the actual situation of the world shows at the same time that the essential *contingency*, which is a fundamental feature of being-in-the-world as existence, is rooted here. No one is master of the situation that sets him into the world. We *find ourselves* as part and parcel of this general situation, and we are placed in it by *mood*, characterizing the whole but concealing the particulars. That we acquire, in the course of differentiated experience, a situation which we have not chosen and cannot justify, yet which is nonetheless *ours*, and for which we bear responsibility—this is one of the fundamental characteristics of human finitude.

The original world of anchoring loses its bliss in this differentiation. Another loss is linked with the development of the fact, or rather the primal trait, that we are not only discovered in our neediness, but come to possess the being which mediates and provides for us in occupying it wholly with and for ourselves. With the differentiation of the primal cave, we awaken from this dim slumber into equally vague antagonisms, jealousies, and hatreds. The golden age is the age of these eventful, albeit originally speechless dramas. They are intense but non-thematic, non-objective, and tend thus to escape attention, though they are what determines the meaning of the whole movement—for the same reason, they are liable to be easily repressed, overlooked, forgotten.

What do we gain in mastering our receptive and active, perceptual and motoric, permeable and permeating body? Nothing other than the possibility for existent things to show themselves to us in what they are; our every movement in connection with the perceiving body gives the perceived the possibility of unfolding, of showing itself from a new side; we read out of the present and the immediate that which is absent, mediated, turned away from us; no doubt, things view us as the center of a perspective around which they are disposed in circles of proximity and distance, defined with regard to our reach, but, on the other hand, we are ourselves included in what we see, we "see ourselves" as seen, glimpsed, experienced especially in the eyes of others. Just as our own lived movement is experienced immediately *without perspective*, the other in his movement is also nonperspectively given—the expression and gestures which translate his *acceptance* of me, those gestures of which I am originally the object, give the other immediately in his living essence, in his character of inwardness that either accepts or rejects me, repels or encourages bonding. Just as I myself am not only seeing but also, inseparably, seen, the others, too, are not only seen but seen as seeing. My being is originally a being which lets itself be accepted, whose passivity calls for the other's activity, whose radiating demands the other's inwardness—the understanding of inwardness, of activity, of life appears initially in the form of a *you*. If it is at all possible to understand this primacy of the *you* over the *I*, so often empirically observed and stressed, then it is only out of an understanding of the movement of anchoring, of its starting point in acceptance and being-accepted: in a gesture, a smile, a mimic, an act, there is an "I can," a control over what I feel in passive helplessness, which signifies a nucleus, a center, a living being . . .

We thus learn to read, from perspectives, the connections of things and, from movements, the holding sway and expression of a living being. Hence, our own lived movements are not purely objective, facts among other facts; rather, they are "ontogenic" movements, movements that make manifest, phenomenalize, uncover. Our movements are an expression of our freedom—not in the sense of indeterminacy but in the sense of being able to uncover existents in what they are, to "let them be," to decipher ever further and deeper characteristics in those faces which they show to us. Our perceptual-motoric life is so rich, profound, inexhaustible, and interesting precisely because it is in actual fact much more than the subjectivity of innumerable impressions—it is this living with existing things, accomplishing for them what they are themselves indifferent to, i.e., their unconcealedness in the fact that, and what, they are. This faculty of phenomenalization, this understanding of the world and beings in it, would not be possible if it were not, in germ, already somehow contained in the primal cell, in the acceptance of our own being by that which can hold sway over it, protect it, bring it to completion and fulfill it.

In the movement of anchoring thus takes shape the primal structure which belongs to the human world as an overall framework: the you—the I—the shared environment, the you and the I being both equally bodily, not merely as objects but in a phenomenalizing sense, as manifesting embodiment. Here lies the source of the structure home/alien, which can be regarded as one of the essential dimensions of the natural world.

We have already seen that a universal nonindividuated power rules over life from the first moment of the "acceptance" which is the starting point of the entire movement of anchoring. Following the example of certain contemporary thinkers, we might call this nonindividuated power, this possibilizing universal, *the earth* and contend that the earth dominates the movement of anchoring and, hence, also all the partial, singular movements in which it explicates itself, in which life mediates and provides what it needs from outside itself in order to exist. Of course, once the individual acquires sway over his body, once he becomes master of his own movement, the universal power itself must appear phenomenally as the immobile referent of all his movement—as that with respect to which all movement is ultimately movement: indeed, *we* are not the center to which we relate things (though things appear to us in relation to ourselves and though we are, in all and everything, bound to our own life); rather, we ourselves relate to things in the world, and first and foremost to the "universal thing" (Hegel), the Earth.

The movement of anchoring does not end with the individual's gaining independence and acquiring all the power he can have over himself and the world, insofar as he needs the world in order to exist. Acceptance is originally an act indispensable for life, it is that without which life cannot exist, either in terms of meaning or purely physically, the basis of the very preservation of life. Yet the need for an anchorage does not disappear in ceasing to be linked to the survival of a dependent being. Though the independent being is no longer needy as concerns its survival, though it no longer requires a mediator between its needs and the world, it does not cease to feel need precisely in the independence which heightens its separation, its individuation. Precisely in this detachment, in this revolving around and within the self, which could mean prima facie that the individual in his independence is a closed world unto himself, that for himself he is everything, we feel an emptiness, a want—a need to be accepted and supported in the whole of our being, and not merely in our functions, in whatever our life happens to be materially lacking at this or that moment. This need has an immediate, instinctive character, it is nothing "thought up" but rather an elementary need which, seen from the outside, can be put on a level with individual needs, necessary in order to maintain individuation. In actual fact, it is a matter of overstepping individuality, called for by individuation as such. Individuated being does not cease to feel its incompleteness, it does not cease to understand its finitude, its being as a lack. This is all the more perceptible the more man is a being of the world—the being which has the possibility of letting everything else be and, precisely in this "letting be," distinguishes itself, singles itself out, delimits itself from what it lets be—this is *our* mode of individuation: being in the world, relating to it by uncovering individual things. In performing our ordinary functions, we do not feel that we exist, and this lack of the feeling of existing is in turn perceived as a void. The lack disappears when we are accepted by an other being for whom the mere being of the other is a fulfillment. I myself begin to exist in the eyes of the other, and the reciprocity culminates in an ecstatic bliss in which I feel myself only as accepted by the other and the other as accepted by me; there is a crossing over from life to life—the other, the outside world, has embodied itself in a being capable of accepting me in its name. Precisely this mutual support, this overcoming of our exposure to the freezing cold of the alien throws the span by means of which the world—the other, that which I am not—answers the call of my deepest, of my total neediness. Our finitude radiates as neediness, and is accepted precisely in its state of need. We do not love aspects or features of the other, but the whole of him in his being—and a profound, authentic relationship can be threatened by no disappointment or betrayal. An authentic relationship is no less constant, "eternal," than a mother's relationship to the child rejected by all.—Spanning the gap is thus an end in itself, it has no ulterior purpose; yet, at the same time, it must be in order for a new being to be accepted. Human life necessarily drops anchor in the shelter of this span—it is under this factual and sense-giving condition alone that man can live, growing into individuation out of the bliss of its spanning, the warmth of which screens him from the icy breath of the universe. The movement of anchoring thus shows itself to be an authentic coming forth from dark night into the light of day where life has its while in which things—no less than we ourselves—can appear as what they are.

Reflection on the sphere of anchoring shows that its element is the fortuitous and, consequently, its natural ideal *happiness*.[35] Happiness is at once fulfillment and contingency. Happiness is not in our power; it is a matter of the situation, which we do not control. Reflection on the contingency of happiness generates the ambition to while away life's fleeting moments in full enjoyment of all they can give. Thus is born the aesthetic ideal, which grows already in the soil of disappointment, delusion, and self-enclosure.

All in all, it can be said that, in the movement of anchoring, being binds us to the existent in its singularity. The bond used here is the bond of pleasure. The bliss which gives a feeling of unity and fusion in which all things singular disappear is, paradoxically, what ties life most deeply to itself in its individualized finitude, compensating its incompletion, showing that life has in it an overwhelming, irresistible moment of wholeness, a wholeness in unwholeness, everything in one instant, making up for all want, all separation and one-sidedness. Thus is life bound at once to itself and to the contingency of that being which quenches our inner thirst for the fulfillment of pleasure and warmth. Thus, before itself appearing, being *binds* us to our own and to an alien being in its singularity and contingency.

2. The Movement of Self-Extension

From this follows the necessity of the second fundamental overall movement, which forces the whole primary sphere into the dark, while the possibilities opened and handed down in it are put to use in the service of individuation and its domain of bright day. The whole sphere of the dramas of primitive bonding with its attachments and hatreds, its fusionality and harshness is now relegated into the darkness to which it pays allegiance; the entire realm of dream, imagination and its play is repressed, pushed into the underworld, the sub-earthly. It is no longer the overall relationship to what is *already* but rather a relation to this or that present matter which requires our whole commitment. It is a matter of nothing less than transforming the present given in the sense called for by the service of life. The service and bondage of life to itself is the tacit assumption of the second movement, the movement of reproduction, or self-extension. This movement *renounces* satisfaction, ecstasy, fascination with that which has been attained and is the indispensable starting point as well as the goal of the movement of anchoring. The movement of self-extension is concerned only with things, sees only things, be it purely in their utensility and not in their independence. In this movement, we understand ourselves as providers, endowed with skill and know-how, dealing with tasks, entrusted with a function and a "role"; these possibilities, directly realized as such, then throw light on the provided, on the *pragmata*. In this movement, there is no *object* properly speaking, nothing existing in counterposition to us as independent, closed in itself; there are always only networks of instrumental references, every "here" serving merely to refer beyond itself, to the connections—both personal and object-connections—of the undertaking. At the same time, this referring is a movement from presence to presence, always similarly unfulfilled, purely instrumental. Mediating unfulfillment, with its resting point in the means of life, is characteristic here. Since the tissue of references in which life moves makes it possible for us to continuously understand our own activity as well as the things we come across in it, it can seem that all possibilities of encountering realities and giving them meaning are exhausted in this circle of praxis—that this is the authentic and original human world. It is certainly true that the things which surround us as a nonpersonal environment are originally articulated by the possibilities of providing, know-how, function, and role, that they are part of the pragmatic, utensil world. But it is equally certain that we share this utensil world with au-tonomous personal and quasi-personal beings, with our fellow men and animals, since this entire world of the movement of extension is natu-rally a shared world, a world not only of work but of cooperation, organi-zation, or hierarchy, as the case may be. The other beings have the same independence, the same individuated autonomy as we have, be it merely an average typicality, the individuality of a specimen. While our original understanding of *pragmata*, as means toward our possibilities, proceeds from these possibilities, it is certain that we originally understand other individuals *as we understand ourselves*, i.e., as possibilities being realized and, hence, as movements of existence. We do not understand other human beings out of their utility for *our* possibilities but as independent centers of possibilities. In our sphere, however, these possibilities are all and only possibilities to provide and take care of things, so that while, on the one hand, we are that "for the sake of" which the *pragmata* function, on the other hand, we ourselves exist solely for the *pragmata* to be able to function.

The élan toward things which takes hold of us in this movement and causes us to take flight from, and to be unaware of, ourselves—we have always already overlooked ourselves, put ourselves aside—is essentially a deferred instinct, deprived of satisfaction. The surrounding world does not form with us a blissful unity in which we forget our separation and live our fusion; rather, it becomes, so to say, part of us, our nonorganic body. My original holding-sway over my organic body makes it possible for me to transform my surroundings into a nonorganic body, something no less mastered, separate, visible, and manipulable than my own organism. Or, rather, even *better* mastered, since my surroundings are *before me*, unlike the body over which I hold sway, in original nongivenness and darkness reigning on the stage thus made to unfold. In working, our comportment always already presupposes a holding-sway over the body and movement, not a mechanical control, but a mastery constantly oriented by means of our perceptual impressions. These original possibilities must be already given, and they are, of course, taken over from our anchorage, sphere of the "already." Henceforth, they are put to the service of instrumentality, continuation, self-projection into things, and self-reification.

The movement of reproduction, which we are now tracing, is thus both an extension of the movement of anchoring and a *reversal of its mean-ing*. Not that anchoring is annulled—self-projection is possible only on its basis—but it becomes a *deferred* satisfaction. To accomplish this move-ment now means to bear the burden of the *satisfying*, to be seen, not with the kind and loving eye of acceptance, but rather in a cold appraisal of the way in which we can be *put to use*. We are now "usable," and in this usableness, at others' disposal. As usable, we are, at the same time, put at the disposal of users. We are a community of mutually using users.

This is imposed on us by life's bondage to itself. Life is not mere indifferent duration; rather, it is constant neediness, dependence on vital functions which must be repeatedly satisfied either by oneself or by others. The task of satisfaction, initially one-sided, now becomes reciprocal; we mediate for each other the outside which we put to use, while at the same time using one another. There is an unfree link binding us to one another and to things; a complexly mediated and, for the most part, asymmetrical bondage. The most important is the last link in the chain: that which directly mediates between human needs and the outside, things. This mediation, the systematic and permanent expenditure of life and its energies in intervening in the outside so as to adapt it to human needs and thus make life possible, is *labor, work in the primary sense.* Of course, life can also be systematically expended for organizing the human relations required by work in this primary acceptation; here, too, one can speak of labor, but only in a mediated sense.

In this movement, man is reified from the very beginning in being nakedly inserted into the system of providing for needs. As needy, man is always already reified: things are vitally contained within him, as that which he essentially lacks and has to provide. On the other hand, for this very reason, they appear to him essentially in the form of *pragmata.* The system of providing is permeated by the primitive fact that someone has to provide primarily, and that the product of this primary providing can be taken from him. The other can be exploited, turned into a provider on a one-time temporary basis or enduringly and systematically. Man can be put to death. Or, again, life's bondage to itself can be exploited in order to shackle him to the task of mediating with things.

The second movement runs its entire course in these tacitly present assumptions. It is, for this reason, characterized by the reduction of man *to his social role* and, in connection with this, by the seeking and keeping of distances. All the phenomena analyzed under the heading of "distantiation" stem from this diffuse fear, from this ever-present impulse to exploit the other wherever possible, since we ourselves are under the same pressure. Nothing independently disinterested and dedicated, neither the authentic self nor an authentic undertaking, can develop in this sphere. Nonetheless, no undertaking or conception whatever would be possible without it. The material of all human formation lies here.

The thingness which is at home in this sphere has to do with the fact that those who partake of this movement are most sensitive to the understanding of being which uncovers the objectivity of things in their manipulability, in the forces that can thus be made available, in their potential for transforming both objective and human reality. What arises here is a quest into the inside of things which is also, correlatively, a discovery of the possibilities of man, of human activity and human capacities. Every practical discovery, every modification of things modifies at the same time man and his relations to others and to himself. His community with things, his quest into the inside of things shows itself to be simultaneously a way toward his own modification and self-formation. As if man were the work of the primary pressure brought to bear on him by life's bondage to itself and by the possibility of his using and being put to use by his fellows. As if the collective effort of mankind were shaping an ever more complicated social-natural body, a kind of supraorganic organism in which the currently actual phase of this movement then takes place.

This specific mode of uncovering, along with the mode of open comportment rooted in it, goes together not only with a focus on the existent in its efficacy but also with a particular sort of delusion: interestedness produces a way of seeing whereby we stimulate ourselves and our partners in our social role and disarm our real and virtual opponents by means of ideological fallacies whose inexhaustible variability resists all attempts at exposure and unmasking.

It follows simply from the foregoing that the organized form of the movement of self-projection falls into the categories of *work* and *struggle*. Work and struggle are two fundamentally different principles: in work man confronts things, in struggle he confronts his fellows as virtually enthralled or enthralling. In practice, the two principles combine: the organization of humanity for work is the result of a struggle, and is itself a struggle.

The fundamental situation in which this movement takes place, which it presupposes and in which it continuously remains, is guilt, oppression, and suffering. Guilt, here, does not necessarily signify culpability in the moral sense but rather its precondition—life in a world already full to the brim, where every act of self-assertion necessarily affects others and means virtual damage to them: hence, the necessity of oppression, present not only in its brutal forms but also where it is alleviated. And suffering is inevitable in every unsheltered situation, which goes through work and struggle.

Though the movement of projection and self-extension organizes both the human and the surrounding world to an increasing extent, it still contains an uncontrolled element, a *chaos* inside and out. In its organizing of life into ever more extensive wholes, there is something uncontrollable which is not merely the inadequacy of organization but rather the absence of the essential. The labyrinthine character of this whole movement, often stressed in the past, becomes more and more a dominant life-feeling especially in modern times, when the accumulation of utensils and means for life to extend and multiply its possibilities is palpable, yet the absence of what really matters only escalates.

3. The Movement of Breakthrough

The movement of breakthrough, or actual self-comprehension, is the most important, the most humanly significant of the three; it is also the one which counterbalances the first two and maintains them in upswing as a mere possibility, which is not the full reality of human existence.

What is at stake in this movement is not the encounter with an other but with one's own being, otherwise than in the movement of anchoring, where I find myself in the factual possibilities and impossibilities of active comportment, or in the movement of self-projection, where I am my role and my task, whether I make good in it or fail. In the last movement, the true movement of existence, the point is to see myself in my ownmost human essence and possibility—in my "earthliness" which is, at the same time, a relationship to being and to the universe. The point is not to encounter *in life* something that I can uncover in my comportment, through its openness for what is, but rather not to let the mass of these particular possibilities conceal the essential—the possibility to come to terms with the fact that I am precisely also as a whole this possibility either to disperse and lose myself in particulars or to find and realize myself in my properly human nature. In the first two movements, I am bound to a particular activity by the very nature of life, by its universality, its relation to being— bound to the performance of life-functions, to relating to the existent, i.e., to particulars. In the third movement, it becomes apparent that I can open myself for being in yet another way, that I can modify this bondage to the particular and transform my own relationship to the universe. This transformation goes hand in hand with a transformation of what binds me to my own life; it is not mere insight, pure reflection or contemplation, though these are all assuredly present as stages on the way; here, too, living in a possibility means grasping and realizing this possibility, it is a mode of praxis.

Already the primitive ritual representational comportment is thus no mere expression, depicting a life-feeling in the relationship of life as a whole to the cosmos as a whole. Rather, it is a change of life, partaking of the marriage of heaven and earth, celebrating their explicit presence and encounter. It is not a relation to any one thing, but rather something that is here to attract the eye of all those powers without whose mutual presence the world would be unthinkable. And this presence of the world is what makes it possible too for us to see ourselves in the world, to see our connection and our dependence, the "part" we play in the world. Human life thus experienced in festive rapture retains a glint of the suprahuman, the divine. In this light, it is then easier to take up our lot, which is an indispensable part of the world, though the most arduous and most finite of all—the lot of a mortal being.

Myth, the ritual representational comportment that accedes to language and takes on narrative form, belongs also to this context. It is nothing other than the same assembly, the same encounter of the world called forth by ritual behavior, but as given through the transparent medium of language.—Long before there arises any question, with the explicit reflection which goes with it, the answers are provided by myth; myth is an expression of the primordial relations we know from the movement of anchoring, the mysteries of individuation and primal unity, the dramas of division and duality, hatred and resentment in the protective shade of life's primal warmth, the tragic blindness through which this warmth conceals cruel reality. Or, again, the fundamental tale of banishment from paradise, from blissful anchorage, with its whole atmosphere not only of misfortune and misery but also of guilt, neediness, mercy, and "redemption" from the slavery into which man sinks by the mere fact of existence.

Myth penetrates the secrets of human life with admirably deep clairvoyance. So sharp is its sight that it calls for assuagement, and it is assuaged by the narrative form, the mock history transposing it into the past. Transposing into the past provides the unreality fitting for presentation as something depicted, but it is purely formal. Once we understand the intention of myth, we realize that it does not only see clear in man's present reality, but also contains a standpoint, an attitude, an openness for the future in which we disclose our ownmost possibility.

Let us take a look, from this angle, at the myth of creation in Genesis, analyzed in part, with great acumen, by Bröcker.[36] This myth depicts man's existence in the Garden of Eden where, in security and unaware of mortality, he works as a ward of God, knowing no shame, obeying the voice of instinct, above all of sexuality, ignorant of the distinction of good and evil, since he has as yet no relationship to time and to the future—is this not a perfect picture of the movement of anchoring, as we have attempted to elucidate it above? As for the knowledge of good and evil, linked with the realization of nakedness, the need of covering, the expulsion from the divine garden and its safety, the loss of ignorance of mortality—is this not the passage into the second movement and its unshelteredness, but also, at the same time, the relegation of the instinctual sphere into the domain of censorship, indispensable in a world of organized activity, work, effort, and pain?

Yet this is still not all. In its account of the eating of the forbidden fruit of the tree of knowledge, the myth has grasped human life not as a fact but rather as an *event* which disrupts the calm of indifferent nature, the peace of man's indifference to his own being, and deviates from the hitherto existing world order. In connection with this, the human condition is understood as responsible for this event, a responsibility manifest inasmuch as existence in the shackles of the second movement, the movement of coming to terms with things, is viewed as a *punishment.* As punishment, it is not something that simply is but rather that is *borne,* and in this bearing lies the disclosure of our own being, glimpsed face to face in its mortality, disdaining flight and claiming responsibility, i.e., owning up to its lot.

This responsibility for one's own lot is the theme of myth's groping exploration of life's bondages, at the basis of a speculative and experimenting investigation of existence which fills centuries. Speculatively interpreted, responsibility for one's own lot inspires the idea of the wheel of reincarnations—guilt is here projected into the past and anticipatively determines the future as an implacable law of destiny.

This "groping exploration" can be understood as the practical effort to inwardly act against those life-structures which force existence into a situation incompatible with its character as a free possibility. In Buddhism, an example of such inward praxis, or inner action, is the intuition of the fundamental function of the correlation between want and pleasure, this primitive principle binding life to itself, which we have attempted to elaborate in dealing with the movement of anchoring. Buddhism attacks this fundamental bondage, which contemplation shows to be the prime origin of all the joints of reality as an endless cycle of *appearance,* the protofoundation of the phenomenon, viewed thus in the light of the movement of anchoring. The result is then necessarily the canceling of the phenomenon, with the disappearance of the first condition of all consciousness of a singularized, individualized existent in its separation, and there remains only to return to pristine undifferentiated being, lacking all distinction—a peaceful, nonviolent retreat into the primordial night. Life's bondage to the other and to itself is indeed severed, but at the cost of individuation, at the cost of the simultaneous disappearance of the world, of being in its manifest form.

In his interpretation of the myth of the tree of knowledge, Bröcker remarks that the Pauline, New Testament conception of sin as having come into the world through one single person, and being removed likewise, by one alone, has no basis in the myth itself. No less alien to it is the Enlightenment notion of man as called to found, on his own, his own sphere of freedom based on his coming of age, though he at the same time bears responsibility for his minority.[37] In Paul's strangely legalistic version as well as in the form of Enlightenment titanism, the problematic of the atonement of guilt is alien to the myth of Genesis—on this point Bröcker is right. There is nonetheless, in the conception of our life in the second movement as a *punishment*, in the idea that we are responsible for our life in finitude, a pang of discontent and an urge to investigate the shackles that fasten man here.

The bondage uncovered by this investigation is life's bondage to the antecedent self, regarded as a given reality, to the self whose content is determined by its interests, basically by instinct, traditions, and consideration of others, by leveling distantiality. It stands to reason that life entangled in finitude only becomes more obdurate in gaining awareness of death. Finitude is, for such a life, merely a confirmation of its banal carpe-diem truth. But the investigating life would not seek if it had not already found. Its truth consists in showing life in bondage to be a mere possibility, and by no means a reality which is there like a stone in the road or a piece of lava on the moon.[38] As a possibility which, as such, is responsible, it is as it is not by any "natural" necessity, emanating from the sphere of the existent indifferent to its being, but by virtue of its own freedom, though motivated by fundamental human possibilities.

In this new attitude, confronting finitude does not mean self-attachment, binding and relating everything we encounter to our accepted, obdurate self. This confrontation has now the meaning of devotion. My being is no longer defined as a being for me but rather as a being in self-surrender, a being which opens itself to being, which lives in order for things—as well as myself and others—to be, to show themselves as what they are. This means: life in self-surrender, life outside oneself, not a mere solidarity of interests but a total reversal of interest—I no longer live in that which separates and encloses, but rather in that which unites and opens, being openness itself. To be in devotion is to devote oneself to being, it is a perfectly unbiased, "objective" existence.

This turn is not accompanied by a *loss of the world* but, on the contrary, by its full discovery; it is, in a certain sense, a mundane turn, since the world here lives more deeply, a cosmocentric and luminocentric life. And it brings with it a new myth, one of the most profound and most widespread, a myth endowed, like all myths, with an inexhaustible meaning: the myth of the divine man, the perfectly true man, his necessary end, and his inevitable "resurrection."

Truth—the word—has become flesh: the event of being, which has chosen man as the locus of its appearing, has found its fullness in a fully "true" man, living entirely in devotion, beyond the concern for his interests, not however like the animals of the field and the birds of the sky, on the ground of instinct which binds only one existent to another, but rather in the light of being. If the event of being is conceived as that with which divinity is inseparably associated, then it can be said that such a fully true man is rightly called the God-man. The apparition of such a man will, of course, necessarily be understood as an attack upon the world's powers-that-be, upon the self-understanding which avoids itself and closes itself off, founding its entire ascendancy over the world and the sense of its every act on this closure within the given present, into the organization, the power of what is. It is therefore logical for it to interpret the God-man as a rival for the rule of the world—though, of course, this is also an error, for he is no pretender, nor is it a matter of replacing one person with another in the machine of human society; the question is *what* is to rule in general—the existent in its superior force, or, rather, the truth of being. And there is more connected with this: all and sundry are now placed in this crisis, confronted with this distinction, for all and sundry there suddenly opens a future from which a new self is forthcoming, the self given in dedication, the kingdom of God already come, already among us—but in such a way that each must *accomplish* his conversion to it: it is not here after the manner of the phone booth around the corner, present whether I want it or not, and indifferent to my presence. The God-man will, therefore, inevitably be made to perish: such is the only radical way for "the world," which has eyes only for what is, to be quit of him. But he will just as inevitably rise from the dead: truth against which the deadly weapon was wielded, truth from which we were to be deterred by the most appalling imaginable torture and death, cannot be struck down by that weapon, truth is no *thing*, nothing within the reach of an innerworldly force of destruction.

Life given in dedication is, in a certain sense, everlasting. Not that human mortal finitude is eliminated and replaced by the fruits of the tree of life. But the life that gives itself up lives outside itself, and the authenticity of this "outside itself" is attested precisely by what it gives itself up to. It thus begets a community of those who understand each other in surrender and devotion, and, through the negation of separate centers, cement a fellowship of dedication, a fellowship in devoted service, which transcends every individual. The goal Husserl meant to attain with his phenomenological reduction as a fact achievable in philosophical reflection is in reality a result of the communication of existences: their transcending into a chain of beings united not merely by an external link, of beings which are not mere islands of life in a sea of objectivity, but for whom things and objects emerge from the ocean of being in the service of which they commune.

The third movement of existence, which is to the first two in a relation of integration and repression, i.e., a dialectical relation, discovers here a fundamental dimension of the natural world, a dimension which is not *given*, which escapes both perception and recollection, eludes objective identification, and yet essentially determines this world. This is a sphere overlooked by both Husserl and the positivists in their descriptions and analyses of the "natural" life-world. We have attempted here to indicate its basic importance and, at the same time, to show that there is nothing "mystical" about it, unless one wants to call the world itself mystical, as well as being, and even man, this being-of-the-world, relating essentially to both.

Afterword to the First French Translation (1976)

Why publish today the translation of a book that appeared in Prague in 1936?

First of all, the book was chronologically the first to attempt a comprehensive review of the problem put by Husserl under the heading of *natürliche Welt* (later, *Lebenswelt*, the life-world or world of our life). The author of this summary of Husserlian ideas lays no claim to originality, but neither would he want Husserl to be held responsible for all the statements put forward in his book; it is an attempt at a synthesis of the analytical studies scattered throughout Husserl's works and, as such, is not without personal risk. The form chosen is not that of an elaborative "commentary" or an essay *on* Husserl but rather a systematic presentation. At a time when this manner of setting the problem (referring to the analyses of other thinkers as well, but with a view to synthesis)[1] appears to be undergoing a renewal, and the problem of a life-world to be once again becoming topical (there are a number of authors who should be cited here, from Landgrebe, Schütz, and Gurwitsch to their many disciples and others still), it can be useful to recall that, already in the 1930s, the "disquieting problem" of the "natural world," though perhaps not progressing, was not wholly neglected.

Secondly, present-day philosophy is largely focused on a reflection on formalization and formalism. Husserlian phenomenology, in the last great unfinished work of the founder of this discipline—*Die Krisis der europäischen Wissenschaften und die transzendentale Phänomenologie*, which grew out of the Prague lectures of 1935 and was first partially published in Belgrade, in 1936,[2] before being edited by Walter Biemel in 1954 as volume VI of the *Husserliana* series[3]—is one of the modalities of this reflection. (It is in this work and in this context that Husserl speaks of the *Lebenswelt*.) Admittedly, what Husserl and his disciples have in view is not the technique but rather the philosophy of formalization; his undertaking is nonetheless useful and legitimate in its way.

Thirdly, this slim volume can be regarded as a kind of introduction to philosophy for students. In composing these pages, the author was indeed striving to find access to philosophy for himself. He looked for help to several thinkers of his time who are perhaps still unknown in the French-speaking world, at least from the viewpoint he was then concerned with. The sincerity of his endeavor may possibly prove inspiring to other philosophical apprentices.

A second enlarged edition was published in Czech in 1971,[4] with a supplement of a few dozen pages intended to clarify and update our view of the problem. Written in haste, under the pressure of circumstances, the added text falls short of this aim. We have therefore chosen not to include it in the French edition: it is too long for an outline but too brief to even begin to fully deal with the matter. For those interested in the views which more or less clearly inspired this supplement, we venture to propose rather the following remarks.

Our first doubt concerning Husserl's approach to the problem has to do with the noesis/noema duality, which we have come to see as fundamentally insufficient, its two elements now as indistinct, now as duplicates. But this is a dualism inseparably linked to the whole conception of the constitution of objectivity in transcendental subjective life. Giving it up thus entails a fundamental reform of phenomenology. Our skepticism does not go so far as to postulate a purely noematic phenomenology but concerns rather the allegedly apodictic evidence of that which is given in reflection. This then leads us directly to question the possibility and the scope of reflection as conceived by Husserl, as an immediate act of perception turned "inward."

Another point directly touching the problem of the natural world is the concept of horizon (the world being defined as the "ultimate horizon," "horizon of all horizons"). What is the place of this concept in the theory of consciousness as intentionality, the place of a concept that admits none of the classic characteristics of intentionality (consciousness of an object) yet is not an object concept? A nonintentional subjectivity, which extends beyond the framework of the polarity of empty intention and fulfillment, does not turn toward an object-pole, though making possible its understanding, and remains itself in the dark—is this still intentionality in the classical sense of the term, as in the *Ideas I*? Is it still possible to tackle the problem of the natural world with the conceptual means of Husserlian transcendentalism?

But is phenomenology—the study of appearing, the study of the phenomenon as such—possible only in the guise of this subjective objectivity, as the "reflection" grasping absolute being in which Husserl's *Ideas,* and so many of his other works, wanted to found it once and for all? Does it not have in itself the means of overcoming this stage, which is only *one* of the possible phenomenological philosophies, the one supposed to lead to the absolute spirit? Husserl's insights and analyses seem to reach beyond it in all directions. Not only the idea of things accessible in the original, not only the broadening of traditional views of the idea of truth, but even the central theme, which Husserl himself held to be the true starting point of phenomenological considerations, the concept of *epochē*, seems conducive to the surpassing of transcendental phenomenological idealism. Should not the *epochē*—this act of suspending "belief in the world" without which, according to Husserl, there can be no true phenomenology, no study of the phenomenon as such—be interpreted as the "step back from being as a whole" which Heidegger speaks of in his lecture *Was ist das—die Philosophie?*[5] Of course, Husserl explicitly limited the application of the *epochē* to objectivity alone. He deemed this necessary, on the one hand, to preserve an object for phenomenology, but also because, guided by Cartesian tradition, he considered the subjective, taken in its purity, as the absolute givenness of an absolute being, so that its remaining outside the *epochē*—which he claimed to be apodictically necessary—would be a confirmation of its progress toward the infinity of spirit. Admitting that the *epochē* manifests the freedom and power of thought with respect to everything contained in the world, the question remains whether it is indeed right to put a halt to this "step back" at the limit of the "subjective." Does not this freedom go beyond? Does it not encompass the totality of all that is? In certain considerations concerning the *epochē* contained in his lectures on phenomenological psychology[6] Husserl speaks of a split, a kind of schizophrenia affecting the consciousness which performs the act of *epochē*: I am free with regard to the act of belief that I let the mundane subject carry out, while I concentrate on the consideration of his act of belief, on a reflection that is no longer to be surpassed in the same way. But does this new version of the Cartesian *cogito* truly support the edifice Husserl proposes to erect on its foundation? Where does this negative force of freedom originate? What is the source of this *de*-tachment, of which the *epochē*, the very most speculative idea of the master of phenomenology, is itself the most striking expression? If the act of belief in the world can be surpassed in a reflective *cogito*, cannot this *cogito*, which is part of my fundamentally finite life, be likewise surpassed, for example, in an act of *Vorlaufen* (advance to the limit) as discussed in Heidegger?[7] From a purely formal viewpoint, Husserl's quasi-Cartesian consideration is correct. The reflective act cannot free itself from the thesis of the reflected act. Since the reflective act is however the act of a finite life, inwardly determined, as phase of an "opening," by such an advance to the limit, it is not only the affirmation of the reflected act but also, at the same time, its negation. It follows that an infinite consciousness can be affirmed on the basis of the finite *cogito* only so long as we fail to recognize its ontological character. Husserl gave in to this temptation, but the act of *epochē* attests to an "un-thought" in his thinking that goes beyond traditional ontology. Despite the opinion of so eminently qualified an interpreter as Eugen Fink,[8] we see not only a rupture but also a continuity between Husserl's phenomenology and a phenomenology of fundamental finitude, and we believe that continuity has the last word.

If this is indeed the case, the problem of the natural world is freed from fixation on the subject-object dualism and cumbersome schemes such as that of noema/noesis, and it calls upon us to apply the concept of world, "the wherein as that 'for which,'"[9] classically analyzed in *Sein und Zeit*. We can then pass over the question of intersubjectivity and the overcoming of solipsism, since our being-in-the-world is at the same time a being-with, but we shall have to look for a guideline other than Husserl's object for our analyses of the natural world. At the same time, the ontological problematic emerges with incomparably greater depth than in the somewhat hazy initiatives exemplified by the "Fundamental Considerations" of Husserl's *Ideas I*, distinguishing an absolutely given being and the being given through its agency (a sort of ontology defining two categories of being profoundly different in their mode of *givenness* if not in their mode of being, but which could be seen as announcing two ways of relating to being, since Husserl's absolute being is that which makes both itself and the other of itself appear). We have to acknowledge that what lies at the ground of the natural world is not "internal time-consciousness," but rather care and temporality.

On the other hand, Heidegger's analyses as presented in *Sein und Zeit* go far beyond the problem of the natural world (since their primary aim is to prepare the renewal of the problem of being), and, for that very reason, seem inadequate to reveal its major structures. Husserl's idea that there is a zone of home, correlative and opposed to the alien (farther and farther removed in the style of its structure), that there is a private sphere as opposed to what is more or less public, cannot be explained by Heidegger's analyses. The phenomena discerned by Husserl remain; phenomena are phenomena. In *Sein und Zeit*, we see where the "things" we take care of at home and at work are situated, but we do not see the source of the opposition between "at home" and "at the workplace." We can rightly ask whether the family hearth and the workshop or office are ontologically "on the same page," whether the fact that the former is primarily a place of solicitude (toward human beings), the latter rather a place of handling things (*pragmata*) does not have a deep enough foundation to be taken into account.

It seems, consequently, that the masterly analysis set forth in *Sein und Zeit*—analysis of the recovery of the authentic self against the backdrop of anxiety, in echo to the voice of conscience which is none other than the voice of care calling itself back into its ground permeated with negativity—sees only part of the problem. What is here termed recovery is the genesis of a self born in the solitude of anxiety, where the "world" has ceased to perform its signifying function. This solitude is, of course, yet another modality of the "being-with" characteristic of human being. The authentic self once recovered, does it not, however, in addition to facing the world as a historical being solving the problems of its situation, necessarily acquire a "being-with-others" which is no longer that of anonymous leveling?

Where does anonymous leveling originate, if not in the fact that human being, in its being toward things, is at the same time a being toward anonymous and interchangeable others? Is the anonymity of this alienated self—subordinate to others and subordinating itself through the competitive tendency which takes hold of it and ultimately makes possible flight into the world, blinding it to its fundamental situation as a finite being permeated with negativity—possible otherwise than by virtue of the fact that human being is a being toward others? And this anonymity, with its focus on things, is what makes possible the bad faith of a misunderstanding of human being and the fallacious preontology of objectivity. Does not the movement of the everyday, this possibility of irresponsible and leveling anonymity, also mean the preponderance of a particular dimension of temporality, namely, the dimension of presence to things in which the vulgar notion of time has its source? Does it not conceal not only the fact that the authentic self needs to be won back, but that the same is true of the nonanonymous and irreplaceable "with-others"? The fact that, beyond the everyday manipulations which are subject to the power of leveling anonymity, there is this possibility of a renewal, rooted in the co-presence of human beings situated among the things of the universe in such a way that they are not only implicated in one another but *capable* of understanding the uniqueness of this implication?

Moreover, there is the question of the modes of "open" human comportment, such as acts of devotion or the activities of the artist and thinker, which are neither pragmatic manipulations nor solicitude for persons. Where do they belong in Heidegger's analyses from the period of *Sein und Zeit*? These too are activities that shape our surroundings, moving without doubt in the framework of temporal care, where presence to things constitutes a necessary dimension. This notwithstanding, they do this shaping with a view neither to a *hou heneka* immediately comprehensible in the sphere of the everyday, nor to a resolute historical action capable of shaping the face of human masses for more or less long periods of time. These are, however, the only two movements explicitly considered in *Sein und Zeit*: the movement of flight and obfuscation, which seeks refuge and forgetfulness in the world, in an anonymous being-with, and the movement of free and resolute advance which takes the detour over the limits, but solely in order to return to the world as a factor of historical action; both movements lead to mundane being and engagement in it.

Do not the phenomena of the sort just mentioned suggest the hypothesis that temporality, in addition to the movement of engagement in the world (with its two modalities, in which the inner acts of flight and courageous exposure take place, so to say, in silence, with a view to passing over into outward action), allows also for a sort of opposite movement: a movement which, while remaining in the world, is oriented toward the limits that determine the human situation within it? And, if authenticity and its opposite, anonymity, are founded on the dimension *out of* which temporalization takes place, should we not also ask *toward* which dimension it is oriented, where it is going, where lies the center of gravity which, in each case, gives it its form?

We know that the world in which we live (and which we *are*) is determined by the *hou heneka* on which depends the discovery of the "things" we encounter within it. If the everyday is to be overcome, there must come about a change or a restructuring of this *hou heneka*. Such changes are possible only at the limit of the world, at the limits of the life of human being, which the everyday flees and eludes. Heidegger has shown, in the phenomenon of the voice of conscience (in which care recalls itself into its inhospitable ground), such a movement toward the limit serving as springboard for an immediate leap into an active situation. There are, however, movements which, though oriented toward the limits of the beginning, which human being can never control, and of the certain and inevitable end, do not directly lead to action, but rather take, so to say, a step back from all that exists in order to draw from it a noneveryday human possibility, i.e., a change of world, and not of the world's contents. These movements are characterized by a certain resting point where it is possible to dwell; the call of conscience does not have this character, rather it is primarily an impulse toward immediate action. One does not dwell in conscience as one does in philosophical astonishment, in the artist's admiration, in hatred, or in love. These resting points are not without speech (in the broad sense of expression) as opposed to the silence of the call. All this seems to show, not unconvincingly, that the movement of life is capable of differentiating itself according to accents marked by the moments of resting or, on the contrary, of momentum, which are part of it.

We cannot go here into a positive description of the three kinds of movement discernible from this point of view. May we be allowed to offer a quick and extremely simplified outline. The first movement, with a resting point at the limit of *the beginnings*, has a personal character. It is founded on the fact that human being is a "being-with" whose possibilities are not exhausted by anonymous and interchangeable coexistence, nor can it be reduced to the comportments of solicitude for . . . ; rather, its main aspect is disposition, indicating that thrownness into the universe is first and foremost a throwing into the presence, or rather the co-presence of other human beings, and of *certain* other human beings. This is a factual, but by no means interchangeable co-presence; though anonymity tends in fact to encroach upon it, there always remains an essential, perceptible, and analyzable difference. As a mode of solicitude for . . . , it is not a concern about common *activity*, but rather about *being* in common, being-together, a concern which calls for other modalities in addition to those of substitution (leaping-in) and exemplarity (leaping-ahead),[10] though substitution, e.g., for children or for the ill, can play an essential part in it. These are the movements which engage us most deeply in the world (of persons). We believe them nonetheless to be oriented toward the origin, since the breakthrough of the everyday is effected here through the medium of *disposition*, of *being-in*, and the true breakthrough reaches all the way to the roots of being thrown together. This means that man (though not doing away with the helplessness of human being) can become a source of warmth for another thrown existence and transform the dread and anxiety of the uninhabitable into a possibility of acceptance. Without acceptance, there is no human existence; man is not only thrown into reality, he is also accepted, he is thrown as accepted; acceptance is part of thrownness. This is why the bliss of being accepted, though it is not a simple veil, a screen marring the true perspective of the origin, is what it is only on the basis of anxiety; it is an anxious and ambivalent bliss.

At the other extremity, it is not difficult to find a similar structure in the advance toward the end. For brevity's sake, we shall consider here the eloquent example of philosophical astonishment. If it is true that philosophy undertakes to explain beings by being, it can do so only if being somehow appears in its difference from beings, albeit unclearly and nonthematically, an appearance solely for the sake of beings and their understanding. Now it is clear that being can appear only in and through a being capable of radically distancing itself from things and from all that exists, including itself. Human being alone, by virtue of its relationship to the nothingness of things, is able to stand at the extreme limit of all that exists. Philosophical astonishment is thus closely related to the advance toward the extreme and unsurpassable possibility which characterizes the birth of the authentic self;[11] it too takes place against a backdrop of anxiety, but it is different in that it is not a matter of only *one* understanding, *one* opening of the eyes—rather it continues in what Plato's *Seventh Letter* calls *hē pollē sunousia kai tribē peri to pragma auto*.[12]

The third movement, the one that has its "center of gravity" in the manifestation of reality, of things, has already been sufficiently characterized for the purposes of the present outline. It is the movement of alienation and its overcoming, movement in which are anchored both anonymous historical developments and their responsible formation. We would hesitate, however, to call this movement properly historical, since the overcoming of alienation shows that the human being is always a being of truth, and that truth is the ground on which history in the strong sense of the word plays itself out. The movement which generates possibilities such as myth, religion, art, and philosophy is surely entitled to be taken into consideration when it comes to understanding history.—Alienation, a phenomenon understood by Hegel as the key to the return of the absolute spirit to itself, interpreted subsequently by Marx in a purely ontic sense, but on the ground of finite human being, has been placed by Heidegger's analytics of such human being on the plane of "fundamental ontology." What is more, this ontological interpretation has made it clear that the phenomenon of alienation falls within the sphere of truth; in going more deeply into the problem of truth, phenomenology allows us to view human labor, too, as an "open comportment," to discover the fundamental mistake of all theories which regard man and human work from the viewpoint of the biosociological conception of *homo faber.*

In short, we now regard the natural world as the world which accompanies human "being-with" by virtue of its ontological structure founded ultimately on the two major possibilities of temporalization in which human being projects itself in the midst of things or concentrates on its own limits: movement of acceptance which, with its modalities of love and hatred, gives us our center of rootedness, movement of alienation and its overcoming, which wins us a place in human and extrahuman nature, and, finally, movement of truth in the specific sense of the word, which situates us with respect to the great whole and that which reveals it.

This attempt at a renewal of the problem makes possible a revision, too, of our earlier conception of language as a founded stratum resting, when all is said and done, on the perceptual layer. The latent sensualism of Husserl's theory of hyletic matter formed by intention will have to give way to a conception in which language is inseparably bound up with the very foundations of human being, with man's capacity for understanding being, since understanding being means understanding the "is," the "there is" which extends over all things—even where there is as yet no *logos prophorikos* [outward speech]—and is the condition of what we call perception (perception being but one of man's "open" comportments).

In proceeding in the way we have just outlined, we do not mean simply to substitute one phenomenological system for another. Rather we see it as a way of expressing our conviction that phenomenology, the study of the movement of manifestation of all being, is one in its various forms.

If our attempt to avoid the one-sidedness of the systems of phenomenological philosophy is indeed legitimate, does it not, however, entail the disappearance of the problem of the natural world? If the structures of the natural world are given by the movement of understanding of being and its major forms, spread between the two poles of engagement in, and distance from, mundane content, is there still something like the natural world properly speaking, a primordial world presupposed by every "specialized" world, such as that of the sciences? Do we not have to do simply with the world as such? The world would then be, on the one hand, the universe disclosed by the movement of understanding, and, on the other hand, this movement itself. And since this disclosing movement comprises—among the specializations of what we have characterized as the movement of truth—philosophy, on which science is largely dependent, science too appears as one of its components and can probably not be reduced to the role which Husserl seems to assign almost exclusively to it, that of a "garb of ideas"[13] thrown over the natural world, alone capable of being experienced, i.e., (for Husserl) intuited in the original. At the term of our inquiry, we would thus find ourselves in contradiction with our initial problem setting.

But is the problem of the natural world truly that of a specific region? If we look upon it in this way, is it not rather another illusion of the crude realism which even those thinkers commonly considered idealists are not totally free of, and which forgets the understanding lying at its source? Is the problem of the natural world that of a world supposedly existing purely in itself, or rather that of the *order* that understanding must follow so as to understand itself and its position, the position of "man in the cosmos"?[14] It was the unity of this understanding that was in question in our first stating of the problem. It cannot be attained if we follow the path marked out by the manner in which most scientists (as well as the general public schooled by them) interpret this position: the path of scientific realism, explaining the world experienced in the original as a subjective copy determined by objective causality. The idealism of the neo-Kantians and their fellows (including certain positivists) endowed the same vision of reality (reality as a construct, intellectual as opposed to sensible being) with a transcendental foundation. Husserl's genius consisted in forcefully stressing that a founded stratum of our world, such as that of mathematical formulae and the eventually corresponding structures, can never be the world in the original, and that the former presupposes the latter.

But Husserl's position is, at the same time, a no less intransigent intellectualism than that of the neo-Kantians; this is apparent in his demand for objective evidence, to be attained by the specific notion of the reflection performed by the subject, in the certitude of its self-apprehension, at each step of the "constitution" of the world in its accomplishments (both passive and active). But the primordial world, the world we experience prior to all theory, cannot be understood in its disclosure as the world of intuition; it is without any doubt a world of the practical, as Husserl himself admits in the *Krisis*, and it is certainly legitimate to regard this character not as founded in intuition but rather as that which founds it. If the first encounter of "things" is possible in principle only in the form of handling *pragmata*, it would seem inevitable that the problem of the phenomenon, the problem of appearing, will be profoundly affected by this fact. It is not the practical that should be understood on the basis of intuited presentations but, on the contrary, the attitude of disinterested contemplation whose genesis we should attempt to understand on the basis of the interested and engaged understanding proper to human being in its finite life. The problem of the natural world thus shows itself to be that of the primordiality of this practical engagement, inseparable from a nonexplicit, nonthematic understanding of being which Husserl would have termed instinctive. The lesson to be drawn from the natural world is perhaps not what Husserl had in mind, i.e., that the world is an unconscious reason searching for itself and which the philosopher should bring especially scientists to understand. There is nonetheless a lesson (and perhaps an even more forceful one) to be drawn—that human life in all its forms is a life of truth, admittedly finite, but engaging our responsibility no less rigorously than the rationalism of apodicticity. Does not *finite* truth, thoroughly distinct from truth *relative* to something other than itself, mean an everyday struggle against the errings, illusions, and obduracies which go along with it and in which man attempts to relinquish himself and become "a piece of lava in the moon"?[15]

Translator's Note

This volume assembles three texts: (1) *Přirozený svět jako filosofický problém* (Prague: Ústřední nakladatelství a knihkupectví učitelstva československého, 1936), 150 pp. (habilitation thesis); (2) "'Přirozený svět' v meditaci svého autora po třiatřiceti letech," in *Přirozený svět jako filosofický problém*, 2nd enl. ed., (Prague: Československý spisovatel, 1970), 155–234; and (3) the postface to *Le Monde naturel comme problème philosophique*, trans. Jaromír Daněk and Henri Declève, Phaenomenologica no. 68 (The Hague: Martinus Nijhoff, 1976), 168–81. The first two have been translated from the latest Czech edition, in volumes 6 and 7 of the "Complete Works" currently edited by the Patočka Archive in Prague (*Sebrané spisy*, vol. 6: *Fenomenologické spisy I*, ed. Ivan Chvatík and Jan Frei [Prague: OIKOYMENH, 2008], 127–261; vol. 7: *Fenomenologické spisy II*, ed. Pavel Kouba and Ondřej Švec [Prague: OIKOYMENH, 2009], 265–334), the third, as in volume 7 of the "Complete Works," directly from the Xerox copy of Patočka's fifteen-page French manuscript conserved at the Patočka Archive (ms. 1976/4) rather than from the well-intentioned, though in places misleading published version revised by Henri Declève. The dates indicated in the table of contents are those of the first editions. The Czech supplement was actually written in 1969, the afterword to the French translation in July–August 1974. The section headings of the first text are our own shortened forms of the subheads featured in the synoptic contents of the book as published in 1936. Those of the second text have been added by the editors of the Czech "Complete Works." The "Complete Works" are also the source of all editors' notes to the three texts.

As in the third volume of the "Select Works" edited in German at the Vienna Institut für die Wissenschaften vom Menschen,[1] from which we have borrowed Ludwig Landgrebe's introductory study, the English translation thus includes *both* of the author's afterwords, or "supplements," published in the 1970s, despite his openly stated criticism of the first of the two and its omission from the 1976 French edition. "'The Natural World' Remeditated" is also disregarded in the introductory study—not on account of these reservations, but merely because the text was not in 1977 available in translation. Of course, Patočka did more than once express his dissatisfaction with his first attempt at updating or "recanting" his position, not only in his subsequent (as yet unpublished) French letters to Henri Declève, but already in 1969, while working on it, in his correspondence with the Czech art historian Václav Richter.[2] Written "in haste" and "too brief[ly]," it is in fact longer than planned in the 1968 contract with the publisher, far less brief (93 typed pages as against 15 handwritten ones) and less hastily prepared than the new self-critique, which he would find the opportunity to compose only thanks to a few weeks in the hospital with pneumonia. "Unsatisfactory," doubtless, in comparison with the opus (a "great work on the problem of movement as key to manifestation")[3] he planned to write after the publication of his second habilitation thesis, dedicated to Aristotle and the problem of movement,[4] it is nonetheless central to this period of his work. The second chapter can be read as a résumé of the lecture course titled "The Problems of the Natural World," held in the summer semester of 1969. Certain passages of its last section are repeated almost word for word in the penultimate lecture of the longer course given at Charles University during the entire 1968–69 academic year and subsequently published, on the basis of a compilation of students' notes, under the title *Body, Community, Language, World*.[5] The third chapter's description of the three movements (165–85) is also part of another publication, "What Is Existence?"[6]—as if Patočka, far from disowning the text, had been intent on insuring at least the most important part of it against the uncertainties of publishing under the Communist "normalization" regime. In short, it is clear that his later disparagement of his first palinode is but an example of the "immense humility" remembered by Landgrebe and all those who came even remotely into contact with him. The French afterword, initially meant to be no shorter than the Czech, but to go over the same matter in greater breadth and depth,[7] can thus by no means replace the "handful of aporistic reflections"[8] first appended to the 1970 second edition of *The Natural World as a Philosophical Problem* and included in all subsequent reeditions. Like the Czech and German versions of the first four chapters of the *Heretical Essays*,[9] the two drafts of the important essay from 1970–71 titled "Husserl's Subjectivism and the Possibility of . . ." or ". . . Call for an Asubjective Phenomenology,"[10] the two versions of the 1973 Varna lecture,[11] or the two long German essays "Europe and Post-Europe"[12] and "The Post-European Era and Its Spiritual Problems," and their shorter Czech counterpart "Spiritual Foundations of Life in Our Time,"[13] the two afterwords are mutually complementary ways of looking at the same problem from different angles.

The interested polyglot reader will find a more detailed philological analysis in my editor's note to the recently published new French translation (Paris: Vrin, 2016), a more substantial philosophical commentary in Klaus Nellen's and Jiří Němec's presentation of the 1990 German translation. Here, I shall close on Patočka's own summary of his book, printed on the jacket flap of the 1970 Czech reedition:

> The natural sciences, in particular physics and chemistry, purport to show us nature as it is in itself. Our knowledge of nature comes, however, from the immediately given world, which is not only not identical but in many respects contradictory with this "in-itself." Concerning the immediately given world, one can say along with Hegel that, though familiar and "well-known," it is not actually known. The problem of the knowledge of the "natural world" is one man has been aware of ever since the beginnings of modern natural science, but the question has only recently been put in explicit terms.
>
> The present work, published thirty-four years ago, was the very first to explicitly deal with this problem, purporting to unfold and solve it from the viewpoint of Husserlian phenomenology. The author thus attempted to re-encompass the description and analysis of the "natural world" within the subject's lived experience. In reflectively apprehended subjective experience, he believed it possible to grasp the origin of both the originally given world and changes to it in language and objectifying science.
>
> With the passing years, the author has come to critically distance himself from the concept of reflection which, in "transcendental phenomenology," was the starting point for the method as well as for the philosophy of the "absolute subject." Taking up the problem anew, he develops the retrospective overview into a genuine concise history of the question through the present day, then goes on from this critical exposé to describe the life of the finite subject in the world, conceived in terms of three fundamental, interrelating movements, each of which unveils a different essential aspect of the natural world.

Thanks are due to Martin Pokorný and Ludger Hagedorn for their precious help with the preparation of this translation, as well as to Dr. Detlev Landgrebe for permission to translate Ludwig Landgrebe's introductory study.

Notes

Foreword

1. Patočka's correspondence with Landgrebe has been partially published, with an introduction by Ludger Hagedorn, in *Lebenswelten: Ludwig Landgrebe—Eugen Fink—Jan Patočka. Wiener Tagungen zur Phänomenologie 2002,* ed. Hellmuth Vetter (Frankfurt: Lang, 2003), 177–94.—*Trans.*

2. Translated here from the third volume of the German edition of Patočka's "Select Works," to which it serves as introduction (*Ausgewählte Schriften,* vol. 3: *Die natürliche Welt als philosophisches Problem,* ed. Klaus Nellen and Jiří Němec [Stuttgart: Klett-Cotta, 1990], 9–21), Landgrebe's study is in the main an abridged version of an homage published shortly after Patočka's death ("Erinnerung an meinen Freund: Jan Patočka—Ein Philosoph von Weltbedeutung," *Perspektiven der Philosophie. Neues Jahrbuch* 3 [1977]: 295–312). The word "today" refers thus to the 1970s, when the Communist regime was still very much in power in Czechoslovakia.—*Eds.*

3. According to a handwritten German curriculum vitae sent by Patočka to Walter Biemel in 1969 or 1970, the 1967–68 Cologne lectures were on "philosophy in the spiritual life of Bohemia in the nineteenth and twentieth century" (a fragment of four pages has been conserved in the Prague Archive, ms. 3000/336), whereas Prague's role in the spiritual history of Europe had been dealt with earlier, in Aachen and Heidelberg, also on Landgrebe's invitation. See Patočka, *Texte—Dokumente—Bibliographie,* ed. Ludger Hagedorn and Hans Rainer Sepp (Freiburg: Alber, 1999), 452–56, esp. 455.—*Trans.*

4. The Festschrift was planned by Patočka's friends to be published in 1967, as an homage on the occasion of his sixtieth birthday. It was, however, not yet ready to go to print when the "Prague Spring" was prematurely quelled in August 1968 and could thus appear only much later, outside of Czechoslovakia, thanks to Walter Biemel and the Husserl-Archive of Leuven: *Die Welt des Menschen—die Welt der Philosophie: Festschrift für Jan Patočka,* Phaenomenologica no. 72 (The Hague: Martinus Nijhoff, 1976). [For Patočka's "Erinnerungen an Husserl," see pages vii–xix.]

5. Title of a series of lectures delivered by Masaryk to a nonacademic public in 1901; see the English translation by W. Preston Warren, *The Ideals of Humanity* (London: G. Allen and Unwin, 1938).—*Eds.*

6. The Vienna lecture was published in *Husserliana* VI (The Hague: Martinus Nijhoff, 1954), 314–48. [Husserl's visit to Prague in 1935 is documented

(in German) in Patočka, *Texte—Dokumente—Bibliographie*, esp. 227–34. The documentation includes correspondence relating to his visit, schedule, and announcements of his talks, as well as subsequent reviews.]

7. See Patočka, "Edmund Husserl zum Gedächtnis," in the Cercle's first publication: *E. Husserl zum Gedächtnis: Zwei Reden gehalten von L. Landgrebe und J. Patočka* (Prague: Academia, 1938), 20–30; reprint of the two speeches in *Perspektiven der Philosophie* 1 (1975): 287–320.

8. The close relationship between Jakobson's structuralism and phenomenology has been pointed out by Elmar Holenstein in his work *Roman Jakobsons phänomenologischer Strukturalismus* (Frankfurt: Suhrkamp, 1975) [reviewed by Patočka himself, in German, in *Tijdschrift voor filosofie* 38 (1976): 129–35; reprinted in Patočka, *Texte—Dokumente—Bibliographie*, 409–18]. The "Prague school" and its debate with the "Copenhagen school" were at the origin of modern linguistics.

9. Patočka, "Die Kritik des psychologischen Objektivismus und das Problem der phänomenologischen Psychologie bei Sartre und Merleau-Ponty," in *Akten des XIV. Internationalen Kongresses für Philosophie, Wien, 2.–9. Sept. 1968* (Vienna: Herder, 1968), 2:175–84 [reprinted in Patočka, *Die Bewegung der menschlichen Existenz*, ed. Klaus Nellen, Jiří Němec, and Ilja Srubar (Stuttgart: Klett-Cotta, 1991), 545–55, esp. 552].

10. See Ludwig Landgrebe, "Die Phänomenologie als transzendentale Theorie der Geschichte," *Phänomenologische Forschungen* 3 (1976): 17–45.

Chapter 1

1. Compare Plato, *Theaetetus*, 155d: "For this feeling of wonder shows that you are a philosopher, since wonder is the only beginning of philosophy" (trans. Harold F. Fowler).—*Trans.*

2. On the meaning of the ancient recommendation to *sōzein ta phainomena*, see Jürgen Mittelstraß, *Die Rettung der Phänomene: Ursprung und Geschichte eines antiken Forschungsprinzips* (Berlin: Walter de Gruyter, 1962).—*Eds.*

3. Francis Bacon, *De Dignitate et Augmentis Scientiarum Libri IX* (Paris, 1624), book 3, 185. [English: *The Advancement of Learning*, ed. G. W. Kitchin, book 2, chap. 7, sec. 6 (London: J. M. Dent and Sons, 1861), 95–96: "the work which God works from the beginning to the end, the summary law of nature."] Compare also Eccl. 3:11.—*Eds.*

4. See, e.g., František Krejčí, *Svoboda vůle a mravnost* [*Freedom of Will and Morality*] (Prague: Jan Laichter, 1907); Krejčí, *Positivní etika jakožto mravouka na základě přirozeném* [*Positive Ethics as Morals on a Natural Basis*] (Prague: Jan Laichter, 1922); and Krejčí, *Psychologie VI (Psychologie vůle)* [*Psychology VI (Psychology of the Will)*] (Prague: Dědictví Komenského, 1926).

5. It would be a pleonasm to stress that self-alienated man is essentially skeptical.

6. See Berkeley, preface, §2, to *Three Dialogues between Hylas and Philonous* (1713).

7. Compare Bergson's interpretation of Berkeley in his lecture "Philosophical Intuition" ["L'intuition philosophique," *Revue de métaphysique et de morale* 19, no. 6 (1911): 809–27; English in Bergson, *The Creative Mind*, trans. Mabelle L. Andison (Westport, Conn.: Greenwood, 1946), 126–52, esp. 136–39], where he very clearly discerns that Berkeley's theory of "ideas" is basically a theory of matter, a theory of the object, rather than of the mental sphere.

8. See the relevant analyses of our chapter 3.

9. See Thomas Reid, *An Inquiry into the Human Mind*, in *The Works of Thomas Reid*, ed. William Hamilton (Edinburgh: Maclachlan, Stewart, 1846), 103.—*Trans.*

10. See Claude Buffier, *Traité des premières vérités* (Paris, 1724).—*Eds.*

11. See, e.g., Reid's distinction between the mind, the operation of the mind, and the object of that operation in perception, in remembrance, and in "conception"; [*Essays on the Intellectual Powers of Man*, in] *The Works of Thomas Reid*, 292.

12. William Hamilton, "Of Presentative and Representative Knowledge," in ibid., 804–15.

13. See Jacobi's letter to Hamann, June 16, 1783, in Friedrich Heinrich Jacobi, *Werke*, vol. 1 (Leipzig, 1812), 363–67 [esp. 364: "unsere Philosophie ist auf einem schlimmen Abwege, da sie über dem Erklären der Dinge, die Dinge selbst zurück läßt, wodurch die Wissenschaft allerdings sehr deutlich und die Köpfe sehr hell, aber auch in demselben Maße jene leer und diese seicht werden. Nach meinem Urtheil ist das größeste Verdienst des Forschers, Daseyn zu enthüllen. Erklärung ist ihm Mittel, Weg zum Ziele, *nächster*, niemals *letzter* Zweck"—"our philosophy has gone badly astray, turning its back on things themselves in order to explain them, whereby science admittedly becomes quite distinct and heads quite clear, but also, to the same extent, the former void and the latter shallow. In my opinion, the scientist's greatest merit is to uncover what is. Explanation is for him a means to an end, the *proximate*, never *ultimate* goal"].

14. Johann Wolfgang von Goethe, *Zur Farbenlehre I, Einleitung* [(Tübingen, 1810), xliv]. [English: *Goethe's Theory of Colours*, trans. Herbert Aach, ed. Rupprecht Matthaei, (New York: Van Nostrand Reinhold, 1971), 76: "We believe we merit thanks from the philosopher for having traced phenomena to their origins, till the point is reached where they simply appear and are, and beyond which no further explanation respecting them is possible."]

15. Hegel, letter to Goethe, February 24, 1821, in *Briefe von und an Hegel*, ed. Johannes Hoffmeister, vol. 2, 3rd ed. (Hamburg: Meiner, 1969), 250. [English: *Hegel: The Letters*, trans. Clark Butler and Christiane Seiler (Bloomington: Indiana University Press, 1984), 699.]—*Trans.*

16. See Johannes Hoffmeister, *Goethe und der deutsche Idealismus: Eine Einführung zu Hegels Realphilosophie* (Leipzig: Meiner, 1932).

17. Richard Avenarius, *Kritik der reinen Erfahrung*, 2 vols. (Leipzig: Fues, 1888–90).—*Eds.*

18. See §1 of this chapter, p. 9.

19. I remark merely that the notion of "introjection," through which Avenarius wants to explain the fact of the duplication of the world, is inadequate for this task: if introjection, i.e., the projection of life "inside" the objects of

experience, were responsible for it, we should expect the duplication to diminish in the course of historical evolution, yet we see the opposite.

20. See Ernst Mach, *Beiträge zur Analyse der Empfindungen* (Jena: Fischer, 1886); 2nd enl. ed. entitled *Die Analyse der Empfindungen und das Verhältnis des Physischen zum Psychischen* (Jena: Fischer, 1900). [English: *The Analysis of Sensations and the Relation of the Physical to the Psychical*, trans. Sydney Waterlow (New York: Dover, 1959).]—*Eds.*

21. Wilhelm Schuppe, "Die Bestätigung des naiven Realismus: Offener Brief an Herrn Prof. Richard Avenarius," *Vierteljahrschrift für wissenschaftliche Philosophie* 17 (1893): 364–88.

22. Bertrand Russell, *Our Knowledge of the External World as a Field of the Scientific Method in Philosophy*, 2nd ed. (London: G. Allen and Unwin, 1926).

23. Rudolf Carnap, *Der logische Aufbau der Welt* (Berlin: Weltkreis-Verlag, 1928). [English: *The Logical Structure of the World*, trans. Rolf A. George (Berkeley: University of California Press, 1967).]

24. See Ludwig Wittgenstein, *Tractatus logico-philosophicus* [trans. Charles Kay Ogden (London: K. Paul, Trench and Trubner, 1933); first published in German as "Logisch-philosophische Abhandlung" in *Annalen der Naturphilosophie* 14, no. 3–4 (1921): 185–262.—*Eds.*]

25. On the concept of structure, see Vladimír Tardy, "Noetika XX. století" ["Twentieth-Century Noetics"] in *Dvacáté století, co dalo lidstvu*, ed. František Páta et al., vol. 7: *Z duševní dílny lidstva* (Prague: Vl. Orel, 1934), 25–40.

26. Wittgenstein, *Tractatus*, 6.124.—*Trans.*

27. Compare Rudolf Carnap, "Überwindung der Metaphysik durch logische Analyse der Sprache," *Erkenntnis* 2 (1931–32): 219–41. [English: "The Elimination of Metaphysics Through Logical Analysis of Language," in *Logical Empiricism at Its Peak: Schlick, Carnap and Neurath*, ed. Sahotra Sarkar (New York: Garland, 1996), 10–31.]

28. Compare Edmund Husserl, *Méditations cartésiennes*, trans. Gabrielle Peiffer and Emmanuel Levinas (Paris: Armand Colin, 1931), 5 [*Cartesianische Meditationen*, in *Husserliana* I, 2nd ed., ed. Stephan Strasser (The Hague: Martinus Nijhoff, 1963), 47–48; English: *Cartesian Meditations*, trans. Dorian Cairns (The Hague: Martinus Nijhoff, 1973), 5–6]; Husserl, *Ideen zu einer reinen Phänomenologie und phänomenologischen Philosophie, Erstes Buch*, in *Jahrbuch für Philosophie und phänomenologische Forschung* 1 (1913): 53 [see also *Husserliana* III, ed. Walter Biemel (The Hague: Martinus Nijhoff, 1950), 63–64; English: *Ideas pertaining to a Pure Phenomenology and to a Phenomenological Philosophy*, First Book, trans. Fred Kersten, in *Collected Works*, vol. 2 (The Hague: Martinus Nijhoff, 1983), 71–73]. —See also Gerhard Krüger, "Die Herkunft des philosophischen Selbstbewußtseins," *Logos* 22 (1933): 225–72.

29. See Dostoyevsky's *Notes from Underground*. ["What can a decent man speak about with the most pleasure? Answer: about himself" (trans. Richard Pevear and Larissa Volokhonsky [New York: Knopf, 1993], 8).]

30. See Nikolaj Onufrievich Lossky, *Transsubjectivity of Sense-Qualities* (Prague: Université libre russe [*Naučno-izsledovatelskoe obedinenie, Zapiski* no. 21], 1936.)—*Trans.*

Chapter 2

1. See René Descartes, *Regulae ad Directionem Ingenii*, VI. [See Descartes, *Œuvres*, ed. Charles Adam and Paul Tannery (Paris: Vrin, 1996), 10:381–87; English: *Rules for the Direction of the Mind*, trans. Dugald Murdoch, in *The Philosophical Writings of Descartes*, vol. 1 (Cambridge: Cambridge University Press, 1985), 21–24.]

2. Ibid., III. [Descartes, *Œuvres*, 10:368; Eng. trans., p. 14: "the conception of a clear and attentive mind, (such) that there can be no room for doubt."]

3. Descartes, *Principia Philosophiae* (1644), part 1, X [quoted in French translation: *Les Principes de la philosophie*, in *Œuvres*, 9:29]: "et lorsque j'ai dit que cette proposition: *Je pense, donc je suis*, est la première et la plus certaine qui se présente à celui qui conduit ses pensées par ordre, je n'ai pas pour cela nié qu'il ne fallût savoir auparavant ce que c'est que pensée, certitude, existence, et que pour penser il faut être . . ." [English: *Principles of Philosophy*, trans. John Veitch (Whitefish, Mont.: Kessering Reprints, 2004), 18: "when I said that the proposition, I THINK, THEREFORE I AM, is of all others the first and most certain which occurs to one philosophizing orderly, I did not therefore deny that it was necessary to know what thought, existence, and certitude are, and the truth that, in order to think it is necessary to be . . ."]

4. Immanuel Kant, *Logik: Ein Handbuch zu Vorlesungen hrsg. von Gottlob Benjamin Jäsche*, in *Werke*, ed. Ernst Cassirer et al., vol. 8 (Berlin: B. Cassirer, 1922), 350. [English: *The Jäsche Logic*, in *Lectures on Logic*, ed. and trans. J. Michael Young (Cambridge: Cambridge University Press, 1992), 544.]

5. Ibid.; compare also Kant, *Kritik der reinen Vernunft* [hereafter *KdrV*], in *Werke*, vol. 3 (Berlin, 1913), A371 [English: *Critique of Pure Reason*, ed. and trans. Paul Guyer and Allen Wood (Cambridge: Cambridge University Press, 1998), 427], where Kant equates consciousness (*Bewußtsein*) with immediate perception of representations (*unmittelbare Wahrnehmung der Vorstellungen*).

6. Kant, *Logik*, in *Werke*, 8:351 [Eng. trans., 545].

7. Ibid., 353 [Eng. trans., 546].

8. Kant, *Prolegomena zu einer jeden künftigen Metaphysik, die als Wissenschaft wird auftreten können* (in *Werke*, ed. Cassirer, vol. 4 [Berlin, 1913]), 38: "es sind uns Dinge als außer uns befindliche Gegenstände unserer Sinne *gegeben*, allein von dem, *was* sie an sich selbst sein mögen, wissen wir nichts. . ." [English: *Prolegomena to Any Future Metaphysics That Will Be Able to Come Forward as Science*, in Kant, *Theoretical Philosophy after 1781*, ed. Henry Allison and Peter Heath, trans. Gary Hatfield (Cambridge: Cambridge University Press, 2002), 84: "There are things *given* to us as objects of our senses existing outside us, yet we know nothing of *them* as they may be in themselves . . ."] (emphasis added).

9. Kant, *KdrV*, A44, A19 [Eng. trans., 186, 155].

10. Kant, "Beantwortung der Frage: Ist es eine Erfahrung, daß wir denken?" in *Werke*, ed. Cassirer, 4:519. [English: "Answer to the Question: Is It an Experience That We Think?" in *Notes and Fragments*, ed. and trans. Paul Guyer (Cambridge: Cambridge University Press, 2005), 289.]

11. Kant, *KdrV*, A20 [Eng. trans., 155].

12. Kant, *Anthropologie in pragmatischer Hinsicht*, in *Werke*, ed. Cassirer, 8:47. [English: *Anthropology from a Pragmatic Point of View*, ed. and trans. Robert B. Louden (Cambridge: Cambridge University Press, 2006), 53.]

13. Kant, *KdrV*, A77 [Eng. trans., 210].

14. Ibid.

15. Ibid., A124 [Eng. trans., 240–41].

16. Martin Heidegger, *Kant und das Problem der Metaphysik* (Bonn: Cohen, 1929), 160ff. [English: *Kant and the Problem of Metaphysics*, trans. Richard Taft, 5th ed. (Bloomington: Indiana University Press, 1997), 112ff.]

17. Kant, *KdrV*, A79 [Eng. trans., 211].

18. Ibid., A126 [Eng. trans., 242].

19. Ibid., B131 [Eng. trans., 246].

20. Ibid., B132 [Eng. trans., 246].

21. Ibid. [Eng. trans., 247].

22. Ibid., B137 [Eng. trans., 249].

23. Kant, "Beantwortung der Frage . . . ," in *Werke*, 4:520 [Eng. trans., 289–90].

24. Kant, *KdrV*, B133–34n, A551/B 579 [Eng. trans., 247n, 542].

25. Kant, *Prolegomena . . .* , §46 [Eng. trans., 125].

26. Kant, *KdrV*, B158 [Eng. trans., 260].

27. Ibid., B158–59 [Eng. trans., 260.].

28. Kant, "Preisschrift über die Fortschritte der Metaphysik seit Leibniz und Wolff," in *Werke*, 8:249. [English: "What Real Progress Has Metaphysics Made in Germany since the Time of Leibniz and Wolff?" trans. Peter Heath, in Kant, *Theoretical Philosophy after 1781*, 362.]

29. Ibid.

30. Kant, *KdrV*, B422n [Eng. trans., 453n].

31. The theories of the person in modern thinkers (Edmund Husserl, Max Scheler, Nicolai Hartmann) are thus a renewal of these Kantian themes.

32. Johann Gottlieb Fichte, "Rezension des Aenesidemus" (1794), in *Werke: Auswahl in sechs Bänden*, ed. Fritz Medicus, vol. 1 (Leipzig: Meiner, 1911), 129–53. [Review of Gottlob Ernst Schulze's anonymously published work *Aenesidemus, oder über die Fundamente der von dem Herrn Professor Reinhold in Jena gelieferten Elementar-Philosophie* (Helmstädt, 1792). English: "Review of Aenesidemus," in Fichte, *Early Philosophical Writings*, ed. and trans. Daniel Breazeale (Ithaca, N.Y.: Cornell University Press, 1993), 59–77.—*Eds.*]

33. Ibid., 1:133–38 [Eng. trans., 63–66].

34. For example, Kant, *KdrV*, B138–39 [Eng. trans., 249–50].

35. Ibid., B146–47 [Eng. trans., 254–55].

36. Fichte, "Rezension des Aenesidemus," in *Werke*, 1:136 [Eng. trans., 64].

37. Fichte, *Grundlage der gesamten Wissenschaftslehre*, in *Werke*, 1:285. [English: "Foundations of the Entire Science of Knowledge," in *Science of Knowledge*, trans. Peter Heath and John Lachs (Cambridge: Cambridge University Press, 1982), 93.]

38. Eugen Fink, "Die phänomenologische Philosophie Husserls in der gegenwärtigen Kritik," *Kant-Studien* 38 (1933), 338 [English: "The Phenomeno-

logical Philosophy of Edmund Husserl and Contemporary Criticism," in *The Phenomenology of Husserl: Selected Critical Readings*, ed. and trans. R. O. Elveton, 2nd ed. (Seattle: Noesis, 2000), 90–91].

39. Compare Fichte, *Über den Begriff der Wissenschaftslehre*, in *Werke*, 1:203. [English: "Concerning the Concept of the *Wissenschaftslehre*," in *Early Philosophical Writings*, 128.]

40. Fichte, *Grundlage der gesamten Wissenschaftslehre*, in *Werke*, 1:288–93 [Eng. trans., 95–99].

41. Fichte, *Über den Begriff der Wissenschaftslehre*, in *Werke*, 1:201 [Eng. trans., 126].

42. Fichte, *Grundlage der gesamten Wissenschaftslehre*, in *Werke*, 1:317–19 [Eng. trans., 119–20].

43. Ibid., 1:319 [Eng. trans., 121].

44. Ibid.

45. Fichte, *Über den Begriff der Wissenschaftslehre*, in *Werke*, 1:166–74, esp. 172 [Eng. trans., 101–6, esp. 105].

46. Ibid., 1:191 [Eng. trans., 119].

47. Ibid.

48. See on this point Nicolai Hartmann, "Hegel et le problème de la dialectique du réel," *Revue de métaphysique et de morale* 38 (1931): 285–316.

49. Hegel, *Enzyklopädie der philosophischen Wissenschaften im Grundriße* (1817), §39. [English: *Encyclopedia of the Philosophical Sciences in Outline*, in *Encyclopedia of the Philosophical Sciences in Outline and Critical Writings*, ed. Ernst Behler, trans. Steven A. Taubeneck (New York: Continuum, 1990), 68.]

50. Fichte, *Über den Begriff der Wissenschaftslehre*, in *Werke*, 1:170–71 [Eng. trans., 103–4].

51. Friedrich Wilhelm Joseph Schelling, *System des transzendentalen Idealismus*, in *Sämmtliche Werke*, ed. Karl Friedrich August Schelling, vol. 3 (Stuttgart: Cotta, 1858), 378. [English: *System of Transcendental Idealism (1800)*, trans. Peter Heath (Charlottesville: University of Virginia Press, 1993), 34.]

52. Patočka's recently discovered personal copy of his habilitation thesis includes here a penciled note: "Meaning here only 'egoity' in itself, not self-consciousness as the apprehension of the *essence* of egoity; only 'I is I,' not = absolute activity, instinct, etc. In short, *Ich = identisches Bewußtsein*. [Fichte, *Grundlage der gesamten*] *Wissenschaftslehre* [in *Werke*, ed. Immanuel Hermann Fichte, vol. 1: *Zur theoretischen Philosophie I* (Berlin: Walter de Gruyter, 1971)], 106" = ed. Fritz Medicus, *Werke*, 1:301. See Eng. trans., 106.—*Eds.*

53. Schelling, *System des transzendentalen Idealismus*, in *Werke*, 3:380 [Eng. trans., 36].

54. Ibid., 3:383 A. aa [Eng. trans., 38].

55. Ibid., bb–dd.

56. Ibid., 3:343 [Eng. trans., 8].

57. Ibid.

58. Hegel, *Enzyklopädie der philosophischen Wissenschaften im Grundriße* (1817), §36 [Eng. trans., 67].

59. It is a total misunderstanding to regard this reductive process as an

"abstraction from all objectnesses," in the words of František Krejčí (*Filosofie posledních let před válkou* [*The Philosophy of the Last Prewar Years*] [Prague: Laichter, 1918], 301). How it can be, then, that the world despite this abstraction "does not collapse into nothing" but is "further maintained as an object of reflection," is incomprehensible. In point of fact, the reduction does not bracket things, what Krejčí calls objectnesses, but rather theses. Krejčí was doubtless misled by the phrase "suspension of the world," but in Husserl this concerns the thesis.

60. Concerning this whole passage, see Husserl, *Méditations cartésiennes*, 16–23, esp. §10 [*Husserliana* I:58–65; Eng. trans., 18–26].

61. It is interesting to note that, among Czech philosophers, this quite widespread misunderstanding is shared by representatives of opposite camps. Both the positivist František Krejčí and a thinker as mystically attuned as Vladimír Hoppe regard the method of reduction as a moment of essential intuition (*Wesenserschauung*). This opinion, totally incorrect, has been explicitly refuted once and for all by the explanations given in the *Cartesian Meditations*. It is no longer possible, in particular, to *identify* the "phenomenological method" with "eidetic intuition," as both Krejčí (*Filosofie posledních let před válkou*, 303) and Hoppe (*Úvod do intuitivní a kontemplativní filosofie* [*Introduction to Intuitive and Contemplative Philosophy*] [Brno: Filosofická fakulta, 1928], 93) do. To mention but one example of the very incomplete knowledge of Husserl on which Krejčí bases his criticism [309]: the example he attributes to August Messer ("Husserls Phänomenologie in ihrem Verhältnis zur Psychologie. Zweiter Aufsatz," *Archiv für die gesamte Psychologie* 32 [1914]: 52–67) commenting on some of Husserl's propositions that are difficult to conceive is actually taken from Husserl's own seminal work, *Ideen zu einer reinen Phänomenologie I*, §88, 182–83 [*Husserliana* III:203–4; Eng. trans., 214–16].

62. Aristotle, *Metaphysics*, I.2.983a9–10 ["such a science either God alone can have, or God above all others" (trans. William David Ross)].

63. Though they remain unable to exactly prove it, many critics (including Czechs such as Krejčí) see here something Husserl has in common with Hegel. For our part, we have drawn a parallel between the tendencies of German idealism and phenomenology, and we hope to have succeeded in pointing out the fertile aspects of German idealism but also its difference in method from that of phenomenology; German idealism is to phenomenology as the intuitive anticipation of an idea is to its methodic, scientific realization or, as concerns procedure, as synthesis is to analysis.

64. Schelling, *System des transzendentalen Idealismus*, in *Werke*, 3:382 and 412ff. [Eng. trans., 37 and 61ff.].

65. According to Nicolai Hartmann, the meaning of the cognitive phenomenon suggests that the real object lies "in the extended direction of the objection" [see Hartmann, *Grundzüge einer Metaphysik der Erkenntnis*, 5th ed. (Berlin: Walter de Gruyter, 1965), 52]; it is clear, however, that the *content* of transcendence is here taken for its *essence*.

66. This confusion is then an easy source of arguments against idealism (e.g., Nicolai Hartmann: in order for a relation such as that of consciousness to exist, there must exist the terms of the relation).

67. Husserl, *Ideen I*, 315–16 [*Husserliana* III:371–72; Eng. trans, 361–63]; Husserl, *Méditations cartésiennes*, 44–45 [*Husserliana* I:88–89; Eng. trans., 51–53].

68. František Krejčí speaks of pure consciousness as "constructing" transcendences within itself. Since the construction of the object is most often referred to in a sense radically different from that of constitution, this statement should be taken with reserve. (See Krejčí, *Filosofie posledních let před válkou*, 302.)

69. Husserl, *Méditations cartésiennes*, §15, 30: "dédoublement du moi" [*Husserliana* I:73; Eng. trans., 35].

70. See Husserl, *Logische Untersuchungen*, vol. 2 (Halle: Niemeyer, 1901), "Investigation II," 136–66 [also in *Husserliana* XIX/1, ed. Ursula Panzer (The Hague: Martinus Nijhoff, 1984), 142–70; English: *Logical Investigations*, 2nd ed., ed. Dermot Moran, trans. J. N. Findlay, vol. 1 (London: Routledge, 2001), 277–88].

71. We encounter this reading, e.g., in Johannes Volkelt, *Gewißheit und Wahrheit: Untersuchung der Geltungsfragen als Grundlegung der Erkenntnistheorie* (Munich: Beck, 1918), 453–54. Other representatives of it are Rickert's disciples Rudolf Zocher (*Husserls Phänomenologie und Schuppes Logik* [Munich: Reinhardt, 1932]) and Friedrich Kreis (*Phänomenologie und Kritizismus* [Tübingen: Mohr, 1930]). In Czechoslovakia, the same line of interpretation is followed by Josef Tvrdý (*Nová filosofie* [*The New Philosophy*], [Prague: Nákl. Volné myšlenky, 1932], 42–43) and, with somewhat naive benevolence, by Vladimír Hoppe (*Úvod do intuitivní a kontemplativní filosofie*, 93). It is undeniable that certain thinkers, generally regarded as phenomenologists, do themselves suggest a correspondence between ideation and the Platonic-Aristotelian *noēsis* (e.g., Max Scheler, *Philosophische Weltanschauung* [Bonn: Cohen, 1929], 11–12 [English: *Philosophical Perspectives*, trans. Oscar A. Haac (Boston: Beacon, 1958), 10–11]). Husserl's formulations in the article "Philosophie als strenge Wissenschaft" [*Logos* 1 (1910–11): 289–341; also in *Husserliana* XXV: *Aufsätze und Vorträge (1911–1922)*, ed. Thomas Nenon and Hans Rainer Sepp (Dordrecht: Martinus Nijhoff, 1987), 3–62; English: "Philosophy as Rigorous Science," in Husserl, *Phenomenology and the Crisis of Philosophy*, ed. and trans. Quentin Lauer (New York: Harper and Row), 1965] also lack precision and have often proved misleading.

72. Husserl, *Logische Studien*, §73. [See Husserl, *Erfahrung und Urteil*, §87e, ed. Ludwig Landgrebe (Prague: Academia, 1939; 2nd ed. Hamburg: Classen and Goverts, 1948), 419 (English: *Experience and Judgment*, trans. James S. Churchill and Karl Ameriks [Evanston, Ill.: Northwestern University Press, 1975], 346–47). The manuscript *Logische Studien* was written when Husserl was working on *Formal and Transcendental Logic* (compare Paul Janssen, "Einleitung des Herausgebers," in *Husserliana* XVII [The Hague: Martinus Nijhoff, 1974], xxii ff.). It was communicated to Patočka in January 1935 by Felix Kaufmann (see Karl Schuhmann, *Husserl-Chronik* [The Hague: Martinus Nijhoff, 1977], 457). Husserl later used this manuscript in composing the volume *Erfahrung und Urteil*, posthumously edited by Ludwig Landgrebe (*Husserl-Chronik*, 482–84). The eventful destiny of this book is evoked in the 1967 interview "S Janem Patočkou o filosofii a filosofech" ("With Jan Patocka on Philosophy and Philosophers"), in *Sebrané spisy*, vol. 12: *Češi I*, ed. Karel Palek and Ivan Chvatík (Prague: OIKOYMENH, 2006), 621; see French translation by Erika Abrams, "Entretien avec J.P.," in *Jan Patočka: Philosophie,*

phénoménologie, politique, ed. Marc Richir and Étienne Tassin (Grenoble: Millon, 1992), 23.—*Eds.*]

73. See his intervention at the Congress of Philosophy in Prague (separate no. 77, 5). [Felix Kaufmann, "Die Bedeutung der logischen Analyse für die Sozialwissenschaften," in *Actes du 8ᵉ Congrès international de Philosophie à Prague, 2–7 septembre 1934* (Prague: Orbis, 1936), 213.—*Eds.*]

74. As shown by Vladimír Tardy in his 1931 thesis *Logický rozbor matematického poznání* [*A Logical Analysis of Mathematical Knowledge*]. See also Tardy, "Noetika XX. století," 32–33.

75. Light is shed on these problems by Eugen Fink's *Transzendentale Methodenlehre* [= *VI. Cartesianische Meditation,* part 1: *Die Idee einer transzendentalen Methodenlehre,* ed. H. Ebeling et al. (Dordrecht: Kluwer, 1988); English: *Sixth Cartesian Meditation: The Idea of a Transcendental Theory of Method,* trans. Ronald Bruzina (Bloomington: Indiana University Press, 1995)].

76. Fichte, *Grundlage der gesamten Wissenschaftslehre,* in *Werke,* 1:315 [Eng. trans., 118].

77. Husserl, *Méditations cartésiennes,* §52, 96: "L'apprésentation comme expérience ayant une manière propre de se confirmer." (See the whole "Fifth Meditation" [*Husserliana* I:121–77, esp. 143; Eng. trans., 89–150, esp. 113: "Appresentation as a kind of experience with its own style of verification"].)

Chapter 3

1. Compare Kurt Grube, *Wilhelm von Humboldts Bildungsphilosophie: Versuch einer Interpretation* (Halle: Akademischer Verlag, 1935), 68–97, esp. 70ff.

2. Cf. Wilhelm Dilthey, *Gesammelte Schriften,* vol. 8: *Weltanschauungslehre: Abhandlungen zur Philosophie der Philosophie,* ed. Bernhard Groethuysen (Stuttgart: Teubner, 1931); partial English translation by William Kluback and Martin Weintraub, *Dilthey's Philosophy of Existence: Introduction to Weltanschauungslehre* (New York: Bookman, 1957).—*Trans.*

3. Georg Simmel, *Lebensanschauung: Vier metaphysische Kapitel,* 2nd ed. (Munich: Duncker and Humblot, 1922), 27–28. [English: Simmel, *The View of Life: Four Metaphysical Essays with Journal Aphorisms,* trans. John A. Y. Andrews and Donald N. Levine (Chicago: University of Chicago Press, 2010), 19–20: "World in the full sense is . . . a sum of contents freed by spirit from the isolated existence of each piece and brought into a unitary coherence, into a form that is capable of including known and unknown."]

4. Ibid., 29. [Eng. trans., 20: "Now for any particular thinker, the choice of which leading concept creates his world as such evidently depends upon his characterological type, upon his way of existing in relation to the world which grounds the way his thinking relates to the world."]

5. Husserl, *Ideen I,* 48ff. [*Husserliana* III:56ff.; Eng. trans., 51ff.].

6. Max Scheler, *Probleme einer Soziologie des Wissens,* in *Die Wissensformen und die Gesellschaft* (Leipzig: Neuer Geist Verlag, 1926), 58ff. [English: *Problems of a So-*

ciology of Knowledge, ed. Kenneth W. Stikkers, trans. Manfred S. Frings (London: Routledge and Kegan Paul, 1980), 74–76.]—*Eds.*

7. Scheler, *Philosophische Weltanschauung*, 13 [Eng. trans., 11].

8. Heidegger, *Sein und Zeit*, §18, in *Jahrbuch für Philosophie und phänomenologische Forschung* 8 (1927): 86. [English: *Being and Time*, trans. Joan Stambaugh (Albany, N.Y.: SUNY Press, 1996), 80–81: "the wherein of . . . understanding as that for which one lets beings be encountered."]—*Eds.*

9. See Jakob von Uexküll, *Bausteine einer biologischen Weltanschauung: Gesammelte Aufsätze*, ed. Felix Groß (Munich: Bruckmann, 1913), 71ff.—*Trans.*

10. Compare Henri Bergson, *Matière et mémoire*, 28th ed. (Paris: Alcan, 1934), 217–18 [English: *Matter and Memory*, trans. N. M. Paul and W. S. Palmer (Mineola, N.Y.: Dover, 2004), 256–57]; Bergson, *L'Évolution créatrice*, 17th ed. (Paris: Alcan, 1914), 11–12 [English: *Creative Evolution*, trans. Arthur Mitchell (New York: Henry Holt, 1911), 11].

11. Patočka may be referring here to the manuscripts A VII 10, 25a–38b (1932); A VII 23 (1933); A V 3 (1933); A VII 9 (1933); A VII 4 (1933); A VII 2 (1934); see the recently published vol. XXXIX of the *Husserliana* series: *Die Lebenswelt. Auslegungen der vorgegebenen Welt und ihrer Konstitution: Texte aus dem Nachlaß (1916–1937)*, ed. Rochus Sowa (Dordrecht: Springer, 2008).—*Eds.*

12. See Oswald Spengler, *Der Untergang des Abendlandes*, vol. 1: *Gestalt und Wirklichkeit* (Vienna: Braumüller, 1918). [English: *The Decline of the West*, ed. and trans. Charles Francis Atkinson (New York: Knopf, 1926).]

13. See Georg Misch, *Lebensphilosophie und Phänomenologie* (Bonn: Cohen, 1930).—*Eds.*

14. See Bernhard Groethuysen, *Die Entstehung der bürgerlichen Welt- und Lebensanschauung in Frankreich* (Halle: Niemeyer, 1927). [English: *The Bourgeois: Catholicism vs. Capitalism in Eighteenth-Century France*, trans. Mary Ilford (New York: Holt, Rinehart and Winston, 1968).]

15. See Erich Rothacker, *Einleitung in die Geisteswissenschaften* (Tübingen: Mohr, 1920).—*Eds.*

16. See Lucien Lévy-Bruhl, *La Mentalité primitive* (Paris: Alcan, 1922). [English: *The Primitive Mentality*, trans. Lilian A. Clare (New York: Macmillan, 1923).]—*Eds.*

17. See Jean Piaget, *Le Langage et la pensée chez l'enfant* (Neuchâtel: Delachaux et Niestlé, 1923) [English: *The Language and Thought of the Child*, trans. Marjorie Warden (New York: Harcourt Brace, 1926)]; Piaget, *La Représentation du monde chez l'enfant* (Paris: Alcan, 1926) [English: *The Child's Conception of the World*, trans. Joan and Andrew Tomlinson (New York: Harcourt Brace, 1929)].—*Eds.*

18. Edmund Husserl was the first to recognize the fundamental significance of this fact. See his *Méditations cartésiennes*.

19. The term "horizon" is first frequently encountered in Husserl's 1913 *Ideas*. Objectively, the concept is however already present in the 1905 lectures on the consciousness of time (published only in 1928), where, moreover, we find terms such as *Vergangenheitshorizont* (389). [See Husserl, *Vorlesungen zur Phänomenologie des inneren Zeitbewußtseins*, §10, in *Jahrbuch für Philosophie und*

phänomenologische Forschung 9 (1928)—hereafter cited as *Zeitbewußtsein*; also in *Husserliana* X, *Zur Phänomenologie des inneren Zeitbewußtseins (1893–1917)*, ed. Rudolf Boehm (The Hague: Martinus Nijhoff, 1966), 28; English: *On the Phenomenology of the Consciousness of Internal Time (1893–1917)*, trans. John Barnett Brough (Dordrecht: Kluwer, 1991), 29.]

20. Kant, *Logik*, in *Werke*, 8:356–57 [Eng. trans., 550–51].

21. Johann Gustav Droysen, *Grundriß der Historik*, §43, ed. Erich Rothacker (Halle: Niemeyer, 1925), 23 [see English translation of the 1875 edition: *Outline of the Principles of History*, trans. Elisha Benjamin Andrews (Boston: Ginn, 1893), 31]. Droysen in his historical views is close to Wilhelm von Humboldt.

22. Characters such as "old" and "new" are also of such origin. A "new pen" does not mean a "younger" one but one that is unused and suitable.

23. As Husserl, for instance, did in his *Zeitbewußtsein*.

24. Husserl speaks of the "source-point" (*Quellpunkt*), of the "production of the enduring object" (*Erzeugung des dauernden Objekts*). Compare *Zeitbewußtsein*, 390 [*Husserliana* X:29, §10; Eng. trans., 30]. These formulations directly invite a comparison of the phenomenological conception of original time with Bergson's.

25. The level of intersubjective time, constituted on the basis of the apperception of the other, also belongs in this context. See Husserl, *Zeitbewußtsein*, 427ff. [*Husserliana* X:71ff., §33; Eng. trans., 73ff.].

26. Heidegger, *Sein und Zeit*, 421ff. [Eng. trans., 386ff.].

27. See Bergson, *Durée et simultanéité*, 6th ed. (Paris: Alcan, 1931), 54ff. [English: *Duration and Simultaneity*, trans. Leon Jacobson (Indianapolis, Ind.: Bobbs-Merrill, 1965), 72ff.]

28. Compare Aristotle's *ouk an ezēteito ho topos, ei mē kinēsis tis ēn hē kata topon*—*Physics* IV.4.211a12–13 ["place would not have been thought of, if there had not been a special kind of motion, namely that with respect to place" (trans. R. P. Hardie and R. K. Gaye)].

29. As concerns the complex character of animal perception, see also Heinz Werner, *Einführung in die Entwicklungspsychologie*, 2nd rev. ed. (Leipzig: Barth, 1933) [English: *Comparative Psychology of Mental Development*, trans. Edward Ballard Garside (New York: International Universities Press, 1980)]. Max Scheler attempted to construct a life-form of the kind outlined here in *Die Stellung des Menschen im Kosmos* (Darmstadt: Reichl, 1928) [English: *Man's Place in Nature*, trans. Hans Meyerhoff (Boston: Beacon, 1961)].

30. Bergson, *L'Évolution créatrice*, 12–13. [Eng. trans., 12: "The bodies we perceive are . . . cut out of the stuff of nature by our *perception*, and the scissors follow . . . the marking of lines along which *action* might be taken."]

31. On horizon, see Husserl's manuscript "Horizon" from the period after 1930. [Patočka is probably referring here to the manuscript kept in the Husserl Archives in Leuven under the signature A VII 9, substantial parts of which have been published in *Husserliana* XXXIX.—*Eds.*]

32. On counting time, see Heidegger, *Sein und Zeit*, 404–20 [Eng. trans., 371–85].

33. As concerns this passage, see Fink's dissertation *Vergegenwärtigung und Bild*, in *Jahrbuch für Philosophie und phänomenologische Forschung* 11 (1930): 239–309.

34. See Husserl, *Méditations cartésiennes*, "Fifth Meditation."

35. As Filip Karfík has pointed out (*Unendlichwerden durch die Endlichkeit* [Würzburg: Königshausen and Neumann, 2008], 72), it is no coincidence that the phrase used here by Patočka (*hlubina bezpečnosti*) is, word for word, the Czech title of one of the important spiritual works of Johann Amos Comenius, *Centrum securitatis* (Leszno, 1633).—*Trans.*

36. Conflict in human society is not the same as struggle in nature: the object here is to submit the *will* of the opponent and not simply to seize a prey, though an animal struggle for prey is, of course, also possible among human beings.

37. Compare Aristotle: *hē men oun technē archē en allōi, hē de phusis archē en autōi*—*Metaphysics*, XII.3.1070a7–8 ["art is a principle of movement in something other than the thing moved, nature is a principle in the thing itself" (trans. William David Ross)].

38. George Dalgarno, *Ars Signorum, vulgo Character Universalis et Lingua Philosophica* (London, 1661). [English: *The Art of Signs*, in *George Dalgarno on Universal Language*, ed. and trans. David Cram and Jaap Maat (Oxford: Oxford University Press, 2001), 137–290.]—*Eds.*

39. See Louis Couturat, *La Logique de Leibniz d'après des documents inédits* (Paris: Alcan, 1901), 171.

40. Compare Bergson, *La Pensée et le mouvant* (Paris: Alcan, 1934), 69ff. [English: *The Creative Mind*, 65–71.]

41. Ibid., 67–68 [Eng. trans., 64].

Chapter 4

1. Compare Johann Leo Weisgerber, "Die Stellung der Sprache im Aufbau der Gesamtkultur. Zweiter Teil," *Wörter und Sachen* 16 (1934): 97–236.

2. The terms "symptom" and "symbol" are borrowed from Karl Bühler, *Sprachtheorie: Die Darstellungsfunktion der Sprache* (Jena: Fischer, 1934), 28. [English: *Theory of Language: The Representational Function of Language*, trans. Donald Fraser Goodwin and Achim Eschbach (Philadelphia: John Benjamins, 2011), 35.]

3. Compare Hegel, *Jenenser Realphilosophie II*, ed. Johannes Hoffmeister (Leipzig: Meiner, 1931), 182–94. [English: *Hegel and the Human Spirit: A Translation of the Jena Lectures on the Philosophy of Spirit (1805–06) with Commentary*, trans. Leo Rauch (Detroit: Wayne State University Press, 1983), 88–99.]—*Eds.*

4. See Hermann Ammann, *Die menschliche Rede: Sprachphilosophische Untersuchungen*, part 2: *Der Satz. Lebensformen und Lebensfunktionen der Rede—das Wesen der Satzform—Satz und Urteil* (Lahr: Schauenburg, 1928), 30.

5. Otherwise there would be no sense in wanting to communicate with

members of another language community, the phenomenon of translation would be absurd, and comparative linguistics impossible.

6. See, e.g., František Krejčí, *Psychologie IV* (*Psychologie myšlení*) [*Psychology of Thought*] (Prague: Dědictví Komenského, 1910).

7. Anton Marty, *Untersuchungen zur Grundlegung der allgemeinen Grammatik und Sprachphilosophie* (Halle: Niemeyer, 1908); see also Marty, *Zur Sprachphilosophie* (Halle: Niemeyer, 1910).—*Eds.*

8. We cannot therefore agree with Krejčí (*Psychologie IV*, 55ff.), who reduces the comprehension of the meaning of a word to simple association and is then incapable of explaining how in actual fact nonaffective speech comes about; it is not clear here why an animal raised in human conditions (as in Kellogg's experiment [see Winthrop Niles and Luella Agger Kellogg, *The Ape and the Child: A Study of Environmental Influence upon Early Behavior* (New York: McGraw-Hill, 1933)] does not create a language. It is also inexact to claim, e.g., that the word "bow" uttered by a child in the presence of a dog means no more than a sound gesture; in particular, it is decidedly not one with which linked with a demonstrative gesture.

9. See William Stern, *Psychologie der frühen Kindheit bis zum sechsten Lebensjahre* (Leipzig: Quelle and Meyer, 1914) [English: *Psychology of Early Childhood up to the Sixth Year of Age*, trans. Anna Barwell (New York: H. Holt, 1924)]; and Milivoïe Pavlovitch, *Le Langage enfantin: Acquisition du serbe et du français par un enfant serbe* (Paris: Champion, 1920).—*Eds.*

10. Even when this is not the case, one can find analogies in adult speech. See Henri Delacroix, *Le Langage et la pensée* (Paris: Alcan, 1924), 301–4.

11. Karl Bühler, *Die geistige Entwicklung des Kindes* (Jena: Fischer, 1918; English: *The Mental Development of the Child*, trans. Oscar Oeser [London: K. Paul, Trench and Trubner, 1930], 58).—*Trans.*

12. Ludwig Landgrebe, *Nennfunktion und Wortbedeutung: Eine Studie über Martys Sprachphilosophie* (Halle: Niemeyer, 1934), esp. 104–8.

13. See Hermann Ammann, *Vom Ursprung der Sprache* (Lahr: Schauenburg, 1929), 17.

14. Maurice Blondel, *La Pensée*, vol. 1: *La Genèse de la pensée et les paliers de son ascension spontanée* (Paris: Alcan, 1934).

15. Ibid., 333ff.—*Eds.*

16. Carl Stumpf, "Eigenartige sprachliche Entwicklung eines Kindes," *Zeitschrift für pädagogische Psychologie und Pathologie* 3, no. 6 (1901): 419–47.—*Eds.*

17. Louis Boutan, *Les Deux Méthodes de l'enfant* (Bordeaux: Société linnéenne de Bordeaux, 1914).—*Trans.*

18. See the account of these experiments given in Henri Delacroix, *L'Enfant et le langage* (Paris: Alcan, 1934), and their interpretation in Blondel, *La Pensée I*, 71ff.

19. Wilhelm von Humboldt, *Gesammelte Schriften*, Prussian Academy Edition, ed. Albert Leitzmann, vol. VII/1: *Einleitung zum Kawiwerk* (Berlin: Behr, 1907), 55. [English: *On Language: The Diversity of Human Language-Structure and Its Influence on the Mental Development of Mankind*, trans. Peter Heath (Cambridge: Cambridge University Press, 1988), 56.]

20. Hegel, *Jenenser Realphilosophie II*, 183. [Eng. trans., 89: "The power of imagination provides only the empty form; (it is) the designative power positing the name as internal. Language, on the other hand, posits the internal as *being*."]

21. Julius Stenzel, *Philosophie der Sprache* (Munich: Oldenbourg, 1934), 36 ["the intended meaning, the inner thought stands equally as a reality in being; the mind stands face to face with itself"].

22. See Hermann von Helmholtz, *Die Lehre von den Tonempfindungen als physiologische Grundlage für die Theorie der Musik* (Brunswick: Vieweg, 1863) (English: *On the Sensations of Tone as a Physiological Basis for the Theory of Music*, trans. Alexander J. Ellis [Bristol: Thoemmes, 1998]); Carl Stumpf, *Tonpsychologie*, 2 vols. (Leipzig: Hirzel, 1883–90).—*Trans.*

23. John Locke, *An Essay concerning Human Understanding*, book 2, chap. 2, sec. 2. See also Locke's comparison of the human mind with a dark room (ibid., book 2, chap. 11, sec. 17).

24. On both these questions, see Werner, *Entwicklungspsychologie*, 81 [Eng. trans., 98–99].

25. Anton Marty, *Die Frage nach der geschichtlichen Entwicklung des Farbensinnes* (Vienna: Gerold, 1879), 40ff.

26. On these problems, see David Katz, *Der Aufbau der Farbwelt* (2nd rev. ed. of *Die Erscheinungsweisen der Farben und ihre Beeinflussung durch die individuelle Erfahrung*, 1911) (Leipzig: Barth, 1930), part 1, §2. [English abr. ed.: Katz, *The World of Colour*, trans. Robert Brodie Macleod and Charles Warren Fox (London: K. Paul, Trench and Trubner, 1935), 7–28.]

27. Erich Rudolf Jaensch, *Untersuchungen über Grundfragen der Akustik und Tonpsychologie* (Leipzig: Barth, 1929), 8, quoted in Katz, *Der Aufbau*, 119. [Passage omitted in the English: "The sense of color exhibits the particular disposition for object-apprehension which is a fundamental characteristic of all cognitive processes and here, in the sphere of the higher psychic functions, is generally labeled as their 'intentional character.'"]

28. See the account of various facts pertaining to this sphere in Werner, *Entwicklungspsychologie*. [Cf. Eng. trans., esp. 59ff., citing Johannes Volkelt, *Über die Vorstellungen der Tiere: Ein Beitrag zur Entwicklungspsychologie* (Leipzig: Engelmann, 1914).]

29. Carl Stumpf, *Die Sprachlaute: Experimentell-phonetische Untersuchungen* (Berlin: Springer, 1926), 254.

30. Ibid., 255 ["each of which marks certain positions in the vowel triangle as salient for the people and period in question, just as certain instrumental timbres and particular intervals of the various usual scales, and even certain absolute pitches, are salient for the hearing of the respective people or period. . . . But, generally speaking, these saliencies are acoustically contingent and meaningless . . ."].

31. Karl Bühler, "Phonetik und Phonologie," *Travaux du Cercle linguistique de Prague* 4 (1931): 22–53; see also Bühler, *Sprachtheorie*, 281ff. [Eng. trans., 319ff.].

32. Compare Evguéni Polivanov, "La perception des sons d'une langue étrangère," *Travaux du Cercle linguistique de Prague* 4 (1931): 80.

33. Stenzel, *Philosophie der Sprache*, 18ff.

34. Bühler, *Sprachtheorie*, 271ff. [Eng. trans., 313ff.].

35. Dmitry Čiževsky, "Phonologie und Psychologie," *Travaux du Cercle linguistique de Prague* 4 (1931): 18.

36. Delacroix, *Le Langage et la pensée*, 291.

37. Oscar Bloch, "Les premiers stades du langage de l'enfant," *Journal de psychologie normale et pathologique* 18 (1921): 697, quoted in Delacroix, *Le Langage et la pensée*, p. 290.

38. Bühler, *Sprachtheorie*, 283 (Eng. trans., 321).—*Trans.*

39. Wittgenstein, *Tractatus*, 4.026–4.03.

40. Ibid., 3.

41. Ibid., 5.4.—*Trans.*

42. See Husserl, *Formale und transzendentale Logik*, §42, in *Jahrbuch für Philosophie und phänomenologische Forschung* 10 (1929): 98–100. [Also in *Husserliana* XVII:115–17; English: *Formal and Transcendental Logic*, trans. Dorian Cairns (The Hague: Martinus Nijhoff, 1969), 111–12.]

43. See ibid., 100 and 259ff. [*Husserliana* XVII:117 and 299ff.; Eng. trans., 112 and 294ff.].

44. Descartes, *Regulae ad Directionem Ingenii*, III, in *Œuvres*, 10:369–70; Eng. trans., 15.—*Eds.*

45. Compare John Stuart Mill, *A System of Logic*, book 1, chap. 2, sec. 1.

46. Compare Delacroix, *Le Langage et la pensée*, 213.

47. Bühler, *Sprachtheorie*, 75 [Eng. trans., 87].

48. See Otto Funke, *Innere Sprachform: Eine Einführung in A. Martys Sprachphilosophie* (Reichenberg: Kraus, 1924), 22.

49. Landgrebe, *Nennfunktion und Wortbedeutung*, 123.

50. Delacroix, *Le Langage et la pensée*, 220 ["any morphological process which can be isolated and corresponds to a notion"].

51. Compare Charles Serrus, *Le Parallélisme logico-grammatical* (Paris: Alcan, 1933).

Chapter 5

1. See p. 6 in this volume, where Patočka speaks rather of "the disanthropomorphization of the world."—*Trans.*

2. Ernst Cassirer, *Das Erkenntnisproblem in der Philosophie und Wissenschaft der neueren Zeit*, vol. 1 (Berlin: B. Cassirer, 1906), 384ff.

3. After the title of Bergson's most widely known major work (see chapter 3, n10 in this volume).—*Trans.*

Supplement to the Second Czech Edition

1. Eugen Fink, "Welt und Geschichte," in *Husserl und das Denken der Neuzeit: Akten des 2. Internationalen Phänomenologischen Kolloquiums, Krefeld, 1.–3. 11. 1956,*

ed. Herman Leo van Breda and Jacques Taminiaux (The Hague: Martinus Nijhoff, 1959), 159.

2. Francis Bacon, *Novum Organum*, Aph. XXXIX–XLIV.—*Trans.*

3. See Gaston Bachelard, *La Formation de l'esprit scientifique: Contribution à une psychanalyse de la connaissance* (Paris: Vrin, 1938). (English: *The Formation of the Scientific Mind*, trans. Mary McAllester Jones [Manchester: Clinamen, 2002])—*Trans.*

4. Compare Bergson, *Écrits et paroles*, ed. Rose-Marie Mossé-Bastide (Paris: Presses universitaires de France, 1957–59), 2:424.—*Trans.*

5. Michel Henry, *Philosophie et phénoménologie du corps* (Paris: Presses universitaires de France, 1965), 78. [English: *Philosophy and Phenomenology of the Body*, trans. Girard Etzkorn (The Hague: Martinus Nijhoff, 1975), 57.]

6. Hans Lipps, *Goethes Farbenlehre* (Leipzig: Keller, 1939).—*Eds.*

7. Hegel, *Hegels theologische Jugendschriften*, ed. Herman Nohl (Tübingen: Mohr, 1907), 379. [English: *Early Theological Writings*, trans. T. M. Knox (Chicago: University of Chicago Press, 1948), 305.]—*Eds.*

8. Compare, e.g., Hegel, *Enzyklopädie der philosophischen Wissenschaften im Grundriße* (1830), part 3: *Die Philosophie des Geistes*, §389 (Berlin, 1845) 46. [English: *Hegel's Philosophy of Mind*, trans. A. V. Miller and William Wallace (Oxford: Oxford University Press, 2010), 29.]—*Eds.*

9. Aristotle, *On the Soul*, III.8.431b21.—*Eds.*

10. Errol E. Harris, "Hegel's Theory of Body and Soul," in *Akten des XIV. Internationalen Kongreßes für Philosophie, Wien, 2.–9. Sept. 1968* (Vienna: Herder, 1968), 2:41–45.—*Trans.*

11. Ludwig Feuerbach, *Kleine philosophische Schriften (1842–1845)*, ed. Max Gustav Lange (Leipzig: Meiner, 1950), 63. [In subsequent references, page numbers in parentheses in the text refer to this edition. For English translations, compare Feuerbach, "Provisional Theses for the Reformation of Philosophy," trans. Daniel O. Dahlstrom, in *The Young Hegelians: An Anthology*, ed. Lawrence S. Stepelevich (Cambridge: Cambridge University Press, 1983), 156–71, esp. 161–63 (trans. mod.) and 170; and Feuerbach, "Principles of the Philosophy of the Future," in *The Fiery Brook: Selected Writings of Ludwig Feuerbach*, trans. Zawar Hanfi (Garden City, N.Y.: Anchor, 1972), 215–16 and 224–26.]

12. See chapter 1, n20 in this volume.—*Eds.*

13. Ewald Hering, *Beiträge zur Physiologie* (Leipzig: Engelmann, 1861–64); see also Hering, *Zur Lehre von der Beziehung zwischen Leib und Seele*, in *Sitzungsberichte der kaiserlichen Akademie der Wissenschaften*, 3rd section, vol. 72 (Vienna, 1875).—*Eds.*

14. Compare Richard Avenarius, *Der menschliche Weltbegriff* (Leipzig: Reisland, 1891).—*Trans.*

15. Compare Franz Brentano, *Psychologie vom empirischen Standpunkte* (Leipzig: Duncker and Humblot, 1874), 115ff. (English: *Psychology from an Empirical Standpoint*, ed. Linda L. McAlister, trans. Antos C. Rancurello et al., 2nd rev. ed. [London: Routledge, 1995], 68 and passim.)—*Trans.*

16. Goswin Uphues, *Psychologie des Erkennens vom empirischen Standpunkte*, vol. 1 (Leipzig: Engelmann, 1893).—*Eds.*

17. Hermann Schwarz, *Das Wahrnehmungsproblem vom Standpunkte des Physikers, des Physiologen und des Philosophen: Beiträge zur Erkenntnistheorie und empirischen Psychologie* (Leipzig: Duncker and Humblot, 1892), 397–98.

18. See chapter 3, n10 in this volume. The original French edition dates from 1896.—*Eds.*

19. Samuel Alexander, *Space, Time, and Deity* (London: Macmillan, 1920). —*Trans.*

20. See, e.g., Max Scheler, "Lehre von den drei Tatsachen" [in *Gesammelte Werke*, vol. 10.1: *Schriften aus dem Nachlaß—Zur Ethik und Erkenntnislehre*, ed. Maria Scheler (Berne: Francke, 1957), 431–502]; and esp. Scheler, *Erkenntnis und Arbeit*, in *Gesammelte Werke*, vol. 8: *Die Wissensformen und die Gesellschaft*, ed. Maria Scheler (Bern: Francke, 1960), 283–379.

21. Patočka is probably referring to the paging of the typewritten copy made by Ludwig Landgrebe, in 1924–25, from Husserl's stenographic notes for the lectures given in October–November 1910. See in Husserl, *Zur Phänomenologie der Intersubjektivität. Texte aus dem Nachlaß. 1. Teil: 1905–1920, Husserliana* XIII, ed. Iso Kern (The Hague: Martinus Nijhoff, 1973), the editor's introduction, notes and commentaries, xxxiii–xl, 245, and 509–10. The lectures were published in this volume as "Text No. 6" under the title "Aus den Vorlesungen Grundprobleme der Phänomenologie: Wintersemester 1910/11," 111–94. [English: *The Basic Problems of Phenomenology: From the Lectures, Winter Semester 1910–1911*, trans. Ingo Farin and James J. Hart (Dordrecht: Springer, 2006).] Patočka refers here to the first chapter, 111–38 [Eng. trans., 1–28].—*Eds.*

22. Ibid., 124–25 [Eng. trans., 15].—*Eds.*

23. Husserl, *Cartesianische Meditationen*, 82 [Eng. trans., 44].

24. Ibid., 97 [Eng. trans., 62].

25. Lecture given (twice) on May 7 and 10, 1935, in the Vienna Kulturbund. Published under the title "Die Krisis des europäischen Menschentums und die Philosophie," in Husserl, *Die Krisis der europäischen Wissenschaften und die transzendentale Phänomenologie, Husserliana* VI, ed. Walter Biemel (The Hague: Martinus Nijhoff, 1954), 314–48. [English: "Philosophy and the Crisis of European Humanity," in *The Crisis of European Sciences and Transcendental Phenomenology*, trans. David Carr (Evanston, Ill.: Northwestern University Press, 1970), 269–300.]—*Eds.*

26. Compare Husserl, *Ideen zu einer reinen Phänomenologie I*, §49, p. 92 (*Husserliana* III:115; Eng. trans., 110); and Descartes, *Principia Philosophiae*, part 1, LI [Eng. trans., 33: "By substance we can conceive nothing else than a thing which exists in such a way as to stand in need of nothing beyond itself in order to exist."]—*Eds.*

27. Husserl, "Naturwissenschaftliche und geisteswissenschaftliche Einstellung: Naturalismus, Dualismus und psychophysische Psychologie," in *Husserliana* VI, 306. [English: "The Attitude of Natural Science and the Attitude of Humanistic Science: Naturalism, Dualism and Psychophysical Psychology," in *The Crisis of European Sciences and Transcendental Phenomenology*, 327.]

28. Patočka uses throughout this text the Czech calque *pobyt*, combining a durative preverb (*po-*) with the root of the verb "to be" *(býti)*. (See his own com-

mentary on this translation in *Plato and Europe*, trans. Petr Lom [Stanford, Calif.: Stanford University Press, 2002], 169.) In the afterword to the 1976 French translation of *The Natural World*, the same understanding has been rendered without recourse to neologism, by the *être*—be-ing—in *être humain*, "human being."—*Trans.*

29. This seems to me to be the meaning of the critiques raised against Heidegger's existential ontology by Gerhard Funke in his book *Phänomenologie— Metaphysik oder Methode?* (Bonn: Bouvier, 1966) [English: *Phenomenology— Metaphysics or Method?* trans. David J. Parent (Athens: Ohio University Press, 1987)].

30. Heidegger, *Sein und Zeit*, §14, 64–65 [Eng. trans., 60–61].

31. We adopt here the translation of Patočka's Czech translation of Heidegger's *Zeug* proposed by Erazim Kohák (in Patočka, *Body, Community, Language, World*, ed. James Dodd [Chicago: Open Court, 1998], 104, n67), confirmed by his own use of the Greek *pragmata* in an altogether analogous sense already in 1936, characterizing the mode of being of things in the "home" dimension of the natural world (see chapter 3 in this volume, p. 57), as well as in his unpublished correspondence with Henri Declève concerning the French translation of *The Natural World.*—*Trans.*

32. Heidegger, *Sein und Zeit*, §18, 86 [Eng. trans., 80–81].—*Eds.*

33. In Czech, as in other Slavic tongues, the word "world" (*svět*) initially meant "light" (*světlo*), as in the verb "to light, to give or shed light" (*svítit*)—or "to explain" (*vysvětlit*)—from the root *svьt-.*—*Trans.*

34. Hegel, *Wissenschaft der Logik I*, ed. Georg Lasson (Leipzig: Meiner, 1932), 67. (English: *The Science of Logic*, trans. George di Giovanni [Cambridge: Cambridge University Press, 2010], 59.)—*Trans.*

35. In the sense both of bliss and (closer to "the fortuitous") of good fortune, or good hap; as in the German *Glück*, the two meanings are equally salient in the Czech word *štěstí* used here by Patočka.—*Trans.*

36. See Walter Bröcker, "Der Mythos vom Baum der Erkenntnis," in *Anteile: Martin Heidegger zum 60. Geburtstag*, ed. Walter F. Otto (Frankfurt: Klostermann, 1950), 29–50.

37. Compare Kant, *Beantwortung der Frage: Was ist Aufklärung?* (1784). (English: "An Answer to the Question: What Is Enlightenment?" in Kant, *Practical Philosophy*, ed. and trans. Mary J. Gregor [Cambridge: Cambridge University Press, 1996], 17.)—*Trans.*

38. Compare Fichte, *Grundlage· der gesamten Wissenschaftslehre*, in *Werke* 1:370; Eng. trans., 162.—*Trans.*

Afterword to the First French Translation

1. See, e.g., Gerd Brand, *Die Lebenswelt: Eine Philosophie des konkreten Apriori* (Berlin: Walter de Gruyter, 1971); or Karl Ulmer, *Philosophie der modernen Lebenswelt* (Tübingen: Mohr, 1972).

2. Husserl, "Die Krisis der europäischen Wissenschaften und die transzen-

dentale Phänomenologie: Eine Einleitung in die phänomenologische Philosophie," in *Philosophia* 1 (1936): 77–176.—*Eds.*

3. See, in this volume, the supplement to the second Czech edition, n25. —*Eds.*

4. Threatened by the censorship of Communist normalization in Czechoslovakia, the second edition of Patočka's *Natural World* was actually made available only in 1971, despite the date of 1970 figuring in both copyright and imprint, in a number of copies reduced from 2,200 to 300.—*Trans.*

5. Heidegger, "Was ist das—die Philosophie?" (1955), in *Gesamtausgabe*, vol. 11: *Identität und Differenz*, ed. F.-W. von Herrmann (Frankfurt: Klostermann, 2006), 23. [English: *What Is Philosophy?* trans. Jean T. Wilde and William Kluback (Lanham, Md.: Rowman and Littlefield, 1956), 85.]—*Eds.*

6. Husserl, *Phänomenologische Psychologie: Vorlesungen Sommersemester 1925*, in *Husserliana* IX, ed. Walter Biemel (The Hague: Martinus Nijhoff, 1962). (English: Husserl, *Phenomenological Psychology: Lectures Summer Semester 1925*, trans. John Scanlon [The Hague: Martinus Nijhoff, 1977].)—*Trans.*

7. See Heidegger, *Sein und Zeit*, §§53, 61, and 62.—*Trans.*

8. See Eugen Fink, "Reflexionen zu Husserls phänomenologischer Reduktion" (1971), in *Nähe und Distanz* (Freiburg: Alber, 1976), 299–322.—*Eds.*

9. Heidegger, *Sein und Zeit*, §18; see chapter 3 in this volume, n8.—*Trans.*

10. See ibid., §26, 122 (Eng. trans., 114–15).—*Trans.*

11. It is clear that philosophy is not the only human possibility born from the movement toward the end. The same is the case with myth, religion, and art. We cannot, however, develop a complete philosophy of the spirit in this mere outline of an outline.

12. "Most diligent and prolonged application and investigation of the subject itself"—compare Plato, *Seventh Letter*, 341c–d and 344b. (Patočka comments on the quotation in an unpublished letter to Henri Declève, October 22, 1974: "You are quite right to point out that my 'quotation' is a sort of collage. What Plato is after is, of course, to introduce by the *tribē* and the *sunousia* the fact that the spark springs up and thereafter nourishes itself, while my quotation means rather that philosophy, which springs up in wonder, subsequently settles down in the uncovering and discussion of the various aspects of being. Plato wants to characterize, by the *tribē*, etc., how *his own* philosophy springs from a movement which in his eyes can just as well lead to sophistry, whereas my quotation aims at characterizing, by means of Plato's intuition, the *gigantomakhia peri tēs ousias* [*Sophist*, 246a] which is philosophy itself in its historical extension, in short, the fact that philosophy is an *Ur-Stiftung* which has its own locus and does not lead *immediately* to 'public' life.")—*Eds.*

13. Husserl, *Die Krisis der europäischen Wissenschaften und die transzendentale Phänomenologie, Husserliana* VI, 51. (Eng. trans., 51.)—*Trans.*

14. The reader will surely have recognized the allusion to the title of Scheler's last work; see chapter 3 in this volume, n29.—*Trans.*

15. Fichte, *Grundlage der gesamten Wissenschaftslehre*, in *Werke*, 1:370; Eng. trans., 162.—*Eds.*

Translator's Note

1. See the foreword to this volume, n2.

2. See Patočka, *Sebrané spisy*, vol. 20: *Dopisy Václavu Richterovi*, ed. Ivan Chvatík and Jiří Michálek (Prague: OIKOYMENH, 2001), esp. 179, 186, 189.

3. Patočka, unpublished letter to Janine Pignet, December 2, 1966 (Patočka Archive, ms. 5000/010).

4. Patočka, *Aristoteles, jeho předchůdci a dědicové: Studie z dějin filosofie od Aristotela k Hegelovi* (Prague: Academia, 1964). See French translation by Erika Abrams: *Aristote, ses devanciers, ses successeurs: Études d'histoire de la philosophie d'Aristote à Hegel* (Paris: Vrin, 2011).

5. See Patočka, *Body, Community, Language, World*, 166–70.

6. Meant for a lecture that could not take place at the Philosophical Union in Brno, published in the journal *Filosofický časopis* 17, no. 5–6 (1969): 682–702. See German translation by Peter Sacher: "Was ist Existenz?" in *Die Bewegung der menschlichen Existenz*, 230–56.

7. See Patočka's unpublished letters to Henri Declève, June 8, 1970, and Ludwig Landgrebe, April 4, 1974 (Patočka Archive, ms. 5000/009 and 5000/018).

8. Patočka, unpublished letter to Walter Biemel, January 21, 1971 (Patočka Archive, ms. 5000/021).

9. Patočka, *Kacířské eseje o filosofii dějin*, in *Sebrané spisy*, vol. 3: *Péče o duši III*, ed. Ivan Chvatík and Pavel Kouba (Prague: OIKOYMENH, 2002), 13–144 (English: *Heretical Essays in the Philosophy of History*, trans. Erazim Kohák [Chicago: Open Court, 1996]); German versions by Patočka in *Sebrané spisy*, 3:517–86 for the first three chapters, and *Philosophische Perspektiven* 14 (1988): 165–84 for the fourth.

10. Patočka, "Der Subjektivismus der Husserlschen und die Möglichkeit einer 'asubjektiven' Phänomenologie," *Philosophische Perspektiven* 2 (1970): 317–34; and "Der Subjektivismus der Husserlschen und die Forderung einer asubjektiven Phänomenologie," *Sborník prací filosofické fakulty brněnské university*, Řada uměnovědná (F) 19–20, no. 14–15 (1971): 11–26. Both texts were reprinted in Patočka, *Die Bewegung der menschlichen Existenz*, 267–309. The 1971 version has recently been translated into English by Ivan Chvatík, Matt Bower, and Kenneth Maly: "Husserl's Subjectivism and the Call for an Asubjective Phenomenology," in *Asubjective Phenomenology: Jan Patočka's Project in the Broader Context of his Work*, ed. Ľubica Učník, Ivan Chvatík, and Anita Williams (Nordhausen: Verlag Traugott Bautz, 2015), 17–40.

11. Patočka, "Die Gefahren der Technisierung in der Wissenschaft bei Edmund Husserl und das Wesen der Technik als Gefahr bei Martin Heidegger." A mixture of the two versions has been published in *Die Bewegung der menschlichen Existenz*, 330–59, an English translation of the first version in Erazim Kohák, *Jan Patočka: Philosophy and Selected Writings* (Chicago: University of Chicago Press, 1989), 327–39.

12. Patočka, "Europa und Nach-Europa. Die nacheuropäische Epoche und ihre geistigen Probleme," in *Ketzerische Essais zur Philosophie der Geschichte*

und ergänzende Schriften, ed. Klaus Nellen and Jiří Němec (Stuttgart: Klett-Cotta, 1988), 207–87.

13. Patočka, "Duchovní základy života v naší době," *Křesťanská revue* 37, no. 1–2 (1970): 12–15, 33–40. Translated into French, German (in *Ketzerische Essais*, 353–78), and Spanish.

Index

Hoppe, Vladimír, 202
horizon, xv–xvi, xvii, xviii, 66, 69–70, 76,
83, 85, 95, 182; concept of before
Husserl, 66–67; Husserl and, 148–
49, 205n19; retention and protention functions, 71–72, 77
Humboldt, Wilhelm von, 61, 101, 206n21
Hume, David, 12
Husserl, Edmund, ix–xvii, 41, 45, 81, 108,
124–25, 143, 151–52, 156–57, 179,
181–84, 189–90, 200n31; on the alter
ego, 80; finitude in, 123; geometry
in, 123; hyletic matter and, in, 188;
intentionality in, 109, 127; on natural
world, 62, xiii, 124–25, 130, 145–50,
180, 190; Patočka's relations with, ix,
x–xv; on reflection, 118; on time, 71

idealism, transcendental, 34, 48–49, 52
ideation. See intuition: eidetic
imagination, transcendental, 25
immanence, 37, 117–18, 120, 126; transcendental, 37, 49
individuation, 116, 158–59, 166, 169–71,
176, 177
intentionality, 42–43, 109, 126, 145, 150,
160, 182; act-intentionality, 63-66;
horizon-intentionality, 66
intersubjectivity, xvi, xvii, 50, 55, 86, 96,
98, 100, 107, 111, 184, 206n25
introjection, 138, 146, 197n19
intuition, 12, 21, 26–27, 29, 36, 44–45,
60–61, 120, 125, 141, 142, 152, 177,
190; in Descartes, 23; eidetic, 46–48,
50; in Kant, 25–26, 60; in Plato
and, 47

Jacobi, Friedrich Heinrich, 14, 15,
197n13
Jaensch, Erich Rudolf, 103
Jakobson, Roman, xiii, 196n8

Kant, Immanuel, xiv, 24–28, 29, 33, 41,
44, 51, 60–61, 66–67, 130–31, 142,
145, 162
Karfík, Filip, 207n35
Katz, David, 103
Kaufmann, Felix, 47
Kellogg, Winthrop Niles, and Luella Ag-
ger, 99

kinestheses, xv, 73–74, 76, 164
Kierkegaard, Søren, 162
Koyré, Alexandre, x
Kozák, J. B., xi, xiii
Kreis, Friedrich, 203n71
Krejčí, František, 202n59, 202n61,
202n63, 203n68, 208n8
Krüger, Gerhard, 198n28

Landgrebe, Ludwig, 97, 181, 192
language and speech, xvii, 86–111, 112,
188, 208n8; children and, 96–98;
origin of, 94, 98
Leibniz, Gottfried Wilhelm, 47, 82, 129;
on language, 107, 109
Leonardo da Vinci, 113
Lévy-Bruhl, Lucien, 63
life, transcendental, xvi, 36, 40
life-feeling, 7, 8, 9–11, 59, 175
life-world (Lebenswelt), Husserl's concept
of, xii–xv, xvii, 145, 148–50, 181–83.
See also natural world
Lipps, Hans, 131
lived-experience, xvi, xviii, 9, 19, 25, 33,
36, 39–44, 49, 55, 84, 117–18, 120,
131, 138–39, 145–47; fictive, 79; intentional nature of, 115, 161
Locke, John, 12, 13–14, 102, 129
logic, xiv–xv, 17–18, 38, 47, 66, 83, 106,
108, 110, 139, 141, 149, 179
Lossky, Nikolaj, 21
Lucian of Samosata, 53

Mach, Ernst, 16, 137
Maine de Biran, François-Pierre-Gonthier,
131, 156
Malebranche, Nicolas, 12
Marty, Anton, 94, 97, 109
Marx, Karl, 162, 188
Masaryk, Tomáš Garigue, xi–xii
materialism, 136–37
mathematics (mathematicism, mathematization), 15, 113, 131–32, 139; Descartes and, 13, 23, 128; direct and
indirect mathematization, 115, 128
Meillet, Antoine, 108
Merleau-Ponty, Maurice, xv, 156
Messer, August, 202n61-
metaphysics, 18–19, 21, 114, 115, 116–17,
123, 128, 135